Asperger Syndrome
and High-Functioning Autism

Asperger Syndrome
and High-Functioning Autism

A Guide for Effective Practice

Third Edition

Richard L. Simpson
Brenda Smith Myles

pro·ed
An International Publisher

8700 Shoal Creek Boulevard
Austin, Texas 78757
800/897-3202   Fax: 800/397-7633
www.proedinc.com

© 1998, 2003, 2011 by PRO-ED, Inc.
8700 Shoal Creek Boulevard
Austin, Texas 78757-6897
800/897-3202   Fax 800/397-7633
www.proedinc.com

Library of Congress Cataloging-in-Publication Data

Simpson, Richard L., 1945–
    Asperger syndrome and high-functioning autism : a guide for
effective practice / Richard L. Simpson, Brenda S. Myles.—3rd ed.
        p. cm.
    Rev. ed. of: Asperger syndrome : a guide for parents and educators /
Brenda Smith Myles, Richard L. Simpson. 2nd ed. 2003.
    Includes bibliographical references and index.
    ISBN 978-1-4164-0489-7
    1. Asperger's syndrome in children. 2. Autism spectrum disorders.
I. Myles, Brenda Smith.   II. Myles, Brenda Smith. Asperger syndrome.
III. Title. [DNLM: 1. Asperger Syndrome.   2. Child Development
Disorders, Pervasive.   3. Child. WS 350.6 S613a 2011]
    RJ506.A9M95 2011
    618.92'858832—dc22
                                                                        2010016439

Art director: Jason Crosier
Designer: Lissa Hattersley
This book was designed in Myriad Pro and Minion

Printed in the United States of America
1   2   3   4   5   6   7   8   9   10   19   18   17   16   15   14   13   12   11   10

Contents

Preface

It was more than 60 years ago that the Viennese physician Hans Asperger published a seminal paper wherein he described a group of children with a unique social disability (Asperger, 1944). The disorder he described continues to be known by his name—Asperger syndrome (AS). For decades, the term *Asperger syndrome* was primarily used in certain parts of Europe, with virtually no mention in the rest of the world. Times have changed. Currently, Asperger syndrome is used worldwide to describe individuals with significant social, language, behavioral, and other peculiarities who simultaneously reveal normal development and functioning in many areas of their lives.

Asperger syndrome is currently classified as an element of autism spectrum disorders (ASDs); as such, it is generally regarded as a complex, neurologically based, developmental disability that typically has its onset early in life. As with other forms of ASD, Asperger syndrome is an increasingly common disability. Indeed, there has been a dramatic increase over the past decade in the number of children and youth identified as having Asperger syndrome or higher functioning autism spectrum disorders. Yet, in spite of a worldwide exponential increase in the diagnostic use of the terms *Asperger syndrome, high-functioning autism,* and *autism spectrum disorders*—and the predictable swell of interest among parents, family members, and professionals—there is a striking lack of understanding regarding these conditions. It is clear that parents and professionals alike are struggling to learn more about Asperger syndrome and high-functioning autism (AS/HFA), especially about effective methods for assisting children and youth diagnosed with these disabilities.

This need for practical information about AS/HFA is the foundation of this book. It is designed to be used by professionals, families, and laypeople. The objectives of this resource are to (a) clearly and succinctly address foundational issues related to the characteristics of children and youth with these disorders and (b) describe utilitarian methods that will facilitate the growth and development of children and youth with Asperger syndrome or high-functioning autism in home, school, and community settings.

chapter one

Understanding Asperger Syndrome and High-Functioning Autism

In 1944, Hans Asperger, a Viennese physician with a particular interest in children with special needs and disabilities, published a seminal manuscript that described four children with an unusual pattern of ability and social behavior. The children had normal cognitive and language abilities; however, they had poor social skills and other atypical behavior. The children had a penchant for social isolation and were generally socially uninformed and awkward. They also displayed a variety of standard autistic-like behaviors, such as self-stimulatory responses and insistence on environmental sameness. However, unlike other children with autism, they generally had average intellectual ability and normal language development, leading Asperger to infer that individuals with this disorder represented a unique and independent diagnostic classification. He termed the condition *Autistic Psychopathy in Childhood* (Asperger, 1944) and concluded that it had a neurodevelopmental origin. Hans Asperger made his discovery shortly after Leo Kanner identified children with *early infantile autism* (Kanner, 1943), commonly described as classic or typical autism. Kanner, who also was Austrian born and received his medical training in Europe before immigrating to the United States in the 1920s, did not know Hans Asperger. The two men independently made their autism-connected discoveries. Today, both disorders are commonly included among the continuum of autism-related disabilities known as *autism spectrum disorders* (ASDs).

Interest in Asperger syndrome (also frequently known as *Asperger disorder*) was slow to develop. Indeed, subsequent to its origin in 1944, little was written or known about Asperger syndrome until the early 1980s (Wing, 1991). Interest in Asperger syndrome continues to dramatically increase, and the disorder is rapidly becoming a part of the everyday lexicon of parents, educators, and other professionals. Moreover, the dramatic increase in the number of individuals diagnosed with Asperger syndrome, including school-age children and youth, has radically affected schools and communities around the world. The exponential increase in interest and the corresponding increase in the number of individuals diagnosed with the disorder are directly correlated with recognition of Asperger syndrome as a subclassification of pervasive developmental disorders in the widely used *Diagnostic and Statistical Manual of Mental Disorders–Fourth Edition, Text Revision* (DSM-IV-TR; American Psychiatric Association, 2000) and the corresponding international classification system, *International Statistical Classification of Diseases and Related Health Problems* (ICD-10; World Health Organization, 2007). In spite of this ever-increasing interest, understanding of this disability, as well as of autism spectrum disorders, lags significantly behind its recognition, leading to (a) significant confusion related to the prominent, defining, and unique characteristics of Asperger syndrome; (b) a lack of diagnostic reliability; (c) debate on whether Asperger syndrome is an independent diagnostic category or simply another dimension of the autism spectrum; and (d) disagreement regarding this disorder and its relationship to other "autistic-like" conditions. For these reasons, this book addresses not only Asperger syndrome but also high-functioning autism (HFA). We are aware that there are arguably subtle differences among individuals diagnosed with Asperger syndrome and those diagnosed with the more generic condition of high-functioning autism. Nonetheless, increasingly these terms are used interchangeably. More importantly, the methods and strategies for individuals with these conditions are generally the same. In this context, this chapter describes characteristics and other issues related to understanding the unique elements of Asperger syndrome and high-functioning autism.

Diagnostic Classification of Asperger Syndrome and High-Functioning Autism

Asperger syndrome, as well as high-functioning autism, has historically been connected with the more widely used term *autism* and more recently with the term *autism spectrum disorder.* Kanner's (1943) original description of children with autism (i.e., that they had relationship difficulties, delayed speech and language development and other speech and language abnormalities, normal physical growth and development, insistence on environmental sameness, obsessive preoccupation with objects, and repetitive and other self-stimulatory responses) has served as a general blueprint for understanding individuals with Asperger syndrome or high-functioning autism.

As Kanner's (1943) original characteristics of autism have been revised and refined, so too have conceptualizations of Asperger syndrome and high-functioning autism. That is, even though the professional community embraces basic elements of Hans Asperger's notions regarding Asperger syndrome, nuances and amendments to the original conceptions of the disorder have occurred over the decades. Moreover, high-functioning autism has increasingly been recognized, and the unique needs of individuals with this diagnosis have been documented. The process of refining the characteristics of Asperger syndrome was particularly stimulated by Lorna Wing (1981), who is widely recognized for translating Hans Asperger's original work into English. Wing attempted to clarify and identify the disorder through extensive clinical descriptions and case examples. Uta Frith (1991) also significantly facilitated this translation and interpretation process. High-functioning autism has followed the trends of the more specific condition Asperger disorder. The two conditions are widely and increasingly viewed as generally encompassing a single classification.

In the United States and North America (as well as in much of the rest of the world), a widely used diagnostic guide for Asperger syndrome and high-functioning autism is the *Diagnostic and Statistical Manual of Mental Disorders–Fourth Edition, Text Revision* (DSM-IV-TR; American Psychiatric Association, 2000). This diagnostic and clinical manual classifies Asperger syndrome as one of five pervasive developmental disorders (PDDs). According to the DSM-IV-TR, the term *pervasive developmental disorder* is used in reference to persons who are "characterized by severe and pervasive impairment in several areas of development: reciprocal social interaction skills, communication skills, or the presence of stereotyped behavior, interests, and activities" (p. 69). Other specific forms of pervasive developmental disorders are identified in the DSM-IV-TR: autistic disorder, childhood disintegrative disorder, Rett's disorder, and pervasive developmental disorder–not otherwise specified. The term *high-functioning autism* is not a separate diagnostic DSM classification. Yet, this term is widely recognized and used, and the term serves as a more general area of classification into which specific forms of pervasive developmental disorders may fall. It is important to note that the DSM subclasses of autism disorder, including Asperger disorder, are slated to be eliminated when the DSM is revised in 2013. Those specific diagnostic elements will be replaced by autism spectrum disorders and the conceptual understanding that autism-related disabilities fall on a continuum and that Asperger syndrome and high-functioning autism constitute functionally similar conditions.

Salient elements of the DSM-IV-TR (2000) diagnostic criteria for Asperger syndrome fall within the general domains of *social interaction impairment* (e.g., eye contact problems, difficulty in understanding body language and facial expression meaning, difficulty in establishing and maintaining peer relationships, problems in relating and interacting with others) and *stereotypical and restricted patterns of interest and behavior* (e.g., limited, stereotypical, and abnormal interest patterns; aberrant and stereotypical movements, such as arm and hand flapping). The DSM-IV-TR diagnostic criteria for Asperger disorder also include an absence of a significant language or cognitive language delay, no self-help skills, a lack of environmental curiosity, and significant occupational or social impairment.

The international counterpart of the DSM-IV-TR (2000) is the ICD-10 (World Health Organization, 2007). This classification also uses the term *pervasive developmental disorders* to refer to autism spectrum disorders, and it conceptualizes and defines autism similarly to the DSM-IV-TR. That is, the ICD-10 includes and similarly defines the same disorders, including Asperger syndrome, childhood autism, Rett's syndrome, other childhood disintegrative disorders, other pervasive developmental disorders, pervasive developmental disorders–unspecified, overactive disorder with mental retardation with stereotyped movements, and atypical autism.

Characteristics of Children and Youth

Children and youth with Asperger syndrome or high-functioning autism share characteristics with children and youth with autism or autism spectrum disorders, as originally described by Kanner (1943) and, more recently, by other researchers and practitioners (e.g., Klin, Volkmar, & Sparrow, 2000; Simpson & Myles, 2008). However, as described below, Asperger syndrome has a number of unique features. These elements are also common elements of high-functioning autism. The characteristics are discussed below and include abnormalities or deficits in social skills and social interaction, in speech and communication, in cognition, in academic performance and learning, in sensory characteristics, and in physical and motor skills.

Social-Skill, Social Interaction, Behavioral and Adaptive Behavior Impairments

Children and adolescents with AS/HFA demonstrate social excesses and deficits, emotional and behavioral challenges, and adaptive behavior struggles that often continue into adulthood. Indeed, the DSM-IV-TR (2000) notes that "the impairment in reciprocal social interaction is gross and sustained" (p. 80). Many such children and adolescents appear to be interested in interacting with others; however, their interactions tend to be unskilled or characterized by an inability to engage in age-expected social interactions, including appropriate play. Indeed, the social deficits of many children and adolescents with AS/HFA may be due more to lack of understanding of the appropriate social customs and poor skill in executing and participating in social interactions than to disinterest or fear of social contact. For example, a child with Asperger syndrome may appear rude or odd because he seems unwilling to take turns in play and conversation or to understand a peer's subtle social cues, in spite of his willingness to seek out others on the playground. It is not unusual for children who appear motivated to interact with others to become less inclined to engage others socially in their teen and adult years, possibly because of a lifetime of being rejected or rebuffed.

In accordance with these behavioral patterns, individuals (including children and adolescents) with AS/HFA can fall anywhere from withdrawn to active on the social-interaction motivation continuum. That is, they can be expected to range from being socially reclusive and preferring isolation to being socially outgoing and interested in having regular contact with others. Regardless of where they fit on this scale, however, they are routinely viewed as socially awkward, socially stiff, emotionally blunted, self-centered, unable to understand nonverbal social cues, inflexible, and lacking in empathy and understanding. Therefore, even when children and adolescents try to seek out others, they frequently encounter social isolation because of their lack of understanding of the rules of social behavior, including appropriate topics for discussion, awareness of give-and-take and reciprocal conversations, eye contact, physical proximity to others, gestures, and posture.

In one of the few studies that attempted to identify the nature of behavior problems and adaptive behavior among students with Asperger syndrome, Barnhill, Hagiwara, Myles, Simpson, et al. (2000) compared behavior rating scale inventories completed by parents, by teachers, and by students. Results revealed that parents had significantly greater concern about the behavior and social skills of their children than did the students' teachers. Responses also revealed that parents perceived their children to have clinically significant problems in a variety of socially related areas, including overall behavioral problems (e.g., conduct problems, aggression, and hyperactivity) and internalizing problems (e.g., withdrawal). In contrast, teachers perceived the children and adolescents in the study to have both fewer and less significant problems than did parents, although they did view the children to be "at risk" in the areas of anxiety, depression, attention problems, and withdrawal. Students' self-evaluations revealed that they did not perceive themselves to have significant problems or to be at risk on any of the clinical components of the scale.

It is not unusual for individuals with AS/HFA to be able to engage in routine social interactions (e.g., greetings) without being able to engage in extended interactions or two-way relationships. Thus, children and youth with AS/HFA are commonly described by families and schoolmates as lacking awareness of social convention and protocol, lacking common sense, tending to misinterpret social cues and unspoken messages, and being inclined to display a variety of socially unaccepted and nonreciprocal responses. In spite of their frequent lack of social awareness, these individuals are aware that they are different from their peers. This commonly leads to self-esteem problems, self-faultfinding, and self-deprecation.

Not surprisingly, many individuals with AS/HFA are poor incidental social learners; that is, they tend to learn social skills without fully understanding their meaning and context. Indeed, many of these individuals attempt to rigidly and generally follow universal social rules, because doing so provides structure to an otherwise confusing, complex, and ever-changing world. Unfortunately, this is often not a successful strategy because there are few, if any, universal and inflexible social rules. Indeed, most social rules come in the form of general guidelines that are applied with nuances and forms that fit particular situations and circumstances.

It is also common for individuals with AS/HFA to become emotionally vulnerable and easily stressed. For example, children may become stressed if there are relatively insignificant breaches in routine, frustrated when demands or expectations exceed their level of comfort, or agitated if they think others are invading their private space when they are in a crowded room or when they find themselves in the midst of social activities that require multiple interpretations and responses. However, unlike many normally developing and achieving peers, many children with AS/HFA do not reveal stress through voice tone, body posture, and so forth. As a result, their agitation may escalate to a point of crisis because of others' unawareness of their discomfort, along with their own inability to monitor and control uncomfortable situations.

It is also significant that children and youth with AS/HFA are relatively easy targets for peers prone to teasing and bullying. Reports suggest that bullying and harassment of individuals diagnosed with higher functioning autism spectrum disorders or Asperger disorder, including adult-age persons, are chillingly common. Such vulnerability and susceptibility for victimization and ill-treatment requires that a significant role for adults working with persons with AS/HFA be in creating safe and supportive school, work, and community settings.

Behavioral and adaptive behavior problems are not universal among individuals with AS/HFA; however, they are not uncommon. As suggested earlier, these problems often involve feelings of stress, anxiety, fatigue, and pressure to perform within set time and expectation parameters, or loss of control or inability to predict outcomes. Accordingly, most children and adolescents with AS/HFA do not have typical conduct problems, but rather behavioral and adaptive behavior problems connected to their inability to function in a world they see as disorganized, confusing, unpredictable, threatening, and often frenzied. In his original (1944) description of children with Asperger syndrome, Hans Asperger described the four prototype children he studied as having significant behavior and conduct problems. These children were described as malicious and mean-spirited. In retrospect, it is likely that Hans Asperger observed the effects of stress and lack of structure in combination with unskilled social skills, which resulted in problem behaviors, the cause and nature of which he likely misinterpreted. To be sure, there is little support for Asperger's

(1944) original description of children with Asperger syndrome as being mean-natured and malevolent. Rather, when persons with the syndrome (as well as individuals with high-functioning autism spectrum disorders) do experience behavioral difficulties, their problems are more likely caused by social ineptness, stress, anxiety, an obsessive and single-minded pursuit of a particular interest, and/or a defensive panic reaction.

As individuals with AS/HFA age, more critical social adaptive behavior and emotional problems often develop (Attwood, 2007; Tantam, 2000). Studies of adolescents (Cesaroni & Garber, 1991; Ghaziuddin, Weidmer-Mikhail, & Ghaziuddin, 1998) have indicated that these individuals experience heightened discomfort or anxiety in social situations, along with a continuing limited ability to interact with peers. Wing (1981) first noted that it is at this time that diagnosable depression and anxiety tend to occur. This pattern has been confirmed by others; for example, clinical reports have revealed that adolescents and young adults with Asperger syndrome appear to be at risk for depression (Barnhill, 2001; Ghaziuddin et al., 1998; Tantam, 2000). Independent living and transitioning to adult roles/activities are often challenges (Attwood, 2007).

Speech, Language, and Communication Characteristics

Unlike children with classic forms of autism, those with AS/HFA typically do not manifest clinically significant delays in language (American Psychiatric Association, 2000; Thompson, 2007). They typically tend to acquire and use words and phrases in general accordance with expected developmental norms, though there may be some language problems and delays in some children with AS/HFA. In this regard, Frith (1991) observed that children with Asperger syndrome "tend to speak fluently by the time they are five" (p. 3). However, she also observed that their language is frequently "odd in its use for communication" (p. 3). Wing (1981) reported that many individuals with AS/HFA display a variety of communication deficits as infants and that many of their perceived "special abilities" could be explained as rote responses rather than as normal or precocious language development.

Disagreement exists among professionals regarding the extent to which children diagnosed with AS/HFA display language acquisition delays and deficits (American Psychiatric Association, 2000; Mesibov, Shea, & Adams, 2001; Wetherby & Prizant, 2000). However, there is no debate that children with AS/HFA manifest a variety of abnormal communication characteristics, particularly in their pragmatic, social, conversational, and related skills (e.g., abnormal voice quality, monotonic voice). Their often egocentric conversational style, one-sided monologues, and narrowly focused interests are independent of their early acquisition and use of words. For example, a child may repeat the same phrase over and over; talk with exaggerated inflections or in a monotonic voice; discuss at length a single topic that is of little interest to others; or have difficulty sustaining conversation unless it focuses on a particular, narrowly defined topic. It is not surprising that there are communication problems associated with these patterns, given that effective communication requires that individuals have shared topics and be willing to listen as well as talk. The often adultlike, pedantic speaking style of some children and adolescents with AS/HFA may further lessen their appeal to their peers.

As might be expected, nonverbal communication deficits and related social communication problems are common among persons with AS/HFA. These include problems during interactions, such as standing closer to another person than is customarily accepted; making unusual gestures or movements while talking; intensely staring at another person for long periods; maintaining abnormal body posture; failing to make eye contact or displaying an inexpressive face, and thereby failing to signal interest, approval, or disapproval; and failing to use or understand gestures and facial expressions.

In school, learners with AS/HFA frequently have difficulty comprehending descriptions of abstract concepts, understanding and correctly using figures of speech (e.g., metaphors, idioms, parables, and allegories), and grasping the meaning and intent of rhetorical questions (Shore, 2003). Because these conventions and language elements are commonly used by teachers and authors of school texts, deficits in this area often have a negative effect on these students' academic success and exacerbate learning difficulties.

Cognitive and Intellectual Characteristics

A salient and defining characteristic of AS/HFA is average or above-average intellectual capacity. Both the ICD-10 (World Health Organization, 2007) and the DSM-IV-TR (American Psychiatric Association, 2000) note that a diagnosis of Asperger syndrome is generally contingent upon an individual's not having a global intellectual or cognitive deficit. However, in spite of this assumption and the recognition of the importance of cognitive profiles in understanding and planning for learners, little is known about the cognitive and intellectual abilities of persons specifically diagnosed with AS/HFA. Indeed, many assumptions regarding the intellectual and cognitive characteristics of children and youth with Asperger syndrome are based on studies of those with high-functioning autism. In this regard, several researchers have reported an uneven cognitive profile pattern on measures of intelligence and cognition (including the widely used Wechsler intelligence scales [Wechsler, 1989, 1991]) among individuals with high-functioning autism.

One such assumed pattern on the Wechsler scales is significantly higher scores on performance items (and thus Performance IQ scores) when compared with verbal performance and Verbal IQ scores (Ehlers et al., 1997; Lincoln, Courchesne, Kilman, Elmasian, & Allen, 1988). More specifically, individuals with high-functioning autism have obtained their highest scores on the Block Design subtest and their lowest scores on the Comprehension subtest. The Block Design element of the Wechsler intelligence scales is a nonverbal, concept-formation task that requires perceptual organization, spatial visualization, and abstract conceptualization. It is believed to be a good measure of general intelligence. In contrast, the Comprehension subtest assesses an individual's understanding of social mores and interpersonal situations and is assumed to relate to one's social judgment, common sense, and grasp of social conventionality. Thus, it is not surprising that individuals with higher functioning autism spectrum disorders (including those with Asperger syndrome) would be expected to score relatively poorly on a test designed to measure social comprehension. Without a doubt, much remains to be learned about the intellectual and cognitive abilities and functioning of persons diagnosed with Asperger syndrome or higher functioning autism spectrum disorders.

In one of the few studies of cognitive abilities of children and youth with Asperger syndrome, Barnhill, Hagiwara, Myles, and Simpson (2000) assessed the cognitive profiles of 37 children and youth with Asperger syndrome, as measured by the Wechsler scales (Wechsler, 1989, 1991). The scores generally fell within the average range of abilities, although IQ scores ranged from intellectually deficient to very superior. No significant difference existed between the Verbal IQ and Performance IQ scores. Consistent with the findings of others, the study also revealed relatively high

Block Design subtest scores, suggesting relatively strong nonverbal reasoning ability and visual–motor spatial integration. Relatively low scores were found on the Coding subtest, suggesting that many of the subjects had visual–motor coordination difficulties, were distractible, were disinterested in school-related tasks, and/or had visual memory weakness. The subjects also obtained relatively low scores on the Comprehension subtest, suggesting poor social judgment. It is important to note, however, that this and other studies have failed to identify a specific cognitive profile among individuals diagnosed with Asperger syndrome. Indeed, patterns of intellectual and cognitive abilities and profiles of persons with Asperger syndrome or higher functioning autism spectrum disorders are increasingly being recognized as similar.

Several theories have been proposed to explain the uneven cognitive performance of individuals with Asperger syndrome or high-functioning autism. Among the most popular of these explanations is the one suggesting that individuals with Asperger syndrome have a "theory of mind" deficit (Baron-Cohen, Golan, Wheelwright, & Hill, 2004; Baron-Cohen, Leslie, & Frith, 1985). Theory of mind refers to an individual's ability to think about and use information related to her and others' intentions, beliefs, and mental states. In accordance with meager theory-of-mind capacity, a weakness in perspective taking and related abilities is used to explain at least some of the problems of individuals with Asperger syndrome or high-functioning autism, as well as to offer a plausible explanation for their irregular profile on certain types of IQ tests.

Academic and Learning Characteristics

In spite of their typically average intellectual abilities and their ability and aptitude to be included in general education classrooms, many learners with AS/HFA can be expected to experience academic performance problems. Indeed, social and communication deficits, in combination with obsessive and narrowly defined interests, concrete and literal thinking styles, inflexibility, poor problem-solving skills, poor organizational skills, difficulty in discerning relevant from irrelevant stimuli, and weak social standing, often make it difficult for these students to fully participate in and comprehend general education curricula and instructional systems. Nevertheless, in spite of these challenges, many children and youth with AS/HFA are able to attend college and have successful careers. That individuals diagnosed with Asperger disorder are increasingly entering and matriculating through higher education systems is clear evidence of this trend (Harpur, Lawlor, & Fitzgerald, 2004).

Some children and youth with AS/HFA are thought to have learning disabilities (Attwood, 2007; Frith, 1991; Siegel, Minshew, & Goldstein, 1996). In fact, this interpretation extends as far back as Asperger (1944) himself, who described the academic performance of the children with whom he worked as irregular. Just as countless parents and teachers have observed, Asperger, too, observed that children with Asperger syndrome, although highly verbal, often fail academic subjects that do not align with their special interests, narrowly defined pursuits, and obsessions.

Students with AS/HFA are widely thought to experience problems related to comprehending abstract materials, metaphors, idioms, and other figures of speech; discriminating relevant from irrelevant information; and understanding inferentially based materials. Strengths among learners with Asperger syndrome tend to be in comprehension of factual material (Church, Alisanski, & Amanullah, 2000). A study of academic achievement undertaken by Griswold, Barnhill, Myles, Hagiwara, and Simpson (2002) revealed that although students' mean academic achievement scores fell within the average range, the scores ranged from significantly below average to significantly above average. Relative strengths were in the areas of oral expression and reading recognition. Students who participated in the study revealed relative weakness in the area of listening comprehension (i.e., comprehending information that was verbally presented). Their written language scores were also significantly lower than their oral expression scores. Low mathematics scores were also found, especially in solving equations and answering mathematical calculation and application problems. Finally, students who participated in the study had significant difficulties in the areas of problem solving and language-based critical thinking. Not surprisingly, this study reported that, in spite of being very verbal, persons with AS/HFA had significant difficulties in understanding the oral language of others and arriving at solutions to routine problems of everyday life.

As previously suggested, children and youth with AS/HFA experience difficulty in generalizing previously learned knowledge and skills. That is, they frequently have problems applying information and skills across settings and situations and with different individuals. Moreover, it is common for students to have difficulty attending to relevant curricular cues and stimuli.

Teachers often fail to recognize the special academic needs of these students because they often give the impression that they understand more than they do. That is, the deficits of some students with AS/HFA are masked by their pedantic style, seemingly advanced vocabulary, and parrot-like responses, as well as by the fact that they may be good word callers without having the higher order thinking and comprehension skills to understand what they read.

Sensory Characteristics

Both Kanner (1943) and Asperger (1944) shared the observation that children with autism and those with Asperger syndrome are prone to peculiar sensory stimuli responses. For example, children with Asperger syndrome are often hypersensitive to certain sounds or visual stimuli (e.g., fluorescent lights) and may respond negatively when overloaded with certain types of sensory stimuli. In fact, parents and teachers have reported behavior problems associated with these children's fear of anticipated stimuli (e.g., fire alarms or chimes that are sounded at certain times). It is common for parents of children with AS/HFA to report that their children have an obsessive preference for certain foods or textures (e.g., a child will wear clothes made of only certain fabrics). Some individuals have been reported to have an extremely high tolerance for physical pain (Dunn, 2008).

Finally, it is not unusual for children with AS/HFA to engage in self-stimulatory responses (e.g., repeatedly spinning an object for extended periods of time). In fact, the DSM-IV-TR (2000) lists "restricted repetitive and stereotyped patterns of behavior, interests, and activities" (p. 84) among the criteria for a diagnosis of Asperger syndrome. Display of these behaviors is most common when the children experience stress, fatigue, or sensory overload (Myles, Cook, Miller, Rinner, & Robbins, 2000).

Physical and Motor Skill Anomalies

Wing (1981) observed that children with Asperger syndrome tend to have poor motor coordination and balance problems. These problems have been confirmed by others (Attwood, 2007; Smith, 2000; Smith & Bryson, 1994). Indeed, parents and educators have found that many children and adolescents with AS/HFA are awkward and clumsy, making it difficult for them to successfully participate in games involving motor skills. Because these are primary social activities for children, problems in this area have significant implications for social and pragmatic language development that go well beyond matters of motor coordination. Moreover, fine–motor skill difficulties have implications for a variety of school activities, such as writing and art. Historically, there has been some dispute over the existence of motor delays and aberrations among individuals with Asperger syndrome (Manjiviona & Prior, 1995). Currently, however, there is evidence that a significant percentage of learners with autism-related disorders, including those with Asperger disorder and high-functioning autism, have physical and motor problems (Todd & Reid, 2007). Thus, this is a problem that requires attention for every child or youth identified with an autism spectrum disorder and necessitates intervention for those students found to have a weakness in this foundational area of education.

Other Considerations

Because research in Asperger syndrome and high-functioning autism is in its early stages, we are just beginning to understand the nature and characteristics of persons with the disorders, as well as important steps that support intervention and treatment. The following section provides an overview of the emergent and current information regarding prevalence, etiology, and comorbidity of the syndrome. Also, the section discusses the prognosis and outlook for individuals with AS/HFA.

Prevalence

The term *prevalence* refers to estimating the number of individuals with a particular characteristic, such as a disease or disability. For a variety of reasons, it is difficult to obtain an accurate count of the number of individuals with autism spectrum disorders. Nevertheless, the Centers for Disease Control and Prevention (2008) estimates that approximately 1 out of every 150 individuals will fall on the autism spectrum. That count is a dramatic increase over the 4 to 5 per 10,000 prevalence estimate of past years (Lotter, 1996). It is also significant to note that a number of professionals and professional organizations estimate that a more accurate and current prevalence estimate is approximately 1 in 100 persons (Autism Society of America, 2009).

Estimating the prevalence of Asperger disorder and high-functioning autism is no less difficult. Use of divergent diagnostic criteria throughout the world, in combination with imprecise diagnostic criteria and the subtle nature of many of the defining characteristics of Asperger syndrome and high-functioning autism, has led to variable estimates. Brasic (2008) notes that "various studies indicate rates ranging from 1 case in 250–10,000 children" and that, not surprisingly, "additional epidemiologic studies are needed" (p. 1). Kadesjo, Gillberg, and Hagberg (1999) estimated that as many as 48 per 10,000 children could have the syndrome. In contrast, Ehlers and Gillberg (1993) estimated the prevalence to be about 36 per 10,000, and Wing (1981) speculated that the number could be as low as 1 per 10,000. Volkmar and Klin (2000) sagely noted that "the lack of a real consensus on the diagnosis of [Asperger syndrome] means that present data are, at best, 'guestimates' of its prevalence" (p. 62). Indeed, the DSM-IV-TR (2000) lacks a prevalence estimate for Asperger syndrome, noting that "definitive data regarding the prevalence of Asperger Syndrome are lacking" (p. 82).

In spite of difficulties in knowing the exact prevalence of Asperger syndrome and high-functioning autism, it is clear that these disabilities are increasingly being recognized and diagnosed. AS/HFA appears to be approximately five times more common in boys than in girls, and it has been identified throughout the world among all racial, ethnic, economic, and social groups. Notwithstanding the debate over the number of individuals who may have Asperger syndrome or high-functioning autism, we adhere to the general range of 1 in approximately 300.

Etiology

There is no known single cause for Asperger syndrome or high-functioning autism. Nevertheless, these conditions are widely considered to be the result of a neurological disorder (Autism Society of America, 2009). The Autism Society of America also strongly supports the position that there are no known psychological or related interpersonal environmental factors (e.g., "refrigerator mother," parental emotional aloofness) that cause the conditions, a position that is shared by virtually every professional and professional organization in the world. Although the etiology of Asperger syndrome, high-functioning autism, and autism spectrum disorders is currently unknown, it is becoming increasingly clear that the disorders are related and that they share at least some of the same causal factors. To be sure, there appears to be a significant hereditary link for cases of AS/HFA (see, for example, Cantor et al., 2005). The DSM-IV-TR (2000) notes that "there appears to be an increased frequency of Asperger's Disorder among family members of individuals who have the disorder. There may also be an increased risk for Autistic Disorder as well as more general social difficulties" (p. 82).

Of course, autism literature—both professional and popular press—is replete with speculation that Asperger syndrome, high-functioning autism, and other autism-related disabilities are the result of environmental factors, such as exposure to environmental chemicals and toxins, metabolic imbalances, and infections. The majority of the attention connected to environmental etiological factors has been linked to autism; nevertheless, this literature also relates to Asperger syndrome and high-functioning autism. The most notable of these purported factors are toxins, such as mercury and vaccination additives. There is no clear scientific evidence that mercury and vaccine preservatives and additives are the cause of any autism-related disabilities. Nonetheless, in recognition of the alleged role of these variables, a resolution was introduced into the United States House of Representatives in 2005 that promoted mercury-free childhood vaccinations (H.R. 881, 2005). Moreover, there continues to be speculation that the phenomenal increase in cases of autism spectrum disorders is the result of unknown environmental factors. Accordingly, speculation and scientific work continue to focus on identifying these purported causal influences and variables.

Comorbidity

Comorbidity refers to an individual's increased risk of developing illnesses and related disorders, in addition to his or her primary disorder. As with many other elements of high-functioning autism and Asperger syndrome, the complete puzzle of whether or not individuals with one of these disabilities experience an increased vulnerability for other mental and emotional/behavioral disorders remains unsolved. Even so, there are strong indications that there is a link between Asperger syndrome and high-functioning autism and obsessive-compulsive disorder, depression, bipolar disorder, Tourette syndrome, affective disorders, attention-deficit/ hyperactivity disorder, and psychosis (American Psychiatric Association, 2000; Volkmar & Klin, 2000).

Prognosis and Outlook

Asperger (1944) opined that most persons diagnosed with Asperger syndrome would experience positive life outcomes based on gainful use of their special interests and unique perspectives. However, he became more guarded in this prognosis in the latter stages of his career. Currently, relatively little is known about the prognosis for persons with AS/HFA. Nevertheless, there is every reason to believe that many children and youth with these conditions will be able to lead relatively normal lives. Gillberg (1992) has voiced perhaps the most optimistic outlook, noting that "oddities of social style, communication and interests are likely to remain, but the majority of this group hold down jobs and it seems that a large proportion get married and have children" (p. 833). Others have been more guarded about the anticipated course for individuals with AS/HFA (Lord & Venter, 1992; Myles, Simpson, & Becker, 1995). They have observed that the long-term prognosis for such individuals is difficult to determine due to myriad social, symptom, severity, intervention, educational, and other factors associated with the disorder. Reflecting this position, the DSM-IV-TR (2000) notes that "Asperger Disorder is a continuous and lifelong disorder" (p. 82) but that "the prognosis appears significantly better than in Autistic Disorder, as follow-up studies suggest that, as adults, many individuals are capable of gainful employment and personal self-sufficiency" (p. 82).

In spite of general agreement that the social, communication, and other characteristics associated with high-functioning autism and Asperger syndrome comprise a significant disability, there is also recognition that with appropriate education, treatment, and support, many of these individuals can lead relatively normal and independent lives (Simpson & Myles, 2008). Underscoring this need for appropriate treatment, Safran (2001) warned that "without appropriate educational supports, students [with Asperger syndrome] may be left to fend for themselves in a world where social cues hold little meaning, [and] where repeated failures in interpersonal relationships create anxiety and social rejection" (p. 154).

Case Examples

The following two case examples illustrate the major characteristics and life experiences of persons identified as having AS/HFA.

 ## Jon

Jon is an 8-year-old boy who lives with his 11-year-old sister and his mother, who is a business education teacher at a high school in their community. Jon and his sister also spend several hours each week with their father and his family.

As a baby, Jon was perceived to be happy, placid, undemanding, and not prone to cry. His parents reported that he was satisfied to lie in his crib for hours and that, although he would acknowledge their presence, he appeared to have little interest in interacting with others or being held. His parents also reported that, unlike his sister, who was assertive in seeking the attention of adults and who talked at an early age, Jon was quiet as a toddler and primarily interested in being by himself, even when around other children. Jon began speaking in single words and short sentences at around 18 months. His parents also noted that he was somewhat delayed, compared to his sister, in walking and developing self-care skills. They were advised by their physician that Jon's delays were mild and thus did not warrant an evaluation. When Jon was 3 to 4 years old, his parents began to be very concerned about his development. They were particularly alarmed that he would wander around their house aimlessly for hours, his head tilted at an odd angle, holding his earlobes between his thumb and index finger while making a high-pitched whining noise. They also reported that he would rhythmically parrot commercials he heard on TV (which he would rarely sit and watch), including one advertisement for a detergent product, a behavior the parents found particularly annoying. Their initial response was to ignore these behaviors, believing that their son was slow in developing and that his peculiar behaviors were satisfying some unknown need and thus should be permitted. However, at the urging of relatives, Jon's parents took him to a child psychiatrist when he was 4. The psychiatrist diagnosed Jon as having pervasive developmental disorder–not otherwise specified and recommended that he attend a specialized preschool for at-risk and delayed children and be reevaluated annually. At a later date, the parents reported that they did not like the psychiatrist's demeanor and thus did not seek reevaluation from him. However, they did enroll Jon in a regular preschool supported by their church. Jon attended this program until he was 6 because his parents thought he was unprepared to begin public school.

Jon's preschool teachers reported that he was compliant, quiet, and placid. He passively participated in most activities and was not considered a behavior problem. He initiated few interactions with peers, although he would respond to peer initiations. At the age of 6, Jon was enrolled in kindergarten at his neighborhood school. Shortly afterward, the parents separated, and they were divorced approximately a year later. The parents reported that the period of separation and divorce was very difficult for their daughter but that Jon appeared to be oblivious to his father's absence.

Jon currently attends a regular second-grade classroom at a neighborhood elementary school. He is eligible for itinerant special education services (his teacher regularly meets with a special education teacher to discuss curriculum adaptations for Jon) and receives weekly 1-hour individualized speech–language services; however, his teacher describes him as an "average" student. His teacher reports that Jon is slow to complete assignments and often appears confused regarding classroom expectations. However, she notes that once he "catches on" to a task, he will obsessively work to complete it. She also notes that he is generally compliant and appears vaguely interested in pleasing her. She also observes that he is extremely orderly in arranging books and other materials in his desk and sometimes appears overwrought when classroom schedule changes occur. For example, a recent rainstorm required that the children complete their recess in the classroom, a change that appeared to be very hard for Jon to comprehend.

Jon typically stands next to his teacher on the playground except when he occasionally obsessively wanders the perimeter of the school grounds. Jon is shy and socially isolated from his peers. He will respond briefly when approached by peers; however, he has yet to be observed initiating contact or joining in any games. Jon tends to be very passive, and, on more than one occasion, he has been bullied by other boys at recess. On these occasions, Jon retreats from the aggressor and stands by his teacher.

Jon's mother reports that his behavior of wandering with his head tilted at an odd angle while holding his earlobes and making high-pitched whining noises has decreased significantly over the past year. However, he sometimes obsessively rubs and flaps his hands when he is agitated or stressed.

Approximately a year ago, Jon was evaluated at a university child guidance clinic. The mother and father were somewhat disturbed by the diagnosis of Asperger syndrome. However, after learning more about the condition, they seemed to be willing to accept their son's disability. They have also voiced a willingness to continue to support their son's continued development.

Terry

Terry is 17 and lives with his mother, father, and younger brother. An older sister attends a nearby state university and lives with the family during the summers. The family is middle class, with both parents holding engineering positions.

Terry was only recently diagnosed with Asperger syndrome by a multidisciplinary evaluation team at a children's hospital. Prior to receiving that diagnosis, Terry had been identified as being learning disabled, "mildly autistic," and schizophrenic and as having attention-deficit/hyperactivity disorder and a developmental expressive language disorder.

Early records reveal that Terry was slightly delayed in starting to walk and in developing expressive language. He spoke using one or two words until about age 3, at which time he almost overnight began speaking in long and complicated sentences. Terry's speech is currently quite pedantic, and other students at his school sometimes call him "professor." However, his conversations are limited to a few set topics, and his overall communication demeanor is marked by an absence of affect and inflection.

Since he was a young child, Terry has maintained an obsessive interest in toilets and related plumbing equipment. His parents reported that when he was as young as 5, he knew the brand name of the toilets in his home, day-care center, father's and mother's businesses, and several of the stores in a nearby shopping center. He also displayed a number of stereotyped repetitive behaviors until he was about 10, including spinning empty 1-liter cola containers and tilting his head and squinting at persons by whom he was standing. He no longer spins cola containers; however, he continues to stare and squint at others with his head tilted.

Terry's family and schoolmates have described him as "odd" since the time he began school. He has never been able to mix with peers, although he daily watches his classmates talk in the hallways between classes. He has occasionally approached classmates; however, his limited repertoire of interests, such as his tendency to describe the plumbing fixtures in the school, has alienated him from his classmates.

According to his parents and teachers, Terry has never had a true friend. In spite of his mother's repeated attempts to arrange relationships with age peers through neighbors and friends and his teachers' development of peer support programs, Terry has remained a loner. Recently, Terry began a program in his special education resource room (where he spends 2 hours daily working on study and social skills) in which general education students participate in social activities with special education students. In this program, Terry is routinely the one with whom the students least want to interact, even though the other special education students have fewer cognitive, language, and academic abilities and skills. When one general education classmate was queried about this circumstance, she responded, "He is such a geek—he gets right in my face and only wants to talk about the sinks in the boys' bathroom."

When asked about his future, Terry responds that he wants to be a plumber (an interest his teachers have recently attempted to cultivate to harness his obsessive interest in plumbing fixtures). He also indicates that he wants to marry and be a member of the community Lion's Club. His parents and siblings worry about Terry's future after he completes school, fearing that he will be unprepared to work or live outside the home.

Concluding Thoughts

Individuals with Asperger syndrome or high-functioning autism are increasingly challenging the resources and capacities of families, schools, and communities. Yet, when provided with appropriate programs and accommodations, these persons routinely experience positive school and postschool outcomes. Understanding individuals with AS/HFA and successfully designing and implementing programs to meet their needs are no routine or easy matters. In spite of these challenges, there is much opportunity for optimism. With suitable supports, these individuals can be expected to succeed and prosper. This process begins with understanding the characteristics and distinctive features of individuals with Asperger syndrome and high-functioning autism.

chapter two

Diagnosis and Assessment of Children and Youth

Broadly speaking, assessment of individuals with Asperger syndrome or high-functioning autism falls within two major categories: diagnostic evaluations and assessment for purposes of programming and instruction. Clinical diagnostic evaluations are most frequently undertaken by professionals such as psychologists, psychiatrists, diagnostic clinical and mental health teams, and so forth. Individuals in these roles typically rely on the diagnostic guidelines of the *Diagnostic and Statistical Manual of Mental Disorders–Fourth Edition, Text Revision* (DSM-IV-TR; American Psychiatric Association, 2000) or an updated version of the DSM. As discussed in Chapter 1, DSM-oriented diagnosticians use the diagnostic template provided for Asperger disorder and the more general diagnostic classification of pervasive developmental disorders to determine whether or not an individual has a high-functioning autism spectrum disorder. As previously noted, the DSM-IV-TR diagnostic criteria for Asperger syndrome include social interaction impairment (e.g., problems in understanding body language and facial expression, difficulty in relating and interacting with others) and stereotypical and restricted patterns of interest and behavior (e.g., abnormal and limited interests, stereotypical behaviors). Relative to Asperger disorder, the DSM also includes caveats that describe an absence of significant language, self-help, and cognitive delays; environmental curiosity deficits; and significant occupational or social impairment.

A DSM diagnostic determination is an important first step leading to services and supports for persons with high-functioning autism or Asperger syndrome. Yet, as important as it is, this process is only a preliminary step. Without subsequent work, a DSM diagnosis will likely have limited utility. Accordingly, additional diagnostic, assessment, and evaluation information beyond an initial diagnostic decision and classification is needed to plan a course of action and to identify and apply appropriate interventions and related resources and services for persons affected by AS/HFA.

It is also important to note that a clinical diagnosis of Asperger disorder does not automatically qualify a student for educational supports and services. The Individuals With Disabilities Education Act (IDEA 1990), subsequently reauthorized in 2004 as the Individuals With Disabilities Education Improvement Act, is the landmark federal law that ensures that all children and youths with disabilities have the right to a free and appropriate public education. IDEA identifies 13 categories of disabilities; each category comes with a definition that a student must meet in order to qualify for services under that exceptionality classification. There is no IDEA category for Asperger disorder or Asperger syndrome. Thus, if a student with Asperger disorder is to receive services under IDEA as an individual with a disability, he or she must qualify under another disability classification. The most closely related IDEA classification to Asperger disorder is autism, although other classifications under IDEA may also be used to make a student with Asperger disorder eligible for educational services.

According to IDEA, students with autism must have characteristics that meet the following definition:

> A developmental disability significantly affecting verbal and non-verbal communication and social interaction, usually evident before age 3, that adversely affects a child's educational performance. Other characteristics often associated with autism are engagement in repetitive activities and stereotyped movement, resistance to environmental change or change in daily routines, and unusual sensory experiences. (IDEA, 2004, as cited in Institute of Education Sciences, 2009)

The differing clinical and educational classification systems are frequently a source of confusion and frustration for parents, families, and professionals (Klin, Sparrow, Marans, Carter, & Volkmar, 2000). It is not uncommon for parents to receive a clinical diagnosis of Asperger disorder for their offspring and yet subsequently find that that determination does not translate into educational services for their child. As a result, even if a child or an adolescent has a DSM diagnosis of Asperger disorder, he or she does not automatically qualify for special education services under IDEA. Those individuals must also be vetted by school personnel using classification guidelines provided under IDEA. School district personnel vary in their interpretation of the IDEA classification most appropriate for serving learners with Asperger syndrome or high-functioning autism. As noted earlier, many school district personnel interpret Asperger syndrome and high-functioning autism as a form of autism, and thus use the IDEA definition listed above. However, some districts may use another classification category, such as learning disability, emotional disturbance, or other health impairment.

Figure 2.1 provides a schematic of the parallel paths that clinical and educational professionals follow in determining whether a child or youth has Asperger syndrome or high-functioning autism. Clinical professionals, for the most part, rely on the DSM diagnostic criteria for Asperger disorder, while educational professionals tend to make their determination of whether a student qualifies for special education services on the basis of IDEA guidelines connected to autism or another disability category of IDEA. In both cases, this determination is vitally important, even though it is only a preliminary step. To be sure, assessment for purposes of program planning and identifying supports must follow both clinical and educational diagnostic evaluations in order for students to receive appropriate services. In almost all cases, the follow-up assessment process, focused on understanding students' needs and on identifying support programs and services, will be the all-important determinant of how successful a child or an adolescent is in his or her school and community.

As displayed in Figure 2.1, assessment and evaluation undertaken for the purpose of identifying a student's unique learning, social, communication, adaptive behavior, and other skill areas is based on both formal and informal assessment methods. Assessment domains include individuals' intellectual and cognitive functioning and capacity; academic skills and knowledge and learning preferences and styles; language and communication performance and needs; sensory functioning; motor

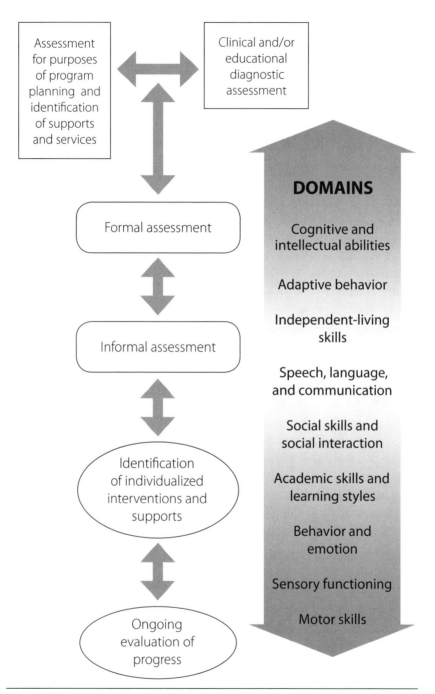

Figure 2.1. Diagnostic and evaluative assessment domains and elements.

skills and challenges; adaptive behavior; independent-living skills; social skills and social interaction abilities and challenges; and behavioral and emotional performance. Relative to Figure 2.1, *formal assessment* generally refers to tests and other norm-referenced measures. In contrast, *informal assessment* includes information and data generated from (a) interviews, (b) review of records and other documents that speak to individuals' unique learning and behavioral characteristics and needs, (c) observations of students, (d) functional behavior assessments and analyses, (e) curriculum-based assessments, (f) portfolio assessments, and (g) informal learning trait assessments.

Figure 2.1 also illustrates the crucial and pivotal role of selecting individualized interventions and supports based on an analysis of formal and informal assessment information. Ongoing systematic evaluation of progress and the utility and outcomes and progress associated with various treatments, interventions, and supports ensures that steps taken to support individuals with Asperger disorder or high-functioning autism are maximally fruitful.

Formal Assessment Measures

Formal assessment measures are typically norm-referenced and are used for both screening and diagnosis. Data and related information generated via use of norm-referenced measures (e.g., standardized tests) can also be used to plan and then later evaluate individuals' support programs and services (Hagiwara, Cook, & Simpson, 2008).

Norm-referenced assessments are designed to statistically compare the performance of an individual with that of similar persons within a particular norm sample. Accordingly, scores on a norm-referenced test are determined by the distribution of responses or performance for a specified norm group. Children of a specific age, for instance, are compared relative to their reading and math skills, intellectual abilities, and so forth. In order to reliably compare individuals with a norm sample, persons administering standardized tests precisely follow testing guidelines such as the wording of questions, time allowed to respond to test items, order of item presentation, and so forth. Norm-referenced measures often yield both a raw score and a standardized score. A particular student's performance on a test or measure is calculated as a raw score. The raw score is subsequently converted into a standard score that permits comparison of an individual's performance with that of a norm group.

In contrast to formal scales, informal assessments rely on a less standardized and rigid protocol. Informal assessments are designed to understand an individual's performance in a particular area rather than to compare him or her with others. Norm groups are thus not required to analyze a person's performance. Rather, an understanding of an individual's strengths and weaknesses is demonstrated through his or her performance in completing typical educational tasks, responding to day-to-day classroom demands and requirements, and responding to conventional situations. By their very nature, informal assessments are more flexible than are norm-referenced methods, and data are often collected in natural settings (e.g., classrooms and homes) rather than in a testing room or clinical setting. An example of an informal assessment is the daily percentage of correctly answered factual comprehensive questions that follow a daily reading assignment. In such a case, a student's teacher records and monitors a pupil's reading comprehension performance over a period of time, albeit without concern as to how the student's performance compares to that of his or her classmates.

Several commonly used norm-referenced tests for individuals with high-functioning autism or Asperger syndrome and/or for individuals suspected of having characteristics similar to those of individuals with these conditions are discussed in the following sections. The tests include (a) diagnostic measures; (b) intellectual, academic, and related achievement tests; (c) tests of adaptive behavior, emotional/behavioral performance, and social skills; (d) neurologically focused measures, such as sensory scales; and (e) speech, language, and communication assessment measures.

Diagnostic Measures

As noted earlier, physicians and psychologists are most often the clinical professionals who make a diagnosis of high-functioning autism or Asperger syndrome (of course, school personnel may also be involved in diagnostic evaluations). Along with application of diagnostic guidelines for Asperger disorder and other pervasive developmental disorders as described in the *Diagnostic and Statistical Manual of Mental Disorders–*

Fourth Edition, Text Revision (2000), these professionals also regularly use diagnostic and screening measures. Two of the most widely used of these scales are the *Asperger Syndrome Diagnostic Scale* (ASDS; Myles, Bock, & Simpson, 2000) and the *Gilliam Asperger Disorder Scale* (GADS; Gilliam, 2001).

The ASDS is a 50-item paper-and-pencil scale that was normed on 227 individuals with Asperger syndrome, attention-deficit/hyperactivity disorder (ADHD), autism spectrum disorders, learning disabilities, and emotional/behavioral disorders. The ASDS can typically be completed in 10 to 15 minutes by any adult who is very familiar with the person being evaluated (i.e., parents, family members, teachers, and so forth). The ASDS has five subscales: (a) language, (b) social, (c) maladaptive behavior, (d) cognitive functioning, and (e) sensory-motor. Respondents (e.g., parents, teachers, or others familiar with the child) indicate the presence or absence of characteristics of the person being evaluated in each of these five areas. Based on their responses, a standard score is derived that indicates the probability that the child or youth has Asperger syndrome. The ASDS scale also differentiates Asperger disorder from ADHD, autism, learning disabilities, and emotional/behavioral disorders.

The GADS was normed on 371 individuals and is designed to differentially distinguish children and youth ages 3 to 22 who have Asperger syndrome from those with other forms of autism-related disabilities and emotional/behavioral disorders. The GADS is built on 32 items that describe observable and measurable behaviors. These behaviors are divided into four subscales: (a) social interaction, (b) restricted patterns of behavior, (c) cognitive patterns, and (d) pragmatic skills. Designed to be completed by parents and professionals, this instrument provides standard scores and percentile ranks to determine the likelihood that an individual has Asperger syndrome. Individuals are able to quickly complete the GADS in approximately 5 to 10 minutes.

Another diagnostic tool appropriate for use with individuals with high-functioning autism or Asperger disorder is the *Autism Diagnostic Interview–Revised* (ADI-R; Couteur, Lord, & Rutter, 2003). The ADI-R uses a standardized, semistructured clinical interview format that focuses on (a) reciprocal social interaction; (b) language and communication; and (c) stereotyped, restricted, and repetitive interests and behaviors. The ADI-R interview generates scores in each of these content areas. A classification of autism is given when scores in all three domains meet or exceed specified cutoff scores. The ADI-R is highly respected; however, it requires significant training to administer and score.

Intellectual, Academic, and Related Achievement Tests

Based on their typically normal cognitive and language capabilities, the vast majority of individuals being assessed for high-functioning autism disorder or Asperger disorder are able to take intelligence and academic tests generally used to evaluate other students suspected of having problems such as learning disabilities and similar high-incidence special needs and disabilities. The *Wechsler Intelligence Scale for Children–Third Edition* (WISC-III; Wechsler, 1991), the *Wechsler Preschool and Primary Scale of Intelligence–Revised* (WPPSI-R; Wechsler, 1989), the *Kauffman Assessment Battery for Children* (K-ABC; Kauffman & Kauffman, 2002), the *Stanford–Binet Intelligence Scale–Fourth Edition* (Thorndike, Hagen, & Sattler, 1985), and the *Stanford-Binet Intelligence Scale–Fifth Edition* (Roid, 2003) are widely used to assess the intelligence and cognitive abilities of persons suspected of having characteristics consistent with AS/HFA. It is important to note that no students with Asperger syndrome were specifically identified in the norm groups for these tests. Nonetheless, these widely used tests yield standardized scores that make it possible to compare the performance of persons with AS/HFA with the test profiles of others.

Because learners with AS/HFA typically experience school difficulties, they are evaluated using a variety of academic scales. There are multiple instruments for assessing learners' academic skills; hence, reading, math, writing, oral language, and other skill areas connected to academic performance may be targeted as a part of an assessment of children and youth for Asperger disorder. Commonly used norm-referenced academic achievement scales include general achievement tests such as the *Peabody Individual Achievement Test* (PIAT; Markwardt, 1998), the *Woodcock-Johnson III Tests of Achievement* (WJ; Woodcock, McGrew, & Mather, 2001), and the *Wechsler Individual Achievement Test* (WIAT; Wechsler, 2002). Each of these tests is a norm-referenced measure with relatively strong psychometric properties. These measures have the capacity to address relevant academic areas such as reading, mathematics, spelling, and language skills. These measures also have the capacity to effectively assist in diagnosing and supporting intervention plans and programs. Tests that focus on particular areas—especially reading, math, written language, and oral language—are also available. These more narrowly focused scales yield specific information that can be used to design instructional programs. For example, the *Woodcock Reading Mastery Tests–Revised* (Woodcock, 1998) reveals students' needs in the areas of word identification, word attack skills, word comprehension, and passage comprehension. Similarly, scales specific to academic areas—such as the *KeyMath* scale (Connolly, 2007), the *Test of Written Language* (Hammill & Larsen, 1996), and the *Test of Early Language Development* (Hresko, Reid, & Hammill, 1999)—respectively provide information in the areas of math, written language, and oral language.

Tests of Adaptive Behavior and Social Skills

Behavioral and social skills are common deficits for students with AS/HFA (American Psychiatric Association, 2000; Wing, 1991; World Health Organization, 2007). Thus, it is important to assess these areas thoroughly. To be sure, if a child does not have behavioral or social deficits, excesses, or other problems, it is unlikely that he or she will be diagnosed with AS/HFA.

Several basic strategies are used to assess the behavior and social skills of students with AS/HFA, including a number of standardized tests. Additionally, a variety of informal measures and methods are used to assess students' social and behavior needs, including reviews and analyses of clinical and school records and documents, interviews of individuals suspected of having AS/HFA and of persons associated with them, direct observations, and nonstandardized scales and tests for assessing students' emotional and social skills.

Aside from the previously discussed *Asperger Syndrome Diagnostic Scale* (ASDS; Myles et al., 2000) and the *Gilliam Asperger Disorder Scale* (GADS; Gilliam, 2001), tests and scales designed to assess behavioral, social, and adaptive behavior skills, deficits, and needs are not exclusively designed for and normed on children and youth with AS/HFA. Yet these instruments are widely used; and when applied by professionals who are knowledgeable of children and youth with AS/HFA and related exceptionalities, they can produce valuable information and assist in productive planning.

The number of available behavioral and social assessment measures far exceeds the capacity for discussion in this chapter. Accordingly, only a few of these measures are discussed.

One potentially productive source of emotional and behavioral information is the *Behavior Assessment System for Children* (BASC; Reynolds & Kamphaus, 1992). The BASC includes a Parent Rating Scale, Teacher Rating Scale, and Student Self-Report. The instrument is designed to examine a variety of areas, including (a) hyperactivity, (b) conduct problems, (c) aggression, (d) anxiety, (e) depression, (f) withdrawal, (g) attention problems, (h) adaptability, (i) leadership, and (j) social skills. The BASC has been shown to be useful in identifying areas of concern relevant to students with Asperger syndrome and as an effective aid in designing treatment plans for these students (Barnhill, Hagiwara, Myles, Simpson, et al., 2000).

Another instrument commonly used to assess the behavioral and social skills of children with AS/HFA is the *Vineland Adaptive Behavior Scales* (VABS; Sparrow, Balla, & Cicchetti, 1984). There are three independent forms of the VABS. Two of the forms, the Expanded Form and the Survey Form, are administered by interviewing the student's primary caregiver. The third form is the Classroom Edition, which is conducted with a teacher. All three forms assess the domains of communication, daily living, socialization, and motor skills. The Expanded Form and the Survey Form also assess a maladaptive behavior domain.

The *Behavior Rating Profile* (BRP; Brown & Hammill, 1990) is another rating scale that allows for a multifaceted and comprehensive view of children via independent input from educators, parents/family members, and students themselves. Peers of students undergoing assessment also provide input via a sociometric element of the BRP instrument. While the BRP is most notable as a measure for children and youth with emotional/behavioral disorders, it also can have a role in assessment and planning relative to students with AS/HFA.

A widely used and potentially valuable source of social skills information is the *Social Skills Improvement System* (SSIS; Gresham & Elliott, 2008). The SSIS has three age-related versions to assess preschool-age children (ages 3-0 to 4-11), elementary-age pupils (Grades 3 to 6), and a secondary age measure to assess students (Grades 7 to 12). The preschool SSIS measure includes a teacher and parent scale; the elementary version of the SSIS accommodates input from teachers, parents, and students in

Grades 3 to 6 themselves. The secondary measure has rating scale measures for teachers, parents, and students. Across the age levels, parents who complete the SSIS focus on rating behavior descriptors relative to their own children within the domains of problem behaviors and social skills. In addition to problem behaviors and social skills, teachers also evaluate students' academic competence. Students themselves evaluate only their social skills. The SSIS is a particularly important source of information because of its focus on social skills (a pivotal and salient element of AS/HFA) and its capacity to connect assessment findings and instruction and related intervention strategies.

Another standardized test for assessing students' social skills is the *Social Responsiveness Scale* (SRS; Constantino, 2009). The SRS, composed of 65 items, is designed to evaluate the severity of autism-related symptoms within naturally occurring social situations and settings. It can be completed by parents and teachers in a relatively brief period of time. The SRS measures various aspects of social behavior within the following domains: (a) Receptive, (b) Cognitive, (c) Expressive, and (d) Motivational aspects of social behavior, as well as (e) Autistic Preoccupations. The SRS is particularly strong in the area of designing and evaluating treatments and interventions. Psychometric properties of the SRS are generally solid.

Sensory Measures

Many children and youth with high-functioning autism, Asperger syndrome, or autism-related disabilities experience sensory problems in basic sensory areas, including tactile, vestibular, proprioception, visual, auditory, gustatory, and olfactory (Dunn, 2008). Accordingly, these areas should be a part of a comprehensive assessment.

The *Sensory Profile* (Dunn, 1999) is a 125-item questionnaire that permits parents to describe children's responses to sensory events. The scale is generally well respected and widely used to assess sensory factors, including the impact of sensory problems on emotions and behavior. The *Sensory Profile* scale is standardized, and items are organized by sensory-system and behavior. This measure has diagnostic utility; however, the most notable strengths of the *Sensory Profile* are in providing explanations for sensory-driven behaviors and offering directions for intervention.

Speech, Language, and Communication

Many children and youth diagnosed with AS/HFA have relatively intact speech and language, and some children with these conditions are very verbal. Nevertheless, because communication deficits, particularly pragmatic and related social-communication problems, are underlying elements of AS/HFA, it is essential that this domain be carefully and fully evaluated.

Because of the nature of AS/HFA, speech, language, and communication assessments must not be limited to evaluations of word pronunciation, vocabulary, sentence structure, and grammar (Ogletree, 2008). Rather, communication and language assessments will frequently focus on pragmatics (the social context of language) and semantics (word meaning and communication via use of words). Without a doubt, understanding a child with AS/HFA relative to his or her ability to understand and apply the social rules of speech, language, and communication is essential. For instance, understanding that a child does not know how close to stand to a peer when talking or that a youth fails to comprehend that his peers will likely not share his strong interest in the idiosyncratic topic of vacuum cleaners is essential in understanding individual needs and directing intervention programs. Insights derived from speech and language assessments can also be used to proactively respond to academic challenges. For example, understanding that a child has difficulty comprehending nonliteral language, the social protocol of small-group classroom activities, abstract information and themes, verbal problem solving and nonverbal communication is crucial to planning an effective program.

There are a variety of norm-referenced speech and language assessment measures that can assist in evaluating and planning for students. While not specifically and exclusively designed for individuals with AS/HFA, these measures are nevertheless applicable and appropriate. Included among the measures are the following: *Clinical Evaluation of Language Fundamentals–Third Edition* (Semel, Wiig, & Secord, 1995); *Comprehensive Receptive and Expressive Vocabulary Test* (Wallace & Hammill, 1994); *Test of Language Competence–Expanded Edition* (Wiig & Secord, 1989); *Test of Pragmatic Language* (Phelps-Terasaki & Phelps-Gunn, 1992); *Test of Problem Solving–Elementary, Revised* (Zachman, Huisingh, Barrett, Orman, & LoGiudice, 1994); and *Test of Problem Solving–Adolescent* (Zachman, Barrett, Huisingh, Orman, & Blagden, 1991).

Informal Assessment

As illustrated in Figure 2.1, an assessment of a child or youth suspected of having high-functioning autism, Asperger disorder, or autism spectrum disorders (ASDs) needs to include informal assessment information and data. Informal assessment findings do not rely on a reference group against which a particular student's performance is compared. Rather, informal information and data are used to estimate functioning of individual children and youth, to identify and describe skills and targets for intervention, and to assess progress. These nonstandardized methods allow for evaluation of a learner's performance relative to a school's curriculum and the demands of a particular program or placement. Data and findings obtained through informal assessment are particularly useful in setting goals, identifying instructional strategies, and measuring outcome behaviors. Informal assessment procedures target what individual students know and learn and how they behave within natural settings without primary regard for how their functioning translates into comparisons with like-age individuals. Informal assessment data are collected in a variety of settings, including schools, community settings, homes, and clinical testing facilities.

The physical environment, the manner in which an assessment task is presented, a child's level of interest, and past learning experience can all influence how well an individual with Asperger disorder or ASD behaves, responds, and performs on a test. Accordingly, informal assessment methods often have advantages over standardized options because they do not adhere to rigid time constraints or uniform procedures. As a result, students with AS/HFA can approach problem solving in traditional or nontraditional ways. Because no time limit is specified, the examiner can start and progress as he or she becomes familiar with the student, allowing time to build rapport (Myles et al., 2000).

Designing an assessment to elicit certain behaviors can also provide information needed to develop a program or gain insight about a student. For example, is the student able to ask for help or indicate that he or she would like to take a break from the test? If not, how does the student communicate needs? Understanding a student's functioning level can lead to an understanding of how the student approaches tasks and indicates readiness skills in academics or social development. This information can aid in establishing realistic goals that are crucial for encouraging learning and building success. Setting multiple goals—those that the student can readily accomplish; those that are more difficult; and those that are challenging, yet motivating—helps to create a best-practice intervention program. Throughout the assessment process, the examiner should informally observe and identify which tasks are easy or difficult for the student and note which activities, materials, and methods receive the most positive response. Behavioral responses should also be observed relative to time of occurrence and triggers that may provoke negative and positive patterns of behavior.

Although it can be used as part of an initial full evaluation, informal assessment is generally best suited for data collection that is ongoing and dynamic. Revising Individualized Education Program (IEP) objectives, selecting instruction and response formats, modifying assignments, setting time frames for performance, and developing individualized curricula can all be enhanced by using informal assessment data.

Informal Assessment Tools and Methods

With the exception of offering standardized initial diagnostic information, informal assessment measures focus on the same domains that formal assessment tools do. Tools for gathering informal assessment information and data include (a) a review of records and related documents, (b) interviews, (c) observations of students, (d) curriculum-based assessments, and (e) informal learning and behavioral trait assessments.

Records and Documents Review

School and clinical records are an invaluable source of information about children and youth and provide archival records of school progress and concerns, medical and social records and treatments, family and social information, and a historical account of concerns about children and steps taken to address these concerns.

Among the most potentially useful types of information in students' records is information about developmental history, including behavior problems, aberrant sleeping patterns, developmental delays, social interests, and social quirks; personal likes and dislikes, hobbies, and unique interests; and historical accounts of past school performance, including measures they have employed to deal with school-related problems. Records of clinical assessments (e.g., by psychologists or speech–language pathologists), as well as nonschool treatments and interventions designed to respond to social, behavioral, and developmental problems, are also a potentially rich source of information.

Interviews

Informal interviews with stakeholders associated with children and youth with AS/HFA (including teachers; related service staff and other educators; parents; clinical professionals; and students, themselves) can also be valuable sources of information and potential keys to successful treatment and support. These interviews often focus on the same areas noted for record reviews (i.e., stakeholders' thoughts and information about a pupil's developmental history; school and nonschool progress and concerns; medical, behavioral, and social concerns and treatments; and family and sociological information that may lend insight into the world and experiences of the student). Goals and expectations for a child held by educators, parents, and the individual being assessed can also be useful sources of information. Finally, interviews are often particularly useful in permitting professionals to understand the unique elements and qualities of students' families. Examples of useful information that professionals may obtain from parents include the socioeconomic status of the family; the family's living arrangements; ethnic, cultural, and/or religious backgrounds and beliefs of the family that may have an influence on educational planning; languages other than English spoken in the home; and parental child-rearing practices and attitudes.

Observations of Students

Direct observations of students not only are an indispensible source of diagnostic and assessment information but also are among the most reliable and utilitarian of the assessment options available to professionals. Structured observations used to collect quantitative data on a specifically defined behavioral target (e.g., number of times within a daily math class that a student talks out without teacher permission; discussed in detail in Chapter 4), as well as more informal qualitative anecdotal notes (e.g., description of a child's initiations with other students at recess relative to comments about his obsessive interest in ceiling fans), provide factual and reasoned information and data that assist in bringing objectivity and insight into the process of understanding individuals with AS/HFA.

Myles, Constant, Simpson, and Carlson (1989) and others (Hagiwara et al., 2008) noted areas germane to understanding learners with Asperger syndrome or related disabilities that are understood via use of informal observational assessment methods: (a) stimulus overselectivity, (b) motivation, (c) self-stimulatory behaviors, and (d) social interactions with peers and others. Functional behavior assessment and functional behavior analysis, discussed in Chapter 4, make up another basic area of diagnostic and assessment observation.

Stimulus Overselectivity. When a student focuses on a limited number of environmental cues and/or eliminates salient environmental cues, he or she is exhibiting stimulus overselectivity. For example, a child may have a particular preference for red items, and independent of teacher instructions (e.g., "Use your red marker to identify the proper nouns in the word passages"), will always select the red marker to complete all assignments. Another example of stimulus overselectivity is a student who has a strong inclination to select items that are placed on his left side. For instance, when shown word cards with the verbal instruction "Point to the card with the word *exit* on it," the student continually selects the card on the left. Understanding this behavioral pattern is essential to successful educational planning. Moreover, once this common characteristic among students with AS/HFA is understood, it can be better managed by varying the presentation of the task, the arrangement of stimuli, or the manner in which the examiner requests the information or structures the activity.

Motivation. Children and youth identified with AS/HFA are well known for having limited motivation for tasks and activities that fall outside a narrow range of individual and highly idiosyncratic interests. Clearly, limited motivation can be confused with inability to complete a task. Students with Asperger syndrome frequently require structure encouragement and/or external motivation to complete a task. To be sure, understanding an individual's interests and willingness to engage in tasks that may be outside a narrow range of interests—and determining whether a child is unable versus unwilling to perform tasks and engage in certain behaviors—is mandatory for the purposes of educational planning and program implementation. Parents, teachers, caregivers, and the student can often provide information about preferences, as well as reinforcers to mitigate limited motivation. Such information is useful not only as an independent evaluation but also as a recommendation tool that others can use to enhance students' willingness to participate and complete schoolwork.

Self-Stimulatory Behaviors. Children and youth diagnosed with AS/HFA are not primarily notable for engaging in significant patterns of self-stimulatory behavior. Individuals with autism and those with more significant cognitive impairments are far more well known for having such behavioral patterns, including hand flapping, rocking, light filtering, and myriad other forms of self-stimulation. Nevertheless, some students exhibit self-stimulatory behaviors (e.g., spinning objects), and more subtle forms of self-stimulation are common, particularly among younger children and when these individuals are in stressful situations. If these repetitive movements are not interfering with test administration or response, they may be ignored during the assessment. If the self-stimulatory behaviors are disruptive, however, it may be necessary to work with the student to achieve appropriate response behaviors. Regardless, anecdotal records regarding the student's self-stimulatory behaviors should be maintained because they can provide valuable information about the student's frustration levels and coping mechanisms.

Social Interaction Analysis. Social behavior plays a salient and pivotal role in evaluating and planning programs for children and youth with AS/HFA. To be sure, social excesses and deficits are the primary challenge facing these learners; hence, assessment-related observations must consider the manner in which children and youth interact with others.

Relative to observations of students' social behaviors and social interactions is the importance of understanding environmental and contextual cues and factors that may support or act as problem triggers for students. This information is potentially useful both in understanding students and their social behavior and in designing social and other programs and interventions. Included is consideration of the types of peers and adults with whom a student may be most and least apt to interact (age, gender, whether or not the peers are known to the person, and so forth). Another variable is the number of persons an individual may be most comfortable being around. Some students are best able to interact with a single person or a small group; others may be comfortable being around larger numbers of peers. A third area of consideration revolves around the types of social situations and demands that students prefer and dislike and the types of activities for which students appear to have a preference. Knowing, for example, that a child prefers to play board games with a small number of same-gender peers with whom he is familiar—and knowing that he has a particular dislike of large-motor ball games that demand knowledge of game rules—will be particularly important in designing peer social support activities and long-range social goals.

Another observational social consideration is analysis of the types of social and social interaction strengths and weaknesses that students display. Such an analysis ordinarily requires that an individual familiar with the student (e.g., a teacher) observe the learner in a variety of natural social situations. According to Gresham (1998), students have three general types of social skill problems: *social skill acquisition deficits* (lack of knowledge needed to execute a social skill or inability to discriminate the appropriateness of particular social behaviors); *social performance deficits* (failure to perform social skills or social behaviors at suitable levels and in needed situations, in spite of possessing the social skill); and *fluency deficits* (lack of ease and skill in demonstrating and performing a social skill at appropriate times). Understanding the type of social interaction or social skill problems a student presents is important, and intervention program planning will need to be based on such information.

Curriculum-Based Assessments

Curriculum-based measurement (CBM) is a progress-monitoring tool for assessing a student's progress in a variety of academic areas, including math, reading, and spelling (Idol, Nevin, & Paolucci-Whitcomb, 1999). CBM is an ongoing direct-assessment method that assesses learners' skill level and progress during regularly occurring probe intervals throughout the instructional process. In many instances, the assessment will occur during the entire academic year. Thus, unlike norm-referenced tests, CBM relies on students' regular classroom curricula and related materials; it directly assesses and helps teachers determine which skills are developing and which skills require additional attention; and it is not designed to compare students' progress in accordance with a standardized norm.

CBM requires that teachers identify samples of academic material taken from the learner's school curriculum. Using these sample materials, teachers regularly (e.g., two to three times weekly) and briefly (e.g., 2 to 3 minutes) probe the student's learning. CBM learning probes are given under standardized or similar conditions. For instance, a teacher who is conducting a CBM probe for reading recognition will sample from among words the student is using in a particular class, apply similar conditions, and give the student the same directions every time the evaluation occurs. The child's performance on a CBM probe is typically evaluated for speed and accuracy. CBM probes are graphed to give teachers and other stakeholders a visual display of a learner's progress in a particular subject. A trajectory showing a trend line for an end-of-year goal is also created and used to monitor a child's progress toward achieving a desired annual target.

An example of a CBM evaluation program for an elementary-age student diagnosed with Asperger disorder was in the area of reading word identification. The student's teacher used words from his regular classroom reading curriculum to create samples of equivalent assessment materials. These materials were used to assess the student's word identification accuracy and speed during 2-minute probes twice weekly. That is, twice weekly, the classroom teacher or teacher assistant asked the student to read orally for 2 minutes using reading materials from his day-to-day curriculum. The teachers evaluated his performance using the number of correctly read words during the 2-minute samples. As shown in Figure 2.2, his CBM reading word identification probe data were graphed weekly to show his reading progress over the course of the academic year.

Informal Learning and Behavioral Trait Assessments

A student's learning, achievement, and behavior are influenced by a variety of factors, including *environmental conditions* (e.g., noise level and peers) and *internal factors*. Internal factors relate to the unique ways that an individual processes and reacts to stimuli. Assessment of learning and behavioral traits is typically undertaken as an informal process of observations and anecdotal note taking. Analysis of observations leads to inferences regarding learning preferences and behavior patterns related to setting demands and identification of response preferences.

Informal learning and behavior trait assessment offers insight as to how a student may learn, react, and behave across educational settings, educational demands, and educational professionals. These assessments are divided into three basic categories: learning style, behavioral patterns/characteristics, and strategies (Myles et al., 1989). A student's learning style is evaluated by observing his or her *memory skills* (short-term, long-term, meaningful, rote, auditory, visual, kinesthetic/motor, and combination memory skills), *skill acquisition* (simultaneous, sequential, or incidental

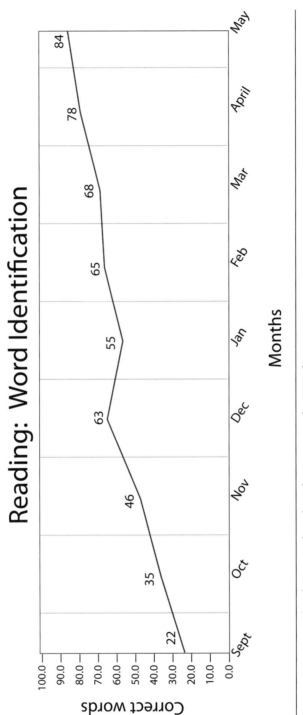

Figure 2.2. Example of a curriculum-based assessment data graph.

learner), *performance rate, generalization skills, independent pacing* or *work habits, stimulus selectivity,* and *presentation and instruction preferences* (auditory, visual, kinesthetic/motor, combination).

Behavioral patterns/characteristic assessments examine a student's *social patterns* (self-concept, peer relationships, and social skills), *task-related behaviors* (motivation, on/off task behavior, independent work habits, and persistence), reactions to *environmental variables* (responses to structure, reinforcement, instruction, distractibility, and stressors), *intra-individual patterns* (echolalia, impulsivity, compulsive behaviors, excessive movement, self-stimulatory behaviors, avoidance behaviors, attention-seeking behavior, flexibility/inflexibility, right or left dominance), and *perseveration.*

Strategy assessment evaluates tactics that a learner uses to respond to academic demands and settings. These strategies include *strategic learner* (innate or learned), *learning preference* (from print, from lecture, from visual aids), *self-verbalization, self-correction, organizational strategies, problem solving* (academic, social, metacognition), *demonstrating competency* (in written work, in oral presentation, on tests), and *memorizing/retrieving information* (words/specific information, conceptual information, relationships). Assessment of a student's learning strategies can also be useful in determining the following: (a) how the student attends and stores information, (b) what level of complexity a student can reach while performing a task, (c) what strategies or techniques a student uses to complete tasks and to solve problems, (d) how novel tasks are approached, (e) how the student solves known problems, (f) how the student organizes information, (g) how the learner applies information to daily functioning, and (h) which behaviors most notably interact with academic requirements and social skills (Myles et al., 1989). Knowledge of strategies can be used to better understand students' preferences for structuring and acquiring information and thus identifying potentially utilitarian ways of teaching students.

Informal Assessment of Academic Skills

Informal academic evaluation of children and youth with AS/HFA includes consideration of three major and essential academic areas: reading, mathematics, and oral and written language. Accurate individualized assessment that encompasses these areas provides basic foundational information required for instructional planning and academic program implementation.

Assessment of academic strengths and weaknesses within the aforementioned areas can be undertaken using commercial tests, a "scope-and-sequence" approach, or evaluation of individual students' skills and knowledge relative to a particular school/school district's curriculum. Commercial items often require little time to administer and often are able to survey a wide range of skills. An example of an informal commercial test is the *BRIGANCE Comprehensive Inventory of Basic Skills II* (Brigance, 2010).

A scope-and-sequence approach involves breaking a skill or concept into its component parts. The first component is taught and practiced until it is mastered. Then the next component is taught, and so on. A scope and sequence can be developed for most academic, functional, behavioral, social, and vocational areas. A scope-and-sequence approach is invaluable for students with Asperger syndrome, especially when they have splinter skills. A student has a splinter skill if he or she can complete a specific step of a task, yet not be able to complete prior or subsequent steps. For example, a student may be able to recite the numbers 1 through 200, yet not be able to understand the concept of one-to-one correspondence. Looking at a math scope and sequence will show where rote counting falls on a continuum of math skills and what skills lie between understanding the concept of one-to-one correspondence and counting numbers up to 200. Consideration should be given to the individual student's learning preferences when selecting a scope-and-sequence approach for assessment or intervention. Students who favor a simultaneous or "big picture" approach do not perform well with a scope-and-sequence approach.

As discussed earlier in this chapter, curriculum-based assessments are based on materials and items drawn from a particular school's curriculum. Students are assessed on skills that are taught in their own school, in the order that they are presented. As previously noted, there are many advantages to using CBM, including enhanced assessment validity and reliability, ease of administration, efficient use of time for conducting assessments, and limited expense. CBM also may have the disadvantage of overemphasizing whether or not students can perform a task rather than how a student approaches the task. The latter, of course, has great instructional implications. As with the scope-and-sequence approach, in curriculum-based assessments, splinter skills and student learning preferences must be considered.

Informal Assessment of Reading

Reading is a complex skill that involves several interrelated skill sets, including word recognition and comprehension. Relative to students with AS/HFA, reading comprehension is a major focus of consideration. To be sure, many students have relatively strong word recognition reading skills (i.e., a number of learners diagnosed with Asperger disorder can correctly decode words and have grade-level sight-word abilities). However, these students' understanding of passages and their ability to relate that understanding to everyday experience may be significantly below grade level. As students progress through the educational system, mechanical reading abilities (i.e., word recognition and word call) become less important, and understanding and generalization of what they read becomes critical. Thus, reading assessment of children and youth must emphasize comprehension, application, and related problem-solving skills.

A composite of specialized reading subareas is key to an individualized and integrated reading assessment plan for each student. Two basic reading levels must be established. First, is the student's independent reading level—that level at which the student can read with 98% to 100% word accuracy and demonstrate comprehension of 90% to 100%. Second, is the student's instructional reading level—that level at which the student can recognize words with at least 95% accuracy and demonstrate comprehension of 75% or higher. These levels should be determined relative to designing oral and silent reading programs.

This information can be gained through a curriculum-based assessment or through a commercial informal reading inventory, such as the *Classroom Reading Inventory* (Silvaroli, 1986), the *Durrell Analysis of Reading Difficulty* (Durrell & Catterson, 1981), or the *Analytical Reading Inventory* (Woods & Moe, 2007).

It is important to select comprehension questions that will evaluate both recognition and recall response levels. Students with AS/HFA may be able to answer general-information questions only understanding the information on a basic level; hence, it is necessary to develop questions that address a variety of comprehension levels. In addition to factual and vocabulary questions (part of most commercial informal reading inventories), inferential and main idea questions must also be included, along with assessment of the ability to predict outcomes, draw conclusions, and distinguish fact from fantasy (Hagiwara et al., 2008).

The ability to sequence visual materials is a prerequisite for more complex comprehension; consequently, any student who has difficulty with passage comprehension may need to be assessed in this area. This ability can be assessed with a series of three or more picture cards (the more cards, the more complex the process) that visually outline the steps of an activity. Commercial sequencing cards can be used; however, if a student has difficulty responding to such materials, the examiner can make an informal series of cards based on a common activity that is familiar to the student (e.g., brushing teeth).

A miscue analysis should be performed on oral reading passages at the student's instructional level. This involves examining the pattern of errors in the passages, emphasizing such qualities as the incorrect word's graphic similarity to the printed word, the occurrence of interclass substitutions (e.g., noun for verb) and intraclass (e.g., noun for noun) substitutions, and the percentage of self-corrections. Such analysis supplements the traditional error marking recommended in many informal reading inventories (i.e., those focusing on differentiating substitutions, omissions, deletions, and repetitions). Miscue analysis may give insight into the student's reading skills as a total process, including use of context, logic cues, word recognition, and analysis (McLoughlin & Lewis, 2008).

The student's listening capacity should also be assessed. This is the level at which students comprehend material read aloud. The examiner reads passages, starting one grade level above a student's established instructional reading level and continuing until a student demonstrates less than 75% comprehension.

The student's contextual analysis strengths and weaknesses may be determined by using a cloze procedure. This involves taking a reading passage of approximately 250 words at the student's instructional level and systematically deleting every seventh or ninth word. The first and last sentences of the passage remain intact. The student then silently reads the passage, filling in the blanks based on the context. Intraclass substitutions that make sense in context should be accepted as correct. Analysis focuses on the types of cues (e.g., surrounding words, pictures, bold or italic print, or the general story plot) used to interpret the material (Sundbye, 2001).

The student's response to certain teaching techniques, such as the language experience approach or morphographic or multisensory reading, can also be examined as a part of the assessment process. For example, to analyze the effectiveness of the language experience approach, the student creates a story and dictates it to the examiner. Different stimuli (e.g., pictures, open-ended sentences, and activities) can be used for story development. The examiner then selects words from the story, writes them on flash cards, and practices with the student. Finally, the complete story is read, first in a choral format (examiner and student reading aloud simultaneously) and then independently by the student. The examiner compares the student's reading abilities using the self-generated stories and published reading materials.

Comprehension is often the major assessment focus for students with AS/HFA. Nonetheless, for some students with word recognition problems, a phonics measure can be used to determine specific phonetic components students use in word analysis (decoding). Many commercial phonics measures are based on the formation of nonsense words, thus isolating consonants, vowels, blends, digraphs, and diphthongs. Two factors must be considered when determining the need to administer a phonics measure. First, for students in mainstream educational settings, phonics training traditionally ends during the early elementary years. Accordingly, phonics instruction is usually recommended only in cases where a student has already acquired and demonstrated the majority of basic phonics skills, thus allowing for training in specific skill areas. The second factor relates to the application of phonetic skills in reading. Some students may exhibit an overreliance on phonics, without regard to non–rule-based pronunciations or contextual clues (Sundbye, 2001). Hence, this area of reading assessment may need to be evaluated for these students.

Word recognition is assessed by determining the student's sight-word vocabulary. This may take several directions, depending on the student's age and reading skills. Core word lists such as those by Dolch (1955) or Fry (1980) can be used to identify words students should know by sight by grade level. These lists are particularly useful with younger students who have limited reading vocabularies or who are in inclusive environments. For older students who exhibit limited vocabulary, sight-word lists stressing survival words (e.g., Brigance, 2010) should be included in the assessment package. Table 2.1 provides an overview of the diagnostic sequence in reading.

Informal Assessment of Mathematics

Mathematics is a hierarchical subject, and math skills are typically learned in a sequential fashion. Thus, learning skills that are more advanced is dependent on acquisition and mastery of more basic skills. Accordingly, learners with AS/HFA, as is the case with other students, must first acquire basic skills in order to progress in a math curriculum.

Some students may have computation skills without having other corresponding prerequisite readiness skills. For example, a student with splinter skills (e.g., computation skills in the absence of numerical understanding) has not mastered a particular skill and will have difficulty moving forward in a curriculum. Instead, the student has probably acquired a rote skill. The skill has limited utility and likely has restricted functional value since it cannot be applied to any simulated or real-life setting. Thus, mathematics assessment for students should be conducted in a fashion that accentuates attention to basic concepts, computation skills, and problem-solving and skill-application abilities.

According to Piaget (1959) and Mercer (1996), basic math skills include the following:

- *Classification*—the ability to judge similarities and differences by color, shape, size, or function
- *Number conservation*—the ability to deduce that amounts remain the same even when appearances change (e.g., the amount of water in two different containers is equal)
- *Ordering and seriation*—the ability to arrange items without considering the quantitative relationship between them or to arrange items based on a change in a property (e.g., arranging items of various lengths from shortest to longest)
- *One-to-one correspondence*—the ability to understand that one object in a set is the same number as one object in another set, regardless of characteristics (e.g., six apples represent the same quantity as six buttons)

Table 2.1
Diagnostic Sequence in Reading

Sequence for Older Elementary Children

    A. Informal reading inventory (silent and oral)

        1. Curriculum-based

        2. Commercial

    B. Miscue analysis

    C. Levels of comprehension (recognition and recall)

        1. Factual

        2. Inferential

        3. Main idea

        4. Predicting outcomes

        5. Drawing conclusions

        6. Fact versus fantasy

        7. Vocabulary

        8. Sequencing

    D. Listening capacity

    E. Cloze procedures

    F. Fluency and rate

Sequence for Younger Elementary Children

    A. Informal reading inventory (silent and oral)

        1. Curriculum-based

        2. Commercial

    B. Miscue analysis

    C. Levels of comprehension (recognition and recall)

        1. Factual

        2. Inferential

        3. Main idea

        4. Predicting outcomes

        5. Drawing conclusions

        6. Fact versus fantasy

        7. Vocabulary

        8. Sequencing

    D. Listening capacity

(continues)

Table 2.1 *(continued)*

Sequence for Younger Elementary Children *(continued)*

    E. Phonics (in isolation and within words)

    F. Sight words (flash and analysis)

    G. Alphabet recognition (particulary if low phonics or sight words)

    H. Language experience

        1. Reads own written stories

        2. Reads own words on flash cards

        3. Comprehends own stories (recognition and recall)

    I. Sequencing of visual material and relating story

Computation involves arithmetic operations and calculations related to addition, subtraction, multiplication, and division. As with other academic skill areas, basic mathematics may be a strength for some students with AS/HFA. That is, these students may be able to answer problems correctly without understanding the process underlying the calculation and math operation. Because this is a foundational matter, it is essential to understand a student's conceptual understanding of various basic math processes. A test that probes comprehension of the proper algorithm, or computational method, is the *Clinical Math Interview* (CMI; Skrtic, Kvam, & Beals, 1983). After working designated problems, a student with Asperger syndrome explains in an interview format how problems were solved. CMI administration reveals (a) a student's current level of arithmetic functioning, (b) how a student works a problem, and (c) whether a student is dependent on incorrect algorithms. Analysis of computation errors can reveal information about a student's mathematical skills in four categories (Roberts, 1968):

- *Wrong operation*—The student performs an operation other than the one that is required to solve the problem.
- *Computational error*—The student applies the correct operation, but the response is based on errors in recalling number facts.
- *Defective algorithm*—The student applies the correct operation but makes errors other than fact.
- *Random response*—The student's response shows no discernible relationship to the problem.

Problem solving is the ability to use computational skills meaningfully to solve word or story problems. Problem solving is dependent on knowledge and application of basic concepts, computation, and generalization. Obviously, other skills, such as reading and written language, may also be involved. Problem-solving assessment must consider a student's ability to (a) identify important features in a problem-solving situation, (b) translate a verbal sentence into a mathematical sentence, and (c) calculate a solution (Shure, 1992). Assessment should reveal a student's competence at each level of problem solving. Learners with AS/HFA commonly demonstrate difficulty with nonrote skills, such as identifying important problem-solving features and translating a verbal sentence into a mathematical sentence.

Functional math skills are those involved in day-to-day living activities; hence, they are essential for all students, including those diagnosed with AS/HFA. Functional skills include calculations involving time, money, measurement, and geometry. These are particularly important to students with high-functioning autism because they are basic life skills. Thus, assessment of these skills is extremely important. Table 2.2 provides an overview of the diagnostic sequence in assessment of mathematics.

Informal Assessment of Oral and Written Language

By definition, students with AS/HFA often have a variety of unique communication and language issues and characteristics, including perseveration, idiosyncratic language, socially peculiar and atypical word use, and so forth. Accordingly, assessment of oral and written language skills is a basic component of an evaluation of students with Asperger disorder. Speech–language pathologists are often involved in these assessments, and these specialists often take a leadership role in the process. At the same time, however, teachers, school psychologists, and other diagnosticians should be involved because many of the oral and written language questions most germane to learners with Asperger disorder are associated with basic classroom-related skills, activities, and issues. In this connection, a particular focus of attention will be students' use of oral language relative to social interactions and communication using written language skills.

Although language acquisition follows a developmental sequence, it is not as clearly hierarchical as math is and thus requires a different assessment approach. Because the ability to communicate is partially

Table 2.2
Diagnostic Sequence in Mathematics

Sequence for Older Elementary Children

  A. Overview of skills
    1. Number/notation
    2. Mathematical language
    3. Ordinality
    4. Place value
    5. Geometric concepts
    6. Fractions
    7. Measurement
    8. Mathematical applications
    9. Word problems
    10. Estimation
    11. Graphing
  B. Probes based on difficulties with overview skills
  C. Informal math inventory
  D. Error pattern analysis
  E. Clinical math interview

Sequence for Younger Elementary Children

  A. Overview of skills based on Piaget's (1959) levels (concrete, semiconcrete, abstract)
    1. Numeration
    2. Mathematical language
    3. Measurement
    4. Place value
    5. One-to-one correspondence
    6. Geometry
    7. Computation
    8. Fractions
    9. Conservation of sets
    10. Graphing
  B. Probes based on difficulties with overview skills
  C. Word problems presented orally
  D. Math facts presentation (flash card fact recognition and analysis)

dependent on the environment, it is necessary to examine a student's language in a variety of settings and conditions.

Normally developing and achieving students typically give teachers numerous opportunities to collect and analyze spontaneous language samples within natural settings. Students tell stories, converse on the playground, and engage in role playing. These samples can be tape-recorded for subsequent transcription and analysis. Students with AS/HFA, on the other hand, may need additional encouragement, stimulus, or preplanning to produce stories or conversations for analysis. For example, a special occasion, such as a field trip or a movie, may be used as a topic of discussion. Also, with some students with Asperger syndrome, a picture or topic, especially related to a special interest, may be used to produce a sample.

Written language samples can be elicited in much the same way; that is, by asking a student to tell a story in writing, with or without prompts. However, examiners must keep in mind the motor skills of a student with AS/HFA. If the student has motor problems (which are common), written samples may be gathered based on handwritten writings and those generated on a computer.

Oral and written language samples can be analyzed and compared on a number of variables. Because oral language generally precedes written language, it is reasonable to expect that most students' oral samples will be more complex than their written work. Thus, oral abilities are most often analyzed to determine initial instructional priorities and to group students for language instruction. If teachers wish to compare a student's language development to that of his or her peers, parallel samples may need to be taken from an average student of the same age and gender. Many of the elements considered in language assessment are subjective; therefore, care must be taken to consider language samples in the context of a student's environment, cultural background, and so forth. As with any student, language differences due to ethnicity, culture, native language, or background must not be confused with language problems.

An initial area of language assessment is communicative content, which focuses on answering the following questions: What type of story did the student relate? Did it have a beginning, a middle, and an end? Was it coherent? Was it interesting and creative? Of course, assessment of communicative content is subjective, albeit a basic element of learning and communication, and hence a necessary element of the assessment process.

Complexity of language should also be considered. Such assessment examines the proportion of simple, compound, and complex sentences. In written language, this analysis focuses on what a student intended rather than on punctuation, for instance. Does the student use only one sentence type or demonstrate ability to use a variety of simple and complex forms? Is there a difference between oral and written sentence length and complexity? Does the student use an effective descriptive vocabulary? Does the student use colorful adjectives and phrases or choose simple words that can be correctly applied and spelled with confidence? Does the student possess a vocabulary adequate to communicate his or her intent?

Grammar is a third area for language analysis. It includes most of the features of language generally taught in English classes, including subject–verb agreement; pronoun usage; and correct usage of word endings to indicate verb tense, plurals, and possessives. As in other areas of assessment, it is important to distinguish between environmental or cultural differences in language and the student's lack of a specific language skill.

Transcription skills are an additional written language consideration. Specifically, this includes appropriate use of capital letters, punctuation, spelling, and handwriting. Spelling errors are analyzed as to type, that is, whether misspelling of words is rule based (i.e., caused by overreliance on rules, such as "*i* before *e* except after *c*"), predictable, or unpredictable.

Additional issues related to understanding language in context may need to be examined in students with language-related learning problems. Some students with Asperger syndrome are extremely literal and inflexible in their use and understanding of language. These individuals may have a limited or single understanding of the meaning of a word. Others have not developed a schema or framework that enables them to relate new words to words already in their vocabulary. A simple way to assess these problems is to devise activities that assess knowledge of common idioms or proverbs. For instance, ask the student to explain "Don't cry over spilt milk"; "A bird in the hand is worth two in the bush"; "A chip on your shoulder"; or "A slap on the wrist."

A final language area to examine is the student's knowledge of school vocabulary, that is, those words that frequently appear in oral and written directions or that are necessary to understand particular subject matter (e.g., in math, *calculate, solve, determine*). If a student cannot understand the vocabulary used to convey instructions or deliver content, appropriate responses cannot be expected. Table 2.3 provides an overview of the diagnostic sequence in oral and written language.

Student Learning Traits

A student's achievement is influenced by a variety of factors. External factors, such as the bus ride to school or where the student's desk is located in the classroom, may have an impact that is often easy to recognize and observe. Internal factors, such as how students perceive or receive information, how they process and store concepts, and how they apply these data to their daily lives, are more elusive; however, this type of variable must be measured subjectively, through direct observation of the student, examination of classroom materials and setting demands, and pinpointing of instructional and response preferences. These indicators of how children learn are called *student learning traits*.

According to Myles et al. (1989), student learning traits offer insight into how students gain information across academic areas. For example, a student may respond to only meaningful stimuli and not to rote stimuli. Some students may be sequential learners, preferring tasks presented in a part-to-whole format; whereas others may favor a simultaneous, "big picture" approach. There are as many learning traits as there are students, and each student possesses specific traits. Student learning traits have been divided into three basic categories: learning and memory, behavioral patterns and characteristics, and learning strategies.

Learning and Memory

Learning and memory refer to those skills that allow students to focus their attention and store information. Sequential versus simultaneous processing, stimulus selectivity, and attention to detail are all in this category. A student's memory skills, including short-term, long-term, visual, auditory, rote, and meaningful memory, play a role in creating the individual's learning style. Tasks that examine students' preferences and strengths within these areas can be contrived and observed for the purpose of shaping instruction.

Table 2.3
Diagnostic Sequence in Oral and Written Language

Sequence for Older Elementary Children

A. Oral language sample (with and without brainstorming)

B. Written language sample (with and without brainstorming)

C. Spelling of known words (looking for organization)

   1. Rule-based

   2. Predictable and unpredictable words

   3. Retest words missed in writing in oral mode

   4. Retest words missed at recall level using recognition level

   5. Retest words missed at recognition level using proofing format

D. Capitalization and punctuation (in contrived sample)

E. Following multistep directions (in written and oral modes)

F. Idioms, synonyms, antonyms, categories

G. Academic language in content areas

H. Near/far point copying

Sequence for Younger Elementary Children

A. Oral language sample (with different stimuli)

B. Language experience story

C. Sequencing

D. Written language sample (one sentence from story or story creation)

E. Writing alphabet (from memory or from model if reversals appear)

F. Personal information (name, address, telephone number)

G. Spelling of known words

   1. Retest words missed in writing in oral mode

   2. Retest words missed at recall level using recognition level

   3. Retest words missed at recognition level using proofing format

H. Following multistep directions (in written and oral modes)

I. Idioms, synonyms, antonyms, categories

J. Academic language in content areas

K. Near/far point copying

A student's rate of performance and task pacing also contribute to learning style. Take, for example, the case of Trudy, a young woman with Asperger syndrome who was being served in a residential treatment center for adolescents with severe behavioral problems. Trudy was thought to be stubborn and oppositional by her house staff, teachers, and therapists because she rarely answered questions or offered input during school and therapy sessions. An examination of Trudy's learning style revealed that she needed a wait time of 20 to 30 seconds to access and process information, rather than the traditional 3- to 5-second wait time experienced in reciprocal conversation. When given adequate wait time, Trudy was able to offer insights and actively participate in her program goals. Incidental learning, independent work habits, and generalization skills round out this category of student learning traits.

Behavioral Patterns and Characteristics

How students act on environmental stimuli and retrieved information and the unique way they apply this information to daily functioning reveal their behavioral patterns and characteristics. All types of interactional patterns are observed, including adult-to-student, student-to-peer, and small- and large-group interchanges. The student's pattern of response to reinforcement, structure, stress, and success should also be examined. Further, avoidance behaviors, attention-seeking behaviors, and self-stimulatory patterns are all part of a student's behavioral profile. Through structured observation of the student in a variety of settings, the examiner can note on-task and off-task characteristics, flexibility in moving from one activity to the next, and the type of events that trigger impulsive or compulsive behavior.

For students with AS/HFA, some specific behavioral patterns must be considered. The use of echolalia as a communication tool, the ability to make and maintain eye contact, and the level of distractibility and perseverance are all important links to successful classroom performance. Eye, hand, and foot dominance, as well as the ability to cross midline, must also be examined to determine perceptual abilities and fine- and gross-motor skills. These areas can easily be tapped by having the student visually track a favorite toy, catch and kick a ball, and draw or write. Midline issues can be addressed by having the student complete a simple shape or interlocking puzzle. The examiner places puzzle pieces on op-posite sides of the puzzle board and observes whether the student reaches across himself or herself to place the puzzle pieces. Any patterns of oral or written perseveration should also be noted. Of course, the important is-sue in examining any behavioral pattern or characteristic is determining which behaviors affect the student's interactions with academic require-ments and social skills.

Learning Strategies

Learning strategies are the techniques, tactics, and rules that learners use to solve problems, to facilitate learning, and to independently complete tasks. It is important to determine what types of strategies a student uses and whether the student can learn or develop new strategies. Sometimes a student may approach tasks very strategically yet elect to use strategies that are ineffective or inappropriate. Students frequently persist in using unsuccessful strategies simply because they know no replacement strate-gies for the situation. For example, on "word problem" math tests, a stu-dent may impulsively attempt to arrive at an answer without reading the entire problem, thus often failing to understand what is being asked.

One specific strategy for consideration is the manner in which stu-dents respond to written and oral directions. Many students with these dis-orders find it difficult to organize or prioritize multilevel instructions and require brief, small instructional steps for successful task completion.

It is also important to consider the types of metacognitive strategies that a student uses when confronted with learning tasks. Metacogni-tive strategies include skills such as self-talk, self-monitoring, and self-correction. For example, a young child who is helping her parent make lunch for her family may use a metacognitive strategy. As she makes sandwiches, she may verbally direct herself by saying, "First I spread the peanut butter on the bread, and then I get out the jelly." Some children may naturally use metacognitive strategies; hence, these tactics can be ex-panded and further trained to facilitate problem solving. In cases where learners lack metacognitive strategies, they may be trained through direct instructional procedures.

Table 2.4 provides a list of several important student learning traits in all three categories.

Table 2.4
Student Learning Traits

Learning and Memory

How students approach instruction by focusing their attention and storing information. How complex a pattern can the student perform?

- A. Sequential learner
- B. Simultaneous learner
- C. Stimulus selectivity
- D. Attention to detail
- E. Memory skills
  - 1. Short-term
  - 2. Long-term
  - 3. Visual
  - 4. Auditory
  - 5. Rote
  - 6. Meaningful
- F. Pacing
- G. Performance rate
- H. Incidental learning
- I. Independent work habits
- J. Generalization

Behavioral Patterns and Characteristics

How students apply retrieved information to daily functioning. Which behaviors affect interactions with academic requirements and social skills?

- A. Group interactions
- B. Peer relationships
- C. Adult relationships
- D. Avoidance behaviors
- E. Attention-seeking behaviors
- F. Self-stimulatory behaviors
- G. Response to reinforcement
- H. Response to structure

(continues)

Table 2.4 *(continued)*

Behavioral Patterns and Characteristics *(continued)*

    I. Response to stressors

    J. Response to success

    K. On-task and off-task behavior

    L. Flexibility or inflexibility

    M. Impulsive behavior

    N. Compulsive behavior

    O. Echolalia

    P. Perseveration (oral, motor, or written)

    Q. Dominance

    R. Perseverance

    S. Distractibility

    T. Eye contact

    U. Excessive movement

    V. Sense of humor

    W. Self-concept

Learning Strategies

Strategies are techniques, principles, or rules that allow students to complete tasks independently and solve problems successfully. How are novel tasks approached? How does the student solve problems already known? How does the student organize information?

    A. Strategic learner

    B. Memory strategies

    C. Problem-solving strategies

        1. Academic

        2. Social

    D. Metacognitive strategies

        1. Organizational

        2. Self-talk

        3. Self-monitoring

        4. Self-correction

    E. Following oral directions

    F. Following written directions

Levels of Skill Acquisition

Levels of skill acquisition align with developmental levels of learning. Individuals, including those with special needs, typically learn and acquire information, knowledge, and skills in a developmental sequence. Initially, individuals become aware of and familiar with some novel skill or information/knowledge, including its meaning, characteristics, and so forth. Subsequent to this foundational learning level, they may expand their learning to using a skill or applying it in some type of applied manner. For example, after initially learning to multiply, an individual may use his or her multiplication skills to calculate the cost of purchasing seven of the same items of the same cost. Levels of learning and skill acquisition are a basic element of assessing students with AS/HFA. Specifically, assessment should occur at the following levels of acquisition: recognition, recall, and application. These levels are hierarchical, with *recognition* representing the lowest level of acquisition and *application* the highest level. If an examiner can determine at which level a student has demonstrated skill mastery, instruction can be more appropriately planned.

To assess the recognition level, an examiner might ask a student to select a stimulus item from similar distracters. At this level of skill acquisition, the student is not expected to generate the correct response without cues but rather to discriminate an item from similar stimuli through a written or oral response. Assessment activities at the recognition level include multiple-choice or matching items. These activities allow students to respond through pointing, underlining, circling, or matching appropriate items. Students need to be able to correctly perform recognition-level tasks before moving ahead to more complex learning activities.

Assessment at the recall level involves asking students to retrieve information or perform tasks without stimulus clues. At this level, students generate thoughts, ideas, or concepts and respond orally or in writing to assessment items. Activities that assess skill acquisition at the recall level include fill-in-the-blank, flash card, or short-answer items. The student who successfully completes a task at the recall level is prepared to apply rote information in a more meaningful manner.

The application level of skill acquisition represents the meaningful use of a skill in a real, simulated, or contrived setting. Assessment tasks are structured so that students can demonstrate proficiency in the classroom or other setting. The importance of application-level assessment was seen in the movie *Rain Man* (Guber, Peters, & Levinson, 1988). In this movie, Raymond Babbitt, a man with autism (played by Dustin Hoffman), demonstrated a unique ability with numbers. He could perform recall-level tasks in mathematics—specifically, adding, subtracting, multiplying, and dividing large numbers without the aid of a calculator or response cues. However, when asked to apply numerical skills to a real-life setting (i.e., use numbers to indicate an understanding of money), his lack of application skills was evident. Assessment tasks at the application level include word problems, theme writing, comprehending and following written directions, and a variety of related problem-solving activities requiring that an individual make functional use of information and knowledge.

Levels of Instructional Representation

Many of the current practices in cognitive development and education are based on the developmental theories of Jean Piaget (1959), and these theories have direct application for teaching children and youth diagnosed with Asperger syndrome or high-functioning autism. From Piaget's description of the type of knowledge displayed by children at various stages of development from birth to adulthood, Bruner (1966) specified three levels of representation through which a child must progress to become an independent learner. The first stage is the concrete, or enactive level, during which the student is actively and physically involved in a learning task. Many children learn best by "doing," whether learning to ride a bicycle or learning the concept of place value in math. In either case, the student interacts with a physical object—the bicycle or place-value manipulatives (e.g., blocks)—to gain a concrete understanding of the process. At this level, the student develops a basic understanding that serves as the foundation for future learning and skill acquisition.

The second, or iconic, stage moves a learner to a more conceptual and abstract level of learning. In this stage of learning, graphic pictures, icons, or images are used to prompt the student to retrieve and apply previously learned skills and prior knowledge to complete a task or solve a problem. A common iconic instructional presentation is the use of pictures or diagrams in math. Most students who used blocks to grasp the concept of place value should be able to respond to items illustrated with drawings of blocks. Bruner (1966) described this stage as governed by principles of perceptual organization.

Symbolic, the highest level of instructional representation, involves representation using symbols, language, or words. Students at this level of representation have developed a schema based on past experiences with a task and are able to respond appropriately to symbols (e.g., words) on a page without further prompts or clues. For instance, a student given a math problem involving regrouping for addition or subtraction will recall his prior experience with place value and apply that knowledge to computing the answer.

As covered in the earlier discussion of the levels of skill acquisition, normal development proceeds sequentially through the three stages. Yet, students may have gaps in their sequentially acquired skills and knowledge, resulting in splinter skills and fragmented information and understanding. For example, they may have developed the ability to superficially use and work with abstract symbols without understanding the underlying concepts needed for successful skill application.

Instructional planning must include an understanding of a student's level of comprehension. To be sure, curricula and instructional strategies must align with concrete, iconic, and symbolic representation. Examiners should also assess students' understanding of underlying concepts, as well as their ability to respond to written problems at an abstract level. Students who have a great deal of rote knowledge or who have developed a successful strategy for test taking may do relatively well on written tests but be deficient in concrete, conceptual understanding needed to build a solid academic knowledge base. Accordingly, teachers and diagnosticians should schedule at least some assessment at the concrete and iconic levels, areas typically not examined beyond the primary grades.

Diagnostic Teaching

Diagnostic teaching is a systematic informal clinical process wherein a student is presented with a task or series of academic tasks. The student is asked to solve a problem or complete an activity while the examiner notes observations and maintains anecdotal records. These notes describe how the student approaches the task, deals with task frustration, modifies and self-corrects errors, and analyzes the problem-solving skills used to complete the task.

Diagnostic teaching also involves presenting a series of similar tasks to the student using a variety of presentation or response modes and under a variety of structuring and support conditions. For example, six spelling words, all unfamiliar to the student and similar in structure and difficulty, are presented for practice using three different modalities. The student practices two words verbally by spelling each word aloud and then using the word in a sentence. The student practices another two words in a written format by writing each word 10 times. The student practices the final two words kinesthetically, or tactilely, by drawing the letters in a box of damp sand. Each practice session lasts approximately 3 minutes. At the conclusion of the practice sessions, the student is tested, using the same type of response required in his or her classroom. The results are then compared to see if different practice modes facilitated the student's memorization of the spelling words. Common presentation and response modes used in this type of diagnostic teaching include visual, auditory, tactile or kinesthetic, and combinations of two or more of these modalities.

Diagnostic teaching sessions are based on the ability of examiners to accurately and precisely observe a student's response patterns and record and analyze patterns of strength. Diagnostic teaching information is used by practitioners to understand a student's strengths, plan instructional strategies, address deficit skill areas, and structure home and school environments to meet the student's specific learning needs.

Translating Assessment Results Into Effective Programs and Practices

A functional and utilitarian assessment involves more than merely determining whether or not a person meets the diagnostic criteria for Asperger syndrome and/or high-functioning autism. It also is more than simply administering and interpreting a variety of formal and informal tests and related diagnostic and evaluation measures. Successful assessment typically consists of data collection using formal and informal assessment methods germane to domains of interest, analysis and interpretation of assessment information and data, identification of strengths and concerns connected to the aforementioned information and data, functional use of this information and data to plan and implement individual interventions and supports, and ongoing evaluation of students' progress and needs.

After data and related diagnostic and evaluation information are organized, students' strengths and concerns should be identified. This process enables clarification of students' current functioning. When making a report of these findings, these elements can be formatted in a two-column table. The left column contains strengths and concerns, and the right column contains observed evidence related to each purported strength or concern. This procedure helps practitioners to focus on salient elements and outcomes of the assessment and to enhance objectivity in the assessment analysis process. The identification of strengths is crucial to planning for learners with Asperger disorder. For example, if a student can use various computer programs, the assessment team could make a recommendation such as "Provide opportunities to use various computer programs and gradually shift the student to helping others use the computer."

The next step of the synthesis process includes analysis, interpretation, and integration of data and findings. Synthesis is an essential part of assessment since this procedure analyzes current functioning and paves the way for identifying plans and intervention steps. Although a synthesis can be summarized in any format, categorizing practitioners' interpretations into several domains is helpful to organize an assessment report. While the synthesis should be thorough and complete, lengthy reports often lose their focus and the attention of readers. Hence, brevity is often a positive quality in an assessment report. A good synthesis contains brief descriptions of test results, concise interpretations matched with markers of strengths and concerns, and recommendations based on the above elements.

Of course, a functional assessment must make clear and utilitarian recommendations. This is an essential process for determining educational interventions for children and youth with AS/HFA. An assessment is only as effective as the information and guidance it provides practitioners, parents, and other stakeholders in designing and implementing individualized programs. Thus, recommendations must logically and clearly align with diagnostic findings and with strengths and concerns identified in the assessment process. A functional assessment report also provides a historical record, as well as useful information for parents, teachers, related service professionals, and other stakeholders.

Ideally, an assessment allows for a thorough and objective investigation of a student's strengths and concerns. It serves as a major source of information leading to the use of maximally effective and utilitarian methods and intervention strategies. To be clear, assessment is a direct link to high-quality services and a pathway for desired outcomes.

Concluding Thoughts

Many types of assessment procedures are available for students with AS/HFA. Professionals must select a battery of measures most appropriate for each individual student, including formal and informal procedures. Norm-referenced tests and formal diagnostic assessments are suitable for initial diagnosis, periodic comprehensive overview, and summative evaluation. Informal assessment techniques can be chosen for ongoing formative evaluation of student skills and progress.

When used appropriately, both forms of assessment identify unique characteristics and results that can be used to identify, implement, and evaluate support plans, unique educational strategies, and individualized interventions. Assessment is not a single process, but part of an ongoing educational cycle that links elements of the educational process. Initial diagnostic and evaluation processes in combination with continuous monitoring of skills, progress, and needs contribute to high-quality educational services that are essential to the education and quality of life of children and youth with high-functioning autism or Asperger disorder and their families.

chapter three

Instructional Methods
for Learners

Children and youth with Asperger syndrome or high-functioning autism, or related disabilities, typically receive all, or the majority of, their education in general education classrooms. Thus, in spite of having a challenging disorder, these learners are generally appropriate and suitable for regular classrooms. To be sure, their cognitive, language, and learning abilities generally bode well for their educational success, contingent on appropriate supports, accommodations, and availability of knowledgeable and committed educators and support staff. At the same time, it is equally clear that in spite of their strengths and assets, they can be expected to encounter myriad educational challenges. These difficulties and obstacles fall not only in cognitive and learning areas but also (and not surprisingly) in social and behavioral areas.

In spite of having a significant disability that clearly affects school adjustment and functioning, most learners with Asperger disorder or high-functioning autism are able to acquire grade-level skills and knowledge that can contribute to school success. Still, it is rare for these children and youth to be successful in school and life without appropriate accommodations and support services. Social difficulties, in combination with learning problems (e.g., organizational deficits) and unsupported cognitive and environmental expectations and demands, all too often mean that children and youth with autism-related disorders fail to achieve in a fashion equal to their potential. Accordingly, it is essential that teachers and related service personnel use maximally effective individualized methods and strategies.

Characteristics Affecting Academic Performance

Students with AS/HFA are typically of average or above-average intelligence. In fact, IQs of persons with Asperger syndrome have been documented in the gifted range (Barnhill, Hagiwara, Myles, & Simpson, 2000). Because of their IQ level, students are often expected to perform at the same level as their peers. Although some students can meet this expectation, many cannot. It is often difficult for teachers to detect that students may not be completing their work in a meaningful way. These students are often able to mask their inability to understand and perform certain tasks. Because their disabilities are usually confounded by their abilities, narrow range of interests, and motivation, these students frequently give the impression that they are competent in many skill areas in which they actually have deficits. Not surprisingly, it is also unmistakable that there is not a consistent pattern of strength and weakness for learners diagnosed with AS/HFA. Just as with other students, their learning assets, abilities, and deficits vary in type and severity from person to person. Hence, there is no easy-to-apply formula for planning and programming for these learners. Yet, there are effective and evidence-based methods that can be used to support these students. When these tools are used consistently, with fidelity, and in an individualized fashion, relative academic success can be expected. Effective use of these tools is contingent on an understanding of the elements of AS/HFA that most typically affect school performance, discussed in the sections that follow.

Distraction and Inattention

It is common for persons with AS/HFA to have received a diagnosis of attention-deficit/hyperactivity disorder (ADHD) at some point in their lives. Relative to school and academic performance, Asperger disorder, high-functioning autism, and ADHD have commonalities, particularly related to distractibility and inattentiveness. Attention often seems fleeting and short-lived. For example, one moment a student with Asperger syndrome may appear to be paying attention, then suddenly seems to withdraw into an inner world and be totally unaware of what is going on in his or her classroom and environment. Teacher directions are not processed; student conversations are not heard. This daydreaming may occur over extended periods, with no predictability. The daydreaming may be so intense that a prompt from the teacher is needed to call the student back to task. Often the antecedent responsible for the lack of attention is unknown.

Even while paying attention, the student may not react to teacher instructions. For example, the student may start to follow a three-step direction but appear to lose focus as he completes the first part of instructions. Rather than looking for a model or asking for help, the student "shuts down" or looks for a way out. The student may remain frozen in that place, wander aimlessly about, shuffle through the desk, stare into space, or begin to daydream. On occasion, the student may cause a distraction or act out. Often these same behaviors are seen when the student is required to engage in nonpreferred work tasks or assignments that fall outside a narrow range of student interests.

Social interactions are often distracting for students with Asperger syndrome or high-functioning autism. Because these students frequently are interested and motivated to interact with others in general, they often focus all of their attention on others in the classroom instead of on their teacher-assigned tasks. If these students have a particularly strong need to interact with a specific classmate, they may attend to those individuals exclusively, staring nonstop at a person or listening to a particular person's conversations. If a student with AS/HFA and a classmate have developed a reciprocal relationship, the student with AS/HFA might unilaterally seek the classmate's approval before beginning a task or addressing the teacher or another student. This gives the peer an enormous amount of power over that person, which can be used in a negative way. For example, the peer may prompt a student with Asperger syndrome to complete assignments for him, prompt the student to break classroom rules, or suggest that the student engage in activities that will harm her academic or social standing.

Students with high-functioning autism or Asperger syndrome are often distracted because they do not know how to discern and discriminate between educationally and socially relevant and irrelevant stimuli. A student might focus on a particular picture or map in a textbook while other students in the class have moved on to the next chapter. This student might focus on the way a speaker's earring dangles when she moves her head instead of listening to the content of her lecture. A student may become highly frustrated when he attempts to memorize every fact associated with Columbus's discovering America as mentioned in the textbook, including an extensive list of food and supplies carried on each ship, while failing to understand salient factors such as the motivation for making the journey.

Tunnel Vision

The school setting requires that students attend to certain stimuli while screening out irrelevant yet competing distractions. That is, at any given time, a student might be expected to attend to a textbook and ignore (a) students talking around her, (b) a teacher offering another student help, or (c) a bulletin board about a favored topic. This is often difficult for students with AS/HFA. On one level, these students often cannot discern what others deem relevant. If the bulletin board contains information on a topic of high interest, the student may consider it far more interesting and important than what is being discussed in the course textbook. If a student has a strong social attachment to someone across the room, interacting with that person might take precedence over any task the teacher assigns. Explanations, rules, and expectations that talking across the room is inappropriate may not affect the student. This student might seem "driven" to interact with his friend.

Tunnel vision also operates in a second way. Students with AS/HFA logically group items or characteristics and frequently make highly idiosyncratic conceptual generalizations so that they make sense to them. That is, they form a schema that makes sense to them without regard to others; and this representation is often very inflexible. For example, a youth might classify houses and cars as falling in the same conceptual grouping because they both have doors and windows. Another example of this pattern is a student who rigidly learns and applies the spelling rule "*i* before *e* except after *c*." The student could be convinced that words like *neighbor* and *weigh* should be spelled *nieghbor* and *wiegh*, not allowing for these exceptions to the rule.

Problems can present themselves when the student is reading for information. This is often a difficult task for learners, including for those who easily learned to orally identify the correct pronunciation of words. Students with these disorders often read for specific information presented in a text study guide while ignoring and simply not processing in a meaningful way information that they were not responsible for. When the student is later tested on the text and given questions that were not in the study guide, he will most likely not answer those questions or answer them incorrectly, even if the information seems obvious to others. This pattern is particularly evident relative to drawing conclusions and making inferential assumptions.

Student obsessions are another hallmark of tunnel vision. Two types of obsessions are frequently shown by students with AS/HFA. The first type of obsession (primary) is one in which the student has an all-encompassing level of interest in a particular topic. It is not unusual for discussion of this topic in class or a social situation to cause the affected student to become very excited and emotional. Rapid speech, increased volume, a high-pitched voice, pacing, and hand-wringing often occur with primary obsessions. Primary obsessions typically do not lend themselves to rational discussions and explorations.

Secondary obsessions, on the other hand, are marked interests about which the student remains lucid, focused, and ready to learn about the particular topic. Students actively seek new information about the topic but can be somewhat redirected. Secondary interests are often used by teachers to motivate students to complete academic tasks. In fact, in some cases, secondary obsessions even develop into career interests.

Rote Memory

While there are exceptions, rote memory skills are frequently well developed in persons with Asperger syndrome or high-functioning autism. Case studies document that some children have learned to recite words they see written by age 3. Others have reported that young children with these disorders have been able to repeat paragraphs of information after seeing them only once. However, the comprehension level of many of these persons does not appear to match their rote skills. Comprehension is often at the factual level. That is, persons with AS/HFA can understand basic facts in written material and either repeat them verbatim or paraphrase them. Many, however, experience difficulty understanding vocabulary in context and reading for information. Thus, these persons may give the false impression that they understand concepts because they are able to parrot responses. As a result, it is easy for a teacher to mistake rote responses for content mastery and urge the student to master more difficult material. Students may be able to repeat algebra equations but be unable to perform them. Similarly, they may be able to answer multiple-choice questions about a novel they have read but be unable to analyze character intent in a cooperative group setting.

Rote memory may be nonproductive: Educators assume that a good rote memory means that students can remember, at any time, pieces of information or events. However, this is not true for many persons with AS/HFA. Although they can store portions of information in memory, they often have difficulty determining how to retrieve the information. Open-ended questions such as "Tell me what the main character in the story did after his brother left home for military service" may not trigger a response, because the student has stored the information under the main character's name and is unable to make the transition from the term *main character* to the character's name. In many students with AS/HFA, therefore, an exceptional memory does not automatically mean that they are able to easily recall and apply information.

A second way in which rote memory may be nonproductive is related to integration of learned material and experience. These students may memorize entire inventories of facts or directions, but these lists often remain unconnected bits of information. For example, a student with Asperger syndrome might memorize the list of supplies to bring to each of his six middle school classes and recite them when supplied with the appropriate trigger or key word. This same student, however, might forget to bring a pencil to class. Another student might remember to bring a pencil to class but arrive with it unsharpened. She knows from past experience that the pencil must have a point to be a useful tool, but somehow she does not connect this bit of information to her present need. These students may be intellectually bright, and frequently they have the ability to memorize elements and bits of academic information, yet their knowledge and functional use of the information is often fragmented and of limited utility.

Visual Versus Auditory Processing

Students with AS/HFA commonly learn and process information in a manner that is generally incompatible with the way academic information is typically presented. Most academic information is presented orally, with auditory input (Ben-Arieh & Miller, 2009). Processing difficulties may occur for one of three reasons.

First, some children and adolescents may be able to comprehend and follow information that is visually presented, especially if they are given sufficient time to review and process the information. In contrast, information that is presented orally—the common communication mode among school personnel—may be difficult to understand and comply with. This pattern is particularly true if students are given little time to reflect on and process orally delivered directions and information.

Second, the student may understand individual words used by a teacher or student but not understand what the words mean when they are used in the context of sentences and paragraphs. The student requires additional processing time to understand the meaning of the words as they are used in sentences. If the student attempts to memorize the words using rote memory skills, it is almost as if there is little cognitive energy left with which to process meaning.

Third, it is commonly believed that students with AS/HFA have difficulty processing visual and auditory information concurrently. Accordingly, information must be presented in one modality or the other to facilitate processing; otherwise, overload occurs.

Structure

Students with Asperger syndrome or high-functioning autism typically fall at the ends of the structure continuum: They either appear to have an inherent ability to provide structure or largely rely on others to help them organize themselves. It is often said that these students have either the neatest or the messiest desks in class.

Not surprisingly, it is easier for most people, including those diagnosed with AS/HFA, to function in an organized environment. Predictable schedules, uniform assignment formats, clearly delivered and consistent expectations, structured physical settings, and so forth help these students devote their time and energy to academic tasks, as opposed to wrestling with variable and unstructured classrooms and schedules. Those who have internal structure often have rigid expectations that schedules be followed and commitments be honored; unscheduled events cause these students great discomfort that can be manifested as disorientation, refusal to engage in the new activity, extended discourse about the canceled or postponed event, or behavioral problems. In other words, these students commonly communicate through language and behavior that change is problematic and almost always unwelcome.

Educators comment that they have seen students with AS/HFA tolerate change in some instances but lose control when the environment was altered in other situations and times. Sometimes these learners can tolerate change if that change occurs in only one dimension. For example, if library time is changed, the student may adjust to the new schedule. However, if library time and the librarian are changed simultaneously, the same student may have difficulty maintaining self-control. Without question, experienced educators have discovered that alerting students to changes and working to clarify expectations and enhance day-to-day structure pay enormous positive benefits for many students with AS/HFA.

Many students with high-functioning autism or Asperger syndrome have limited ability to structure their own environment. For instance, a messy person with Asperger syndrome probably has not made a conscious choice to be that way; rather, he or she lacks good organizational skills. Students can literally lose a paper received only a minute earlier. They might never have a pencil in class. The note that the teacher placed in their backpack never makes it home. Written work is not placed uniformly on a page. Middle school students often cannot locate their locker combination, and when they do, they cannot find what they need inside since their lockers are a mess. They cannot organize their day by bringing both their science and math books to science class, even though math class follows immediately in the room next door. Almost every facet of these students' lives may appear to be in disarray. Teachers and parents often wonder how these students get from one place to another. To be sure, it is a challenge to organize these types of students. Merely providing a schedule or list of supplies is not enough, because these aids may also be lost. Yet, as discussed in this chapter, there are multiple effective strategies that can be used to augment structure and to help students organize their lives.

Problem Solving

It is not unusual to encounter students with AS/HFA who are often able to engage in high-level thinking and problem solving when their area of interest is involved. These very same students, however, may be unable and/or unmotivated to demonstrate these same problem-solving skills in areas that fall outside their narrowly defined special interests. To be sure, many children and youth have extremely weak generalized and consistent problem-solving skills (independent of their abilities). Moreover, many of these students are inconsistent and inflexible in their use of problem-solving strategies. For instance, some students have an extremely limited repertoire of problem-solving options and tend to use it consistently and persistently, regardless of the situation. For example, if the school locker does not open, the student may keep trying the same incorrect locker combination over and over. Such nonfunctional persistence may result in a behavioral outburst if the student does not apply alternative problem-solving strategies, such as asking an adult or a peer for help.

Other students with AS/HFA may have learned several problem-solving strategies but not have generalized their use. For example, a student with high-functioning autism may know to use a dictionary to find the correct spelling of a word but not realize that the same technique may also be effective in understanding its meaning or finding synonyms for the word.

There is also the problem of recall related to problem solving. Although a student may know a host of problem-solving strategies and realize that they can be generalized, he may not be able to recall any strategies or the most appropriate strategy for a particular situation when it is needed. Because the student with AS/HFA often has difficulty searching his or her memory for particular facts, the student may not be able to access a strategy. Even if the student has an effective system for retrieving problem-solving strategies, it is still likely that he cannot consistently use this system. By the time the student cognitively realizes that a problem exists, he may be so frustrated, confused, angry, or disoriented that his reaction is behavioral—a tantrum or withdrawal.

Problem solving becomes even more difficult in academics if abstract concepts are involved. Students with AS/HFA frequently have difficulty with word problems, estimation, algebra, and geometry—all of which require problem-solving skills and often contain a high level of abstraction.

Problem-solving difficulties are also apparent outside the fields of mathematics. Teachers often give assignments that require students to take the role of a historical character. Students may be asked to write papers or plays or make speeches from the perspective of another person or while assuming the role of a historical figure. Tasks of this nature are difficult for those who do not understand the human experience from different perspectives. Persons with AS/HFA frequently have difficulty understanding their own state of mind; therefore, they cannot be expected to easily and automatically imagine the state of mind of others.

Motor Skills

Motor problems that are often seen in persons with AS/HFA affect academic performance. These students are often clumsy, have an unusual gait, have difficulty with pencil grasp, and write illegibly. Gross motor problems may lead to fear of heights and inability to jump over obstacles, to skip, or to catch or throw a ball. These deficits can also further exacerbate a student's poor social standing if the motor problem interferes with game participation and peer acceptance. Fine-motor difficulties may also mean that students may not be motivated to complete work because of the enormous amount of energy required to write. It is not unusual for students who consent to write to turn in assignments that are unreadable. As a result, they are often told to rewrite the page and try to be neater. Requests like this often result in negative reactions. Depending on the student's behavioral repertoire, reactions may include refusal to do the task; withdrawal; ignoring the teacher; daydreaming; or an overt display of anger or aggression directed toward self, peers, or the teacher.

Motivation

Students with AS/HFA are often not motivated to complete a task just because it was assigned by the teacher. If the task does not make sense relative to an individual's interests and perceptions of the world and relative to the scheme of the student's life, chances are he or she will see no reason to invest time and energy. "When will I use algebra, anyway?" is a frequent question. Teacher statements such as "You need to do it because I said so" or "You will need this later in life—believe me" typically fail to motivate these students. Even if the task has relevance to everyday life, the student may not make that connection.

Engaging a student in extensive conversation or "adult logic" or excessive rhetoric to convince him of the importance of the assignment may not be effective for several reasons. Even if the student is apt to listen to the teacher's explanation, he may not understand the abstract concepts used by the teacher to link the assignment with "real-life" needs. Another student with high-functioning autism may like a teacher's rhetoric because the focus is removed from the task at hand and the student does not have to complete the assignment, at least in the short run.

Obsessions, particularly secondary obsessions, often serve as effective motivators for students with AS/HFA. Once a topic of interest is identified, the student may appear to spend the majority of time reflecting and acting on it in a somewhat rational and lucid manner. As a result, the student is frequently motivated to learn more about the area of obsession and is anxious to share knowledge with others. That this information sharing occurs regardless of the interest level of the listeners, however, can sometimes be a problem.

Individuals with AS/HFA are often motivated by people they like; conversely, they may refuse to engage in activities or complete tasks if they involve people with whom they dislike or have no personal interest. Accordingly, and for a variety of other reasons, it is important that to the maximum extent possible, these students be assigned to teachers who have the potential to develop positive, reciprocal relationships with them.

Motivation is also sometimes linked to students' mistaken impression that they have control over a variety of situations or that they are responsible for problems outside their areas of duty. For instance, if a teacher chides her class for performing poorly on a unit test, a student with Asperger syndrome may assume that he or she is to blame. Thus, incorrect perceptions of responsibility and misguided egocentricity may make some students feel personally to blame for the behavior and performance of others.

Effective Instructional Strategies

Learners with AS/HFA have endless potential when educators and support staff recognize and plan for their individual needs and characteristics. Clearly, these are students who can be successful in school and life when provided appropriate structure, program accommodations, and related supports. In this section, we present several instructional support strategies, including priming, assignment modifications, and structuring strategies, that can be used to enhance the performance of learners with Asperger syndrome.

Priming

Priming refers to the introduction of information, assignments, or activities prior to their use in an actual instructional session (Ben-Arieh & Miller, 2009; Wilde, Koegel, & Koegel, 1992). The objectives of priming are particularly well suited for the needs of children and youth with AS/HFA. These learners frequently respond negatively (i.e., with displays of stress, anxiety, aggression, and so forth) to novel or unanticipated information and experiences. Hence, priming (a) familiarizes learners with the material to be used in class before its introduction to a class and (b) introduces familiarity and predictability into the information or activity and reduces stress and anxiety connected to the use of unfamiliar materials and expectations (Ben-Arieh & Miller, 2009; Myles & Adreon, 2001).

According to Wilde and colleagues (1992), the actual materials that will be used in a lesson should, whenever possible, be shown to the student the day, the evening, or even the morning before the activity is to take place. The student is reinforced for attending to the material. In some cases, priming occurs right before the activity, such as when a paraprofessional overviews what will take place during a cooperative group activity immediately prior to the beginning of class. Priming can be done by a parent at home or by a paraprofessional, a resource teacher, or a trusted peer (Myles & Adreon, 2001).

Wilde et al. (1992) also recommended that the actual materials, such as a worksheet or textbook, be used in priming. However, in some cases, a list or a description of the activities to take place may suffice. For students, priming may consist of reviewing an index card that has a reading assignment, identifying the number and type of questions to answer, determining how instruction will occur (in a small group of peers or individually), and defining responsibilities for each class (Myles & Adreon, 2001).

Assignment Modifications

Several basic and important considerations are recommended relative to giving assignments to children and youth with AS/HFA. First, consideration and modifications of the length of the assignment is often warranted. Even though many learners diagnosed with AS/HFA generally have average or above average intelligence, they may require additional processing and/or writing time to complete assignments. In situations in which these students are able to demonstrate competence and otherwise meet the objectives of assignments using shortened assignments, it is recommended that they be permitted to use amended assignments. Of course, it is recognized that some educators, parents, and other students may argue that such accommodations are unfair. However, with due respect to such thinking, we are of the strong opinion that the individual needs of these students and recognition of the difficulty that assignments may present these learners are far more important factors in making such decisions. To be sure, assignments that are modified in length bode well for positive school experiences and completion of learning objectives for many individuals with AS/HFA.

Assignments that require lengthy written documentation can be problematic for some children and youth with AS/HFA. Offering alternatives to paper-and-pencil tasks allows students to demonstrate their knowledge while circumventing a common element of their disability. Winebrenner (2001) listed several alternatives to traditional assignments, including (a) creating a radio or televised newscast, (b) creating a script or mock trial, (c) surveying others and making a graph of the outcomes, (d) creating a diary or journal surrounding an important event, and (e) developing a timeline. Other modifications, centered on changing the format of assignments, include verbal responses instead of written essays and multiple-choice rather than short-answer tests (Myles & Adreon, 2001).

We also strongly recommend that attention be given to the amount of reading required of students with AS/HFA, particularly at the middle and high school levels. Although some of these individuals are strong readers when motivated, they may take significantly longer than their peers do to complete reading assignments. Providing texts that are highlighted and study guides can help students focus and maximize their reading time. Teachers should also identify for students the salient elements within reading assignments, including specific content that they are responsible for learning (Myles & Adreon, 2001). In bringing attention to relevant material, teachers should also consider providing a model of assignments so that students have a visual reminder and model of how their completed tasks should look.

Structuring Strategies

In virtually every situation, children and youth with AS/HFA benefit from enhanced structure wherein there is use of strategies that provide order, safety, predictability, and external organization. These methods help these learners not only attend to and profit from instruction but also manage behavior and promote pro-social peer and adult interactions. These strategies include (a) visual supports, (b) peer buddy programs, (c) early or late classroom and school release, (d) homework assignment notebooks, (e) timelines, (f) Travel Cards, and (g) home base programs.

Visual Supports

Students with AS/HFA generally appear to benefit when information is presented visually rather than orally. While there is clearly a need for additional research on this widely held assertion, there is nevertheless strong initial support for the visual mode being a link to effective learning for the majority of learners with autism-related disabilities. Visual information is more concrete than auditory information and allows for greater processing time. Accordingly, visual schedules, graphic organizers, outlines, and task cards can help these students understand content and more competently carry out assignments.

Visual Schedules. Visual schedules are designed to make abstract temporal concepts and information more concrete and manageable. These tools can yield multiple benefits for children and youth with AS/HFA, who often exhibit visual strengths. For example, visual schedules allow students to anticipate upcoming events and activities; develop a more functional understanding of time, place, and activity; and predict change. Furthermore, they can be used to stimulate communication through discussion of past, present, and future events; increase on-task behavior; facilitate transition between activities; teach new skills; and introduce novel activities and experiences.

Visual schedules are based on the visual strengths and needs of students. We recommend that visual schedules be individualized on the basis of a student's level of visual representation. The more abstract the visual schedule, the higher the level of representation. Table 3.1 shows the hierarchy of visual representation from the highest to the lowest levels of abstraction.

Table 3.1

Visual Schedule Level of Abstraction and Visual Representation

Level of abstraction	Visual representation
Highest	Written phrase or sentence
↑	Written word
	Black-and-white line drawing
	Colored drawing
	Photograph
↓	Miniature object
Lowest	Full-sized object

For young students who require concrete visual cues to understand upcoming and regularly scheduled events and activities, the teacher can design an object schedule that uses the actual materials from each of the scheduled activities. For example, if a math lesson requires the use of colored blocks as manipulative items, then the colored blocks may be used to represent math.

Older and more advanced learners may be able to use schedules that use symbols and representations of events and activities. For instance, drawings or photos of a student completing an activity, icons and symbolic drawings, written words, and even sentences may be suitable. It is essential to determine which level of visual representation is most suitable for each student and then to pair it with the next highest level. This process is useful in moving students along the continuum of being able to use increasingly advanced systems. For example, if a student is functioning at the photograph level, a colored drawing can be paired with the photograph to introduce the higher level concept. Similarly, if a student is functioning at the black-and-white drawing level, written words can be paired with the drawing.

Schedule arrangement and placement options vary in accordance with students' needs and levels of functioning. Schedules can be arranged left to right or top to bottom. Although either arrangement is acceptable, the left-to-right arrangement corresponds with standard reading protocol. Schedules can take a variety of forms, including the following:

- placing the schedule in a photo album or three-ring binder
- hanging the schedule on the classroom wall with Velcro or masking tape
- placing the schedule in a pocket chart
- writing the schedule on a wipe-off board
- writing the schedule on a chalkboard
- typing the schedule on a piece of paper and placing it on the student's desk
- typing the schedule on an index card that will fit in the student's pocket or wallet
- writing the schedule on hole-punched cards that can hang on the student's belt loop with an O-ring

Students may enjoy and sometimes feel more comfortable when participating in the preparation of their schedule. This participation should occur first thing in the morning. Students can assist in assembling their schedule, copying it, or adding their own personal touch. This interactive time can also be used to review the daily routine, discuss changes, and reinforce rules.

Figure 3.1a–b shows sample visual schedules for younger students who require moderate levels of abstraction to understand their respective events. Figure 3.2 was designed for students who have a relatively high level of abstraction but require time and activity cues.

Graphic Organizers. Graphic organizers provide a visual, holistic representation of facts and concepts within an organized framework. Graphic organizers arrange key terms to show their relationship to one another, providing abstract or implicit information in a concrete manner. They are particularly useful with content area material. Graphic organizers can be used before, during, or after students read a selection, either as an advance organizer or as a measure of concept attainment. Graphic organizers often enhance learning for the following reasons:

- Visual modality is often a strength for these students.
- A graphic organizer remains consistent and constant, so when the student "tunes in," it is available.

- A graphic organizer allows for processing time, so the student can reflect on the written material at his or her own pace.
- A graphic organizer presents abstract information in a concrete manner so that the information is more easily understood than it would be through a verbal presentation alone.

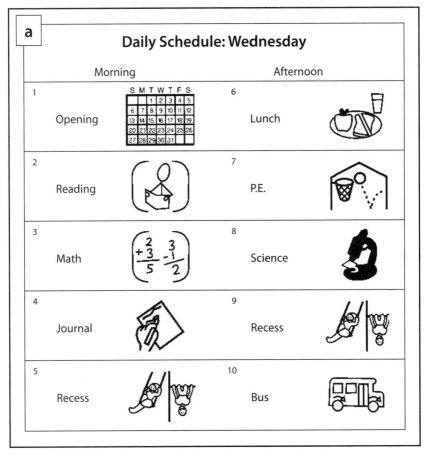

Figure 3.1a–b. Sample visual schedules for a student who functions at a moderate level of abstraction. *Note.* Schedules made with *Boardmaker and Picture Communication Symbols.* © 1987–2001 by Mayer-Johnson, P.O. Box 1579, Solana Beach, CA 92075, 858/550-0084, fax: 858/550-0449, e-mail: mayerj@mayer-johnson.com. Reprinted with permission. *(Figure continues.)*

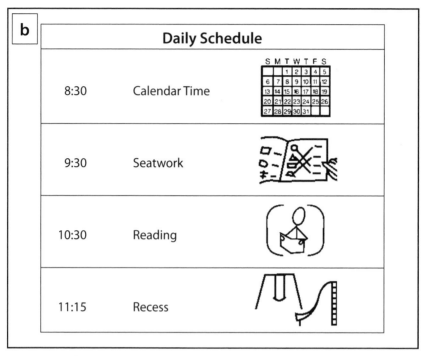

Figure 3.1a–b. *(Continued.)*

One type of graphic organizer is the semantic map (see Figure 3.3). The focal point of the semantic map is the key word or concept that is being instructed or that serves as the conceptual theme. That key word is enclosed in a geometric figure (e.g., circle or square) or is depicted by a pictorial representation of the salient word or concept (see Figure 3.4). Lines or arrows connect this central shape to other words, photographs, icons, symbols, or information related to the central concept. As the map expands, the words become more detailed and specific. That is, the graphic organizer takes the reader from more general conceptual themes to more specific information. For example, if the general theme is "modes of transportation," the graphic organizer might offer a pictorial showing "public transportation" (e.g., buses, trains, commercial airliners, cabs) and "private transportation" (e.g., personal automobiles, bicycles).

Analogy graphic organizers are another strategy that can be used to assist learners with AS/HFA to more easily benefit from instruction. The teacher selects two concepts for which the students will begin to identify attributes. The teacher and the students define how the two concepts

Daily Schedule		
8:00 A.M.	bus routine (put up coat and backpack, use bathroom, review schedule with teacher or paraeducator)	
8:15 A.M.	breakfast	
8:30 A.M.	morning group	
9:00 A.M.	math activities	
10:00 A.M.	reading activities	
11:00 A.M.	adaptive physical education	
11:30 A.M.	lunchtime	
12:00 P.M.	recess	
12:30 P.M.	work time (prevocational activity)	
1:30 P.M.	leisure time	
2:00 P.M.	language group	
2:30 P.M.	recess	
3:00 P.M.	music time	
3:15 P.M.	closing group	

Figure 3.2. Sample visual schedule for a student who functions at a high level of abstraction.

are alike and how they differ, then draw a conclusion. Often the teacher has to assist students in identifying attributes by presenting choices, either written or pictorial, from which the students select. This task can be completed individually, in small groups, or as a class. Figures 3.5 and 3.6 provide examples of two commonly used analogy graphic organizers: the Venn diagram and the compare and contrast chart.

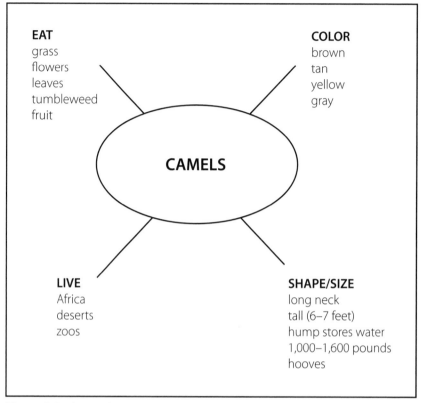

Figure 3.3. Semantic map.

Outlines. Outlines are another visual support that can be effective for students with AS/HFA. Because of motor problems as well as distraction and inattention problems, a number of these students find it challenging to take lecture notes. The first step in helping these students is to teach them how to record notes on lectures and class discussions.

Many students with AS/HFA, as well as other students, may neither understand the concept of a *main idea* nor understand that a teacher's language cues students to salient information or information for which they will be held responsible on tests. Teacher cues related to particularly important information are obvious to many students: The teacher repeats an item or changes voice tone, and so forth. Yet, many learners with AS/HFA miss these cues unless they are taught how to identify which information is most important to write down and learn. In this connection, teachers can assist students by providing the following:

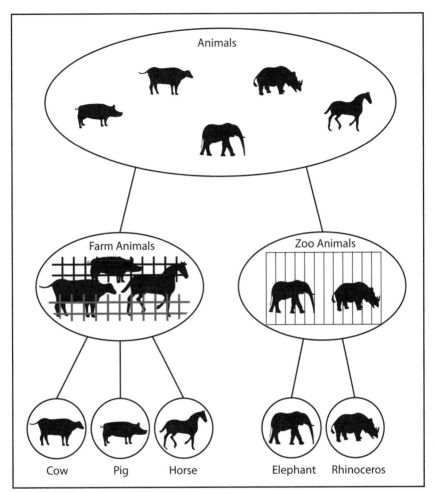

Figure 3.4. Semantic map with pictorial representation.

- *A complete outline*—This outline lists main points and details. It allows students to follow the lecture but frees them from taking notes.
- *A skeletal outline*—This outline lists main points. Students may use this format to fill in pertinent details delivered through lectures.
- *Direct verbal cues*—Verbal cues, such as "This is the first main point" or "This detail should be included in your notes," assist students in knowing which points to include

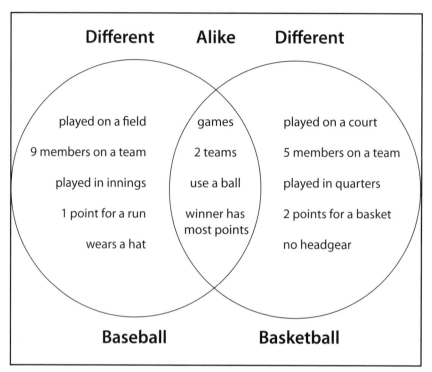

Figure 3.5. Venn diagram.

in notes. At this stage, students may be responsible for taking complete notes. The verbal cues serve as prompts.

- *Subtle verbal cues*—Subtle verbal cues provide clues regarding important information. Students need to recognize these cues, such as "The first branch of the federal government is the *legislative* branch. Did you write that in your notes?" or "You need to remember that the *legislative* branch makes the laws."

The types of note-taking assistance listed above are hierarchical; thus, student level must be considered when selecting the appropriate type of assistance.

When the student has mastered note taking at one level of assistance, the teacher can proceed to the next. Of course, the different types of assistance can be combined to facilitate the student's note taking. For example, a student may be able to work with a skeletal outline but require

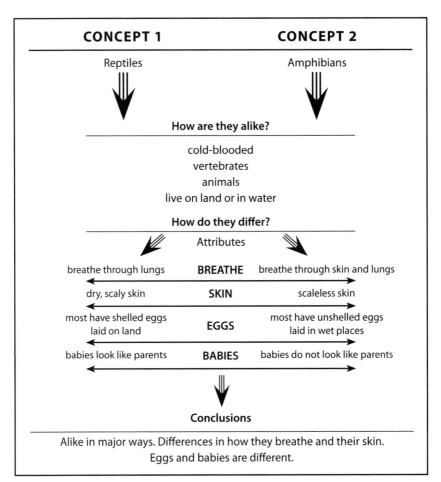

Figure 3.6. Compare and contrast chart.

verbal cues to ensure that he identifies important details. It is important to remember that not all students will proceed up this hierarchy. For instance, some students may always require a complete or skeletal outline.

Other note-taking options include having a peer take notes, with a copy going to the student with AS/HFA. Another alternative is to permit students who have appropriate skills to take notes using a computer.

Task Cards. Task cards are simple cue cards that help individuals recall academic content, routines, social skills, class rules and requirements, and so forth. Typically presented on business-card-size paper, task cards identify the steps that a student must follow. Each statement on the card is a directive. The language on the task card is usually short and concise. For example, a task card for an adolescent might provide an overview of the routines and teacher expectations for each class on his schedule. For younger children, a task card may outline conversation reminders or conversation starters that can be used with peers. Figure 3.7 provides an example of a task card that reviews the daily routine in science class.

Preparation for Changes in Routine

Students with AS/HFA are typically fond of and bound to routines; thus, schedule changes can have deleterious effects on behavior. As a result, changes in these students' schedules must be considered carefully. Students often require advance warning for fire drills, assemblies, pep rallies, or substitute teachers. Some students are so focused on their routine that even relatively minor changes cause behavioral problems. For example, the seriously routine-based student may not be able to adapt easily to a change in the daily reading lesson. This student, who is accustomed to completing a vocabulary exercise, oral reading, silent reading, and comprehension reading, may lose control when the teacher varies the order of the activities or spends reading time playing a game of Jeopardy to test students' recall of the reading material. Such a student may become upset if her teacher varies the order of reading words at a weekly Friday

---

SCIENCE

1. Go to locker.
2. Get green notebook, textbook, pencil, pen, and paper.
3. Go to class.
4. Exchange homework with lab partner and grade it using a pen.
5. Put graded homework in teacher's homework tray and wait for teacher instructions.
6. Do assigned work at the lab station with partner.

Figure 3.7. Sample task card. (This card should be about the size of a business card.)

morning spelling test from the order the teacher listed and introduced the words on Monday.

Visual schedules that clearly outline what the student will be doing on a particular day, including schedule changes, along with what the expectations are for the new activity, can help prepare students for change. Verbal priming and behavioral contracts can also be used in combination with visual schedules to prepare students for variations in routine. Related to using a behavioral contract, a teacher, parent, or staff member can briefly note the change on a contract form, including the nature of the change and why it is occurring; the tasks the student is responsible for completing, along with other expectations; how the student will be monitored; and the reinforcement for appropriate behavior. The student and teacher review the document. After the teacher is certain that the student understands, both sign the document. The student can take the contract to the new situation and refer to it as necessary.

Peer Buddy Program

Typically developing and achieving peers, especially those who have positive relationships and a history of positive interactions with a student(s) with AS/HFA, can be an asset in helping such students navigate and understand school and community settings. That these supporting students make use of normally occurring interactions makes them all the more advantageous. Indeed, many parents and educators have reported that a buddy or mentor has often made the difference in students coping with school situations that would otherwise be problematic.

Buddies can accompany these students during transitions, provide cues for appropriate behavior, and take notes for the students during class. In addition, buddies can provide the social interactions that many students with AS/HFA desire but rarely succeed in mastering without assistance.

Buddies must be carefully selected. They should be volunteers who understand a peer's exceptionality, respect individual differences, and genuinely like the student whom they have been asked to assist. It is important that students understand and accept responsibility for this important role. However, it is equally important that they understand that they are primarily working to support another student as a peer. That is, peer buddy programs should not be presented as opportunities where a student is permitted to assume the role of teacher or of surrogate staff member. To be sure, equality of relationship status is imperative in structuring a peer buddy program. Ideally, peer buddies are responsible and socially adept students who consistently demonstrate behaviors that parents and teachers find positive and favorable. Without question, a number of students with AS/HFA have poor social judgment; hence, they might follow a peer into inappropriate social situations or be led into situations in which unacceptable behavior is modeled or promoted. At the same time, peer buddies do not necessarily need to be "model" students. That is, some students who are the most mature and who are the most academically advanced have no interest in working with classmates with disabilities. Accordingly, while recruitment of good models to work with students with AS/HFA is important, it is even more important to identify and train peers who are motivated to support and interact as friends with classmates who have special needs.

Early or Late Release

Transitions between classes or to special activities (e.g., music, physical education) are often extremely disruptive to students with AS/HFA. Moreover, unanticipated schedule changes may cause these students to experience a high stress level, and when this is combined with unfavorable environmental conditions (e.g., students bumping into one another, the student feeling rushed, a feeling of uncertainty about where the activity is located, or taunting by peers), the student is more likely to succumb to behavior problems, including meltdowns and "falling apart." Because such problems are most apt to occur during periods of transition, simply allowing children and youth with AS/HFA to have a few additional minutes to move to their next class, go to their locker or bus, or otherwise bypass stressful times at school can frequently be a simple solution. To be sure, releasing a student 5 minutes before the bell rings or 5 minutes after the bell rings often results in reduced stress. This strategy may be particularly effective when combined with a transition buddy. Of course, some school personnel may be reluctant to permit schedule changes. Yet, with due respect to school uniformity and group rules, a minor schedule adjustment of this type, if it yields the desired benefits, will likely be a positive experience for everyone.

Homework Assignment Notebooks

One relatively easily implemented and effective organizational strategy for students is an assignment notebook. Such notebooks structure and organize homework assignments and help parents and family members involved in assisting students with homework understand what is expected and how the student will be evaluated. These notebooks travel with students between home and school and identify homework tasks and due dates. Ideally, the assignment notebook also contains a sample of what the assignment should look like. Again, on an ideal basis, teachers inspect and organize students' notebooks daily to ensure that all assignments and all supporting materials (e.g., samples, texts, and worksheets) are included, and parents work cooperatively with the teacher by reviewing the notebook nightly and signing it as the student completes the assigned tasks.

Timelines

Teachers often assign tasks, such as book reports and term papers, that must be completed over an extended period of time. Typically, teachers will announce and/or post the task, explain the steps necessary to complete the assignment, and set a due date. The expectation is that students will budget their time to complete the assignment by the due date. Many learners are able to meet these expectations, and these students work on the assignment in sections or incrementally over days or weeks. However, because of a variety of difficulties (e.g., lack of ability to structure tasks over time, inability to project how long a task will take, general disorganization, or failure to understand the complexity of the task), students with AS/HFA frequently fail to complete these assignments. Encountering a student who thinks he or she will be able to successfully write a 20-page term paper or read a 200-page book and write a report in one evening is of course not limited to individuals who have been diagnosed with high-functioning autism. Yet, this problem is routine among these students. Therefore, they will often require assistance in budgeting time and systematically working to complete assignments on schedule.

Relative to teachers assisting students in budgeting time, teachers should create a list of steps needed to complete the task, help the student set target dates for completing each item, and establish a system to monitor the student over the course of the assignment. Monitoring should include asking to see the project at each stage—because the student with Asperger syndrome or high-functioning autism may indicate that a task is completed when, in fact, it is not. This untruth may not be deliberate; it may be a function of the disability. For example, if a teacher says to a student, "I hope you understand that you should have your book read by now," the student may respond affirmatively, indicating an understanding of the statement but not connecting it to any action that she should have taken. It is ideal for teachers to also enlist the aid of parents in developing and monitoring timelines.

Travel Cards

The Travel Card uses a gridlike format that contains a brief list of the academic, behavior, and social strategies on which the student is working (Jones & Jones, 1995). These are typically listed as column subheadings. Down the side of the card, each of the student's classes is listed.

Students carry the Travel Card from class to class, and each teacher must sign the card and indicate, using a plus (+) or minus (−), whether the student is engaging in the identified targeted behaviors. The student's case manager or resource room teacher prepares the card and gives it to the student daily. The student then carries it to each class. The completed card is left with the student's last teacher, who returns it to the case manager. The student receives reinforcers, such as tokens for carrying the card and engaging in the targeted behavior. The student charts and graphs her points weekly and selects a reinforcer from a menu of preferred items. The student may also choose to "bank" the points to save for reinforcers that require additional points.

Initially, the student may not be able to carry the card from class to class because of organizational problems. Several options exist for introducing the Travel Card system systematically. Initially, general education teachers may have to maintain the card, prompt the student to engage in the target behaviors, and ensure that the card is returned daily to the special educator, lead teacher, or case manager. Alternatively, the Travel Card may be introduced in one setting, with other settings added as the student is successful. The ultimate goal is to have the student maintain responsibility for the card, as well as prompt general education teachers to complete the Travel Card each hour.

The Travel Card increases students' productive behavior across multiple environments. It also facilitates teacher collaboration and improves school–home communication (Carpenter, 2001). Figure 3.8 provides an example of a Travel Card.

Home Base Programs

In his original description of children with significant social shortcomings, Hans Asperger (1944) did a remarkable job of describing a group of

TRAVEL CARD

Name _____

Date _____

Key: $+$ = Yes $-$ = No   NA = Not Applicable

	Did student follow teacher instructions?	Did student bring all materials?	Did student complete assignments?	Did student turn in homework?	Teacher's initials
Reading					
Science					
Geography					
Study Skills					
English					
Spanish					

Bonus Points	Went to nurse after getting off bus?		Has assignment book?	
Total	$+$ $-$			

Teacher Comments/Suggestions/Announcements:

Figure 3.8. Sample Travel Card.

children who were the prototype individuals who had a disability that we now recognize as Asperger syndrome or high-functioning autism. That Hans Asperger was able to describe the salient characteristics of children in a fashion that has withstood the test of time is undeniable. Yet, he likely failed to fully recognize the extent to which these individuals were affected by stress and that a number of the behavior problems and difficulties experienced by persons with AS/HFA in meeting the demands of everyday life are a result of organizational issues, understanding and dealing with environmental changes, and related factors that inflame and rouse stress. To be sure, these students often view school as a stressful environment that presents myriad sources of anxiety and tension, including difficulty predicting events because of changing schedules, understanding and following teacher directions within required time parameters, dealing with and preparing for daily school requirements, and knowing appropriate and socially conventional ways of interacting with peers.

Related to manifestations of stress among children and youth with AS/HFA, it is not unusual for these individuals to fail to communicate that they are under stress or are experiencing difficulty coping with or responding to classroom demands or activities. Frequently, they provide no obvious cues or information that would indicate they are confused, stressed, or in need of support. Because no emotion is conveyed, teachers and staff may fail to take actions that would avoid or forestall behavior problems. Thus, these students are permitted to experience cumulative stress and anger until they reach a threshold where they lose behavioral control.

Some students with AS/HFA do not display these types of behaviors in school. Sometimes teachers report that these students do fine, even with academic and social problems. However, parents report that when these children arrive home, they lose control. They have a tantrum, cry, or are aggressive. It seems as if these students use all their self-control to manage at school, but once they get to a safe environment, they let go of the pressure they have bottled up.

So what can educators do to help these students manage their stress at school and at home? In addition to instructing students on how to recognize and manage stress levels, teachers can create a safe "home base." This is a place where students can go when they feel the need to regain control. Resource rooms or counselors' offices are examples of safe places. When a student feels the need to leave the classroom, he or she can take assignments to the home base and work there in a less stressful environment. School personnel frequently schedule students' days so that they begin at the home base and then have frequent stops there. This gives these students a teacher with whom they have a consistent relationship and a place to go when the need arises (Myles & Adreon, 2001; Myles & Southwick, 1999).

Students need to be trained to use home base programs. That is, they will not naturally be able to recognize that they need respite from the demands of a class or situation. The first step is to assist students to recognize the feelings and thoughts that are signs of significant stress. The second step is to instruct students to communicate to their teachers or others that they are experiencing stress and that they need to leave a situation in order to avoid a problem. The third step is to consistently design environments such that students' requests for home base are honored and that they are not penalized for leaving a class or situation. Some educators may resist the use of home base programs because of a belief that students will exploit the program by leaving and avoiding undesired situations that are unrelated to stressful situations or independent of avoiding behavior problems. In truth, there is little evidence that the vast majority of students with AS/HFA attempt to take advantage of this program. In the vast majority of cases, students prefer to remain in classrooms and generally can be expected to use home base options only to avoid extreme problems.

Instructional Sequence

Learners diagnosed with AS/HFA have a clearly demonstrated capacity for school progress, including, in many instances, acquisition of grade-level knowledge and skills. However, their disability also almost always means that they will require appropriate accommodations and adaptations for optimal learning. Accordingly, their teachers are advised to provide an instructional sequence that facilitates students' learning. This sequence includes effective lesson presentation and, in cases where homework is assigned, consideration of elements that will assist these students in achieving the desired outcomes based on appropriate homework activities.

Rationale

Students often need to understand how or why concepts required for mastery are relevant. Thus, teachers must tell the student (a) why the information is useful, (b) how the student can use it, and (c) where it fits in with the knowledge the student already possesses. As with many other students, including those with and without exceptionalities, students with AS/HFA need to understand lesson rationale before they can or will learn.

Instructional Format

The teacher explains the goals for the content being presented and spells out exactly what the student is expected to learn. Then, using a direct instructional format, the educator teaches the content using various methods, including visual and auditory stimuli. The teacher breaks down the information and presents it in small increments. This type of instruction is active, with the teacher presenting information in an organized and sequential manner, asking questions, and providing corrective feedback.

Modeling

During the modeling phase, the teacher gets the student's attention and shows the student what he or she is supposed to do. The instructor demonstrates how to complete a worksheet, participate in a cooperative group activity, begin a project, and so forth. It is important for the teacher to demonstrate how to correctly complete a task or an assignment, instead of telling the student what not to do. Many students know what they should not do, but have no understanding of what is required of them.

Models should be presented frequently. For some students it may be necessary to present a model of how to put identifying information on a spelling test prior to each exam. The teacher should spell out every direction, preferably with a visual component. The teacher cannot assume, for example, that a student knows to number his spelling paper to 20 just because he has always had 20 spelling words. Anything that is only implied by the teacher or assumed to be understood because it has previously been done in a particular way will often not be understood by these students.

Monitoring and Modified Instruction

Many students with AS/HFA are atypical learners. That is, they have learning styles and characteristics that are highly idiosyncratic and that fail to follow a pattern shown by many students. As a result, teachers must be vigilant about monitoring learning and understanding, including not assuming students have mastered identified skills simply because they "appear" to understand or do not state that they need additional instruction. This pattern is particularly significant relative to abstract or conceptual materials and problem-solving application assignments. Throughout the lesson, the teacher is also advised to closely monitor a student's emotional state. Because students may have a flat, even seemingly negative affect, it may be difficult to tell when they are stressed as a result of not comprehending specific content. The teacher must work with the student to understand how he or she communicates emotional distress and meet that student's needs through additional instruction, modeling, or individual work sessions. If this important step is not completed, the student may tune out teachers' efforts to instruct; have a behavioral outburst; and/or fail to acquire skills, complete application assignments, or finish homework.

Verification

Because of a propensity for tunnel vision, distraction, and inattention, students with AS/HFA must be actively engaged throughout the instructional process. The student may require physical cues to attend to relevant stimuli and be asked frequent questions. A teacher might choose to stay in close proximity and cue the student to respond or attend.

For the student who requires a long processing time, the teacher might want to arrange a strategy so that the student knows when she will be asked a question. For example, the teacher might tell a student that she will be asked a question only when the teacher stands next to her. The teacher can then use this strategy, initially asking the student questions to which she knows the answers. No one else in the class needs to be aware that the student and teacher have this agreement.

A second strategy involves telling the student in advance what questions he will be asked during class. The questions could be presented in written format, oral format, or both, depending on the student's needs. The student will then be able to relax, process, and learn from the lecture without worrying about being unprepared to answer questions.

Verification also includes a generalization component. Teachers should work with students to ensure that they know the content and know how to apply it across multiple settings and with multiple instructors.

Homework

Ideally, teachers, parents, and caregivers should work together to determine whether homework should be assigned, and if so, how much. Because students with AS/HFA have a marked need for structure, it is often best to assign tasks that can be completed at the students' home base or during a study hall. Without a doubt, homework has been a significant source of stress and conflict for many of these learners.

If homework is assigned, it is best to use an assignment notebook and a parent–teacher communication system. This structure is necessary because parents or caregivers will likely need to play an active role in ensuring that the student completes assignments. Parents or caregivers are advised to set up a structure for assignment completion and monitoring similar to what the teachers use in school. In addition, parents will most likely need to assist the student by clarifying and giving an overview of assignments. In some cases, they may need to model the task for the student. Thus, teachers should ensure that the parents or caregivers understand the homework. This is often difficult, because the teacher cannot simply send a note home with the student—it may never reach its destination. The disorganized student with AS/HFA may misplace the note or bury it in the bottom of a backpack and forget that it is there.

To facilitate home-school communication, many schools have established a homework line and school websites that students and parents can use to review assigned work. E-mail is also recommended as a communication tool to ensure that parents and others who are involved in homework activities have an understanding of assignments.

Effective Instructional Methods

Educators have numerous instructional options, curricula, and intervention strategies from which to choose and base their programs. Unfortunately, many of these methods may have little in the way of proven efficacy and utility and thus be of limited educational value. There is also considerable debate within the field as to which methods hold the most promise. Finally, to add to the challenge of choosing those procedures that hold the most promise, there are few resources that are easily accessible and easy to use that direct teachers toward those methods that are most effective. Nevertheless, teachers and other stakeholders are expected to base their programs on those methods that have been objectively shown to produce desired educational outcomes.

One of the recommendations for guiding educators, parents, and other stakeholders in identifying and using maximally effective methods is to rely on the guidelines identified by Simpson (2008). These directing questions, listed below, are intended to assist stakeholders in adopting and appropriately using those tools that have the best chance of producing desired outcomes. Chapter 6 also identifies a number of evidence-based methods, as well as information on choosing maximally utilitarian strategies.

1. What are the proven effectiveness credentials of educational options being considered for a particular student, and are those methods designed to fit the unique needs of that individual student?
2. How will strategy or methods selected for use be evaluated?
3. How well do the selected methods or strategies fit an individual learner's unique educational and family circumstances?

Motivation

Many students with AS/HFA are difficult to motivate. They often see no reason to complete a task and frequently verbalize this to the teacher in a less-than-tactful manner (e.g., "This makes no sense," "No one in the world does anything like this," or "This is stupid"). These students are not necessarily intentionally being rude but are merely stating what they consider to be a fact.

Following are some general ways to motivate these students:

- A rationale will often motivate the student to begin an assignment. However, if the student is one who likes to engage in verbal power struggles, giving a reason for completing an assignment may start a series of "Yes, but . . ." statements or reasons why the rationale is not relevant to the student. In these instances, teachers and others are strongly advised not to engage in back-and-forth arguments and justifications about the logic and need for particular assignments.
- Acknowledge the student's negative statement and then provide a global rule (e.g., "I know you think that no one does work like this, but everyone in this class . . .").
- Assignments that relate to student obsessions are often highly motivating if the obsession is a secondary one. In their desire to discuss, learn, and read about their particular interest, these students may eagerly complete an assignment on the topic.
- Use the Premack principle, or Grandma's Rule. Set a contingency on a visual schedule stating that following completion of a non-preferred task, the student can engage in a preferred activity.
- Allow the student to complete an assignment with a peer. If the motivation for social interaction is strong, the student may complete nonpreferred tasks when allowed to work in pairs or small groups.
- Determine whether the student's resistance is associated with motor skills. Owing to fine-motor problems, the student may balk at an assignment, because the written portion is difficult. Providing a computer for assignment completion or allowing the student to dictate to a peer or into a tape recorder or recording device may be sufficient to prompt the student to begin a task.

Some assignments can be modified from an essay to a multiple-choice format to further reduce written requirements. If the teacher is not testing handwriting, there is often little reason to require that an assignment be handwritten.

Teacher Interaction Strategies

Not surprisingly, parents of students with AS/HFA have often communicated that individual teachers have made a difference to a student's success. Parents have defined a variety of teacher characteristics that seem to match these students' needs. Often these behaviors are not measurable but rather involve personality elements. Overall, these teachers are consistent in the way they structure their classrooms and predictable in the way they act. They tend not to be overly reliant on top–down management approaches, allowing the student options whenever possible. This type of teacher understands students with AS/HFA, detecting their stress level and making accommodations as needed. Some additional effective teacher characteristics include the following:

- has a working knowledge of the characteristics of students with AS/HFA
- works to develop trust between self and student
- accepts student's cognitive and social abilities and learning potential
- accepts the student as he or she is
- understands the student's needs and role in school
- enjoys working with the student and voices that enjoyment
- works to make learning an enjoyable and mutually beneficial experience
- works as an unobtrusive facilitator rather than as a dictator
- reacts calmly to all students
- provides nonthreatening feedback
- is direct and clear without being overly reliant on lecturing
- listens to the student, analyzes the student's needs, and adapts the curriculum accordingly
- avoids asking "why" questions to understand behavior
- states expected behavior and provides examples

- communicates in a fashion that is individually suited for particular students
- limits the number of instructions that are given at one time
- provides instructions in more than one modality, realizing that visual memory is often a relative strength
- uses a matter-of-fact and unemotional tone to redirect
- states rules as universals (e.g., "Everyone in this class needs to listen when I talk")
- behaves in a predictable and dependable manner
- provides adequate wait time for the student to process instructions and comply
- provides a classroom structure that is predictable and organized

Concluding Thoughts

Because of their intellectual capabilities and other educational assets, students with high-functioning autism or Asperger syndrome have the potential to be successful in school. However, intellectual functioning alone is not enough to ensure that these students have the resources, structure, and support they need to acquire the skills and knowledge they need. Educators must develop and implement individualized accommodations and adaptations, including academic supports, environmental modifications, cognitive interventions, and skill-based interventions. Success is also dependent on these students acquiring strategic skills that they can use independently throughout their academic day. Visual, structural, and motivational strategies are integral to these students' success. Just as important to their success is the selection of a teacher whose characteristics match their needs. Supports must be set into place with careful consideration of how these students' needs can best be met. As noted in this chapter, there are multiple methods that bode well for the success of these learners. The current challenge is not only to continue to develop new and better strategies and refine what is currently known about existing strategies but also to systematically implement those methods that are supportive of the unique needs of learners with AS/HFA.

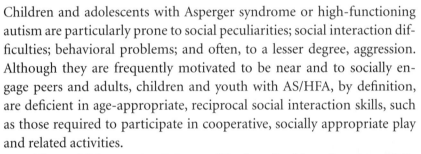

chapter four

Planning and Promoting Behavioral Success and Supportive Management

Children and adolescents with Asperger syndrome or high-functioning autism are particularly prone to social peculiarities; social interaction difficulties; behavioral problems; and often, to a lesser degree, aggression. Although they are frequently motivated to be near and to socially engage peers and adults, children and youth with AS/HFA, by definition, are deficient in age-appropriate, reciprocal social interaction skills, such as those required to participate in cooperative, socially appropriate play and related activities.

These children and youth are often described by others as socially stiff and awkward, emotionally flat, socially unaware, self-absorbed, lacking in empathy, prone to show socially unacceptable behavior, and insensitive or unaware of verbal and nonverbal social cues. Indeed, virtually every educational characteristic is related to their behavior and social skills. Accordingly, professionals and families must provide suitable supports so that these children and adolescents can progress and experience success at school and home. This chapter presents behavior management and behavior support options available to professionals and families.

Social and Behavioral Assessment

The basic model for assessing children and youth with AS/HFA consists of the same general effective-practice elements as for other individuals, with or without disabilities: (a) identify and evaluate important and socially valid behaviors to change; (b) analyze the functions of target behaviors, including environmental and antecedent factors connected to target behaviors, as well as motivational variables that support the response; and (c) based on a thorough understanding of the behaviors, select, implement, and evaluate appropriate interventions and treatments. Each of these components is discussed here as it relates to children and youth with AS/HFA.

Identify and Evaluate Social Behaviors to Change

Identifying and evaluating (including measuring) behaviors that need to be modified requires carefully selecting and clearly defining those target behaviors that have significant social importance. That is, from among the myriad behavioral excesses and deficits that an individual with AS/HFA may have, stakeholders such as parents and educators must target those responses that are most significant. *Significance* in this context means selecting for modification those behaviors that will yield social and quality-of-life benefits if changed. Furthermore, *significance* also means selecting those target behaviors that will create problems for an individual if unaddressed. For example, an individual who stands too close and talks aggressively toward others to gain attention during conversations is likely demonstrating a behavior that will lead to social benefits for the person if improved, and create problems if not changed.

Behaviors selected for evaluation, and subsequently that become targets for change, must also be clearly defined such that different individuals can reliably agree on the occurrence of the response. Accordingly, behavioral terms such as *nonreciprocal social responding, auditory hypersensitivity,* and *sensory and emotional overload* mean different things to different people and therefore are unsuitable as targets for behavioral intervention programs. Instead, target behaviors need to be specified so that they reflect exactly what the behavior is (e.g., one should not say that a child has a problem with auditory hypersensitivity, but rather should identify the target behavior as "loud screaming"). Where and when the behaviors occur should also be specified (e.g., "loud screaming in any classroom or indoor setting during regular school hours"). Specificity helps adults involved in change programs understand and evaluate interventions. It also enables children or youth with AS/HFA to be knowledgeable and involved participants in program efforts on their behalf.

Evaluation of socially valid behaviors for change programs involves collecting and analyzing observational data. Thus, behavior data should be regularly and accurately measured before an intervention is implemented. Such measurement should continue after a strategy is implemented. The most appropriate measurement options include frequency counts (the number of times a particular behavior is observed), duration assessment (the length of time a behavior lasts), and interval and time sampling. Both interval sampling and time sampling involve dividing an observation period into equal time segments and observing whether the target behavior occurs within each segment. Interval sampling requires observation during an entire time segment (e.g., 30 seconds); whereas time sampling requires brief observation of a target response at the end of each segment (e.g., the observer notes whether the child is engaged in a particular behavior at the end of each 30-second segment).

Depending on the nature of the targeted behavior and on resource availability, the appropriate measurement procedure is selected. For example, if the target behavior is tantrums, a duration assessment is selected instead of frequency counts, because the length of time a child throws a tantrum is usually more informative than the number of times he throws a tantrum. Similarly, if the goal of an intervention program is to reduce the number of times a child is out of her assigned seat during a particular class, frequency counts would likely be most suitable.

Analyze Environmental and Antecedent Factors and Motivational Variables

Professionals assess environmental and antecedent variables and motivational factors connected to target behaviors to answer two basic questions: (1) What are the conditions that are most and least apt to be present when the behavior occurs? (2) What is motivating the targeted behavior? For instance, does a child engage in an undesired social behavior as a way of getting peer attention because he lacks more appropriate ways of meeting his need for recognition? Is the behavior more likely to occur at certain times, in the presence of certain people, or in certain settings or environments? Is a target behavior most apt to occur while a student is working on certain types of assignments? Knowing the motivation for a behavior or that a behavior is correlated with particular factors is of obvious assistance in developing an appropriate intervention program. For example, determining that a child primarily engages in argumentative behavior with one paraeducator, as opposed to all teachers and staff, suggests possible causes for the behavior and thus helps in the creation of an intervention program that will have the highest probability of positively influencing the target behavior.

This process of identifying environmental and other antecedents of particular behaviors, along with motivators for those behaviors, is known as a *functional assessment.* In this context, an antecedent is any variable that precedes a target behavior, such as the time of day when particular social problems arise, the instructions given by a teacher prior to a student's displaying a problem behavior, and so on. A related term in this process is *functional analysis.* A functional analysis is a more specific process wherein the persons conducting the assessment systematically evaluate function and antecedent hypotheses about the target behaviors. That is, functional analysis is a more data-based and involved process than a functional assessment, and it typically results in more utilitarian information about factors that are supporting a target behavior and in better intervention program outcomes. Based on an understanding of the variables, factors, and conditions that surround a target response, suitable intervention programs can be developed. Because children and youth with AS/HFA frequently display behaviors that are difficult to understand, functional assessment and functional analysis information is essential. Indeed, it is extremely difficult to craft effective and long-term behavior management programs for these learners without such information.

There are two general assumptions associated with conducting a functional analysis or assessment. First, it is assumed that the behavior of children and youth with AS/HFA, as is the case with all human behavior, serves a purpose. Accordingly, professionals and families who evaluate the behavior and social interactions of individuals with these disorders must assume that the responses, regardless of how nonfunctional they may appear, have a purpose. Thus, these responses satisfy some need or are designed to achieve some goal—communication, escaping an undesired task, and so on—even if form (i.e., how the child communicates) and function (i.e., why the child communicates) appear to be unrelated.

The second assumption associated with functional analysis or assessment is that behaviors are controlled by, or are connected with, antecedent and other environmental factors. Consequences of behaviors are the responses they evoke from others. For example, a child's inappropriate social initiations with peers might routinely have as response consequences verbal reprimands from adults.

Functional analyses are based on indirect and direct procedures. Indirect methods of functional analysis and assessment include (a) review and analysis of student records and files; (b) interviews of professionals such as teachers and physicians; parents; and the students, themselves, regarding specified behavioral and social interaction patterns; and (c) functional assessment scales and questionnaires. In contrast, direct functional analysis methods and procedures rely on (a) direct observations and (b) on-site testing of antecedent and consequent variables thought to be associated with particular responses. Specific direct functional analysis methods include ABC/R charts and scatterplots.

Indirect Functional Analysis and Assessment Methods

Student Files. A primary initial source for understanding the antecedents and motivators associated with a student's behavior are his or her records and files. As shown in Table 4.1, varied sources of information are typically available to help professionals and families understand children and their behavior. For example, a student's file may reflect that noisy settings (e.g., crowded lunchrooms and gyms) are apt to be upsetting to the student and may even provoke tantrums, or that a change of classroom personnel (e.g., a substitute teacher) may be associated with social withdrawal. Analysis of such records independent of other information and data is rarely sufficient to complete an appropriate functional assessment or analysis. However, these data and this information form a foundation for understanding a child or youth and the individual's behavior. Thus, this information serves to provide background and an initial understanding of students and to direct subsequent functional assessment and analysis steps.

Interviews. Another source of indirect functional assessment information is interviews of professionals, parents, and students. Indeed, informant assessment relies heavily on interviews with educators and other professionals and with parents and family members. Furthermore, whenever possible, the student also should be included in these interviews.

Table 4.1

Record Review Information Examples

Medical/ physical	Social history	Response to environment	Classroom and educational
• Growth and development history • Vision and hearing • Medications • Allergies • Health records • Illnesses	• Family socio-economic status • Parent occupation • Siblings • Custody arrangements • Family supports	• Response to environmental changes • Response to noise, various foods, lights, crowds, temperatures, demands, peers	• Peer interactions • Preferred activities • Educational setting • Grades • Individualized education programs • Response to rules • Behavior problems • Response to task difficulty • Response to time demands

Information generated through interviews provides additional background and an understanding of antecedents and motivators associated with a student's social interactions and behaviors. Accordingly, interviews routinely ask such questions as "When is the problem behavior most and least apt to occur?"; "Who is the individual near when the problem behavior is most and least likely to occur?"; "Where is the problem behavior most and least apt to occur?"; and "What typically happens right after the problem behavior occurs?" For example, knowing that a child's aggressive behaviors are shown only in the presence of certain teachers or family members would be extremely helpful in planning an appropriate management and social interaction enhancement program.

The interview form shown in Figure 4.1 offers an example for obtaining information regarding the antecedent conditions surrounding a target behavior. Interview information is most beneficial when a variety of individuals participate in the process, because it provides a means of comparing responses across individuals. Figure 4.1 may also be used to structure direct observations of children.

Scales and Questionnaires. Scales and questionnaires are a third source of indirect functional assessment and functional analysis information. These instruments are designed to identify possible antecedent variables and motivators associated with target behaviors. These instruments vary in quality, with some offering excellent background information and data. For example, Lewis, Scott, and Sugai (1994) provided a simple questionnaire designed to elicit information about specific behavior problems. Based on a "typical episode of a problem behavior," the instrument is used to assess the percentage of time (i.e., ranging from *never* to *always*) each of 15 statements is perceived to be true for a particular student (e.g., "Does the problem behavior occur during specific academic activities?"). The instrument allows individuals conducting a functional assessment to generate information and develop hypotheses related to antecedent variables and peer and adult perceptions of escape and attention functions. A similarly designed scale, the *Motivation Assessment Scale* (Durand & Crimmins, 1992), provides professionals with information needed to conduct an evaluation of four possible functions served by the behavior: sensory, escape, attention, and tangible.

Direct Functional Analysis Methods

In contrast to indirect functional assessment, direct functional analysis involves directly observing students to analyze their behaviors. The first step in conducting a direct functional analysis involves operationally defining and measuring a target behavior. That is, a specific management target, social interaction behavior, or other socially valid behavior is clearly defined by identifying its salient elements. Typically, those elements involve specifying the *who*, *what*, *when*, and *where* components. For example, a desired social interaction behavior such as playing appropriately with other children might be defined as follows: "When on the playground at recess, Walter will approach a peer from his classroom and

Name of individual being observed _____

Observer _____

Target behavior observational definition _____

_____

_____

Timing of target behavior

Target behavior primarily occurs

- ☐ during structured activities
  Explain: _____

- ☐ during unstructured activities
  Explain: _____

- ☐ during lecture times or times of group discussion
  Explain: _____

- ☐ when working or playing with others
  Explain: _____

- ☐ when working or playing alone
  Explain: _____

- ☐ during free time
  Explain: _____

- ☐ during times of transition
  Explain: _____

- ☐ primarily during morning hours
  Explain: _____

- ☐ primarily during afternoon hours
  Explain: _____

- ☐ in specific environments (e.g., classroom, lunchroom, gym)
  Explain: _____

- ☐ other
  Explain: _____

Relation of target behavior to the presence of others

Target behavior primarily occurs

- ☐ when working or playing with another student at school
  - ☐ specific peer
  - ☐ all peers
  Explain: _____

Figure 4.1. Environmental and antecedent analysis interview and/or observation form.

☐ when working or playing with a sibling or peer at home or in the community

   ☐ specific siblings

   ☐ all siblings

   ☐ specific peer

   ☐ all peers

   Explain: _____

☐ when working or interacting with an adult at school

   ☐ specific adult

   ☐ all adults

   Explain: _____

☐ when working or interacting with a parent or other adult at home or in the community

   ☐ specific parent

   ☐ both parents

   ☐ specific adult

   ☐ all adults

   Explain: _____

☐ while a student is working on certain types of assignments

   Explain: _____

Summary analysis of timing of target behavior, presence of others, and other correlates of target behavior:

_____

_____

_____

_____

_____

_____

_____

_____

Figure 4.1. (*Continued.*)

engage in an appropriate cooperative behavior (e.g., play tetherball, jump rope, play tag) for at least 5 continuous minutes." Another example, classroom talk outs, might be defined as "Claudia making any audible vocal sounds during her 9th-grade history class without teacher permission."

Step 2 of the direct functional analysis involves observing and describing the antecedents and consequences that are associated with the behavior's occurrence and nonoccurrence. Two ways of conducting such analyses are to use ABC/R charts and scatterplots.

ABC/R Charts. ABC/R charts offer a structured means of observing and analyzing the antecedents (A), consequences (C), and responses (R) of children relative to a particular target behavior (B). For example, an ABC/R analysis might focus on a child's demonstrating appropriate social behavior in a cooperative group activity with peers. In this scenario, targeting "appropriate social behavior" (B), the antecedent (A) parts of the analysis would include the classroom setting, the teachers and children the child was with, the time of day, the curriculum and classroom activities, the specific instructions and prompts the student was presented, and so forth. The consequences (C) element of the analysis would involve analyzing the reactions or responses of the target child's teachers and peers when he did and did not demonstrate appropriate cooperative group behavior. Finally, the child's responses (R) to these teacher and peer consequences of his behavior would be analyzed. For example, the student's appearing to be pleased by the attention he received from peers for appropriate social behavior would be important information to have in forming hypotheses and developing and implementing an effective intervention program.

For example, a 16-year-old routinely cries and screams in the hallway during class breaks. During these periods (four 5-minute breaks), the school psychologist makes the observations shown in Figure 4.2. The psychologist has determined that the student routinely goes into the hallway outside his classroom during class breaks and begins asking other students if they are aware of various school rules. This student is well-versed in the rules and, in fact, always carries a copy of the school's disciplinary code. He reminds students that it is against school rules to smoke on school property and that security personnel will be called if somebody is observed smoking. In response to these reminders, his peers have begun intimating that it is acceptable to engage in behaviors identified as unac-

Antecedents (A)			Behavior (B), Consequence (C), and Response (R) analysis
Time	Setting	Task	
8:55–9:00	hallway outside class (class break)	none	B: Target student approaches group of students to remind them of school rules. Begins reading various school rules and consequences for infractions.
			C: Peers ignore student; one peer tells student to go away.
			R: Target student retreats and reads class rule book.
			B: Target student repeats rules; reminds peers that security personnel may be called to enforce rules.
			C: Peer informs student that rules don't apply to them: "Mr. Walker [principal] says it's okay to smoke in school."
			R: Target student attempts to show peer the written rule. When peer refuses to look at the rule book and indicates that security personnel are being sent, student begins to cry and scream and continues until quieted by a teacher assigned to patrol hallways.

Figure 4.2. ABC/R chart.

ceptable in the school handbook (e.g., students are allowed to smoke on school property). Confronted with this contradiction, the student tries to show his peers the written rule, but they indicate that they will call security personnel to "arrest" the student. The student consequently becomes upset and starts crying and screaming, much to the delight of his peers. Prompted by the crying and screaming, teachers or administrators attempt to calm or discipline the student.

Use of a functional analysis method such as the one shown in Figure 4.2 does not guarantee an effective intervention program. However, a functional analysis is an efficient and effective tool for understanding variables and outcomes related to student problems and for designing and implementing appropriate intervention programs.

Scatterplots. Scatterplots are used to help identify contextual conditions associated with target responses; that is, they are used to understand a target behavior relative to time, setting, activity, personnel, and so forth. For example, a child might be observed for classroom talk outs and for subsequent removal from class to determine if particular parts of her curriculum are more highly correlated with the target response than others.

Step 3 in the direct functional analysis involves analyzing direct and indirect functional analysis data for possible antecedents and consequences and forming hypotheses to explain the target behavior. For example, in the case shown in Figure 4.2, teachers and staff might hypothesize that the student's peculiar social interactions relating to school rules are associated with one or more of the following: need for peer attention, failure to understand conventional peer interaction protocol, or communication based exclusively on a narrowly defined obsessive interest.

Following identification of possible hypotheses related to a target behavior, Step 4 in the direct functional analysis is testing the hypotheses. Testing involves systematically observing an individual's target behavior under various antecedent and consequent conditions. For example, in the case described in Figure 4.2, the teachers and staff might decide that the student's problem behavior is likely a function of his desire for peer attention in combination with his failure to understand conventional peer interaction protocol. By systematically providing the student with more appropriate ways of gaining peer attention and with alternative topics for peer discussion, they could likely determine whether the hypothesized reasons were responsible for the target behavior. This diagnostic determination would then be used to develop an appropriate intervention program.

A case study of both an indirect and a direct functional analysis of a problematic classroom for a youth with AS/HFA follows. The case illustrates the use of a functional behavior analysis that led to a successful behavior support plan intervention.

Lionel

Lionel is a sophomore who attends public school at a suburban high school. He was diagnosed with Asperger syndrome when he was 11. He also has been diagnosed as having attention-deficit disorder (ADD) and depression. Lionel spends approximately 85% of his school day in general education classes. His special education assignment is three class periods weekly in a resource center classroom for students with mild disabilities. He also has access to the special education learning center if there is a crisis or if he encounters problems that can't easily be dealt with in general education.

Standardized academic assessment measures indicate that Lionel has the abilities to successfully achieve in his general education classes. However, he is frequently frustrated by classroom assignments. When frustrated, he refuses to work. As a consequence, he does not complete assignments and is in danger of failing several subjects. Lionel is very shy and quiet and even when confused about assignments, he refuses to ask teachers or peers for assistance. He is also extremely self-conscious and anxious, and so strives to quietly fit in with his classmates. Lionel becomes outwardly anxious and angry if he is the center of attention or if confronted about his academic difficulties.

Related to the aforementioned problems, Lionel's teachers and support staff identified off-task behavior as the target for intervention. Off-task was operationally defined as behaviors other than those associated with completing classroom assignments, including placing his head on his desk, daydreaming, sleeping, drawing on his assignment sheets, playing with classroom materials, texting, and so forth. Baseline data revealed that Lionel was off-task an average of 65% over a 4-day period during his U.S. Government class. His U.S. Government class was selected for the site of the analysis because it was a class that was representative of his overall functioning. He was particularly prone to being off-task in that class, and his U.S. Government teacher was especially concerned about Lionel's performance and had voiced an interest in better understanding his behavior and in improving his performance.

The functional behavior analysis included the following: (a) a review of school and other records and reports; (b) interviews with Lionel, his teachers and staff, and his parents; (c) assessment using two functional behavior assessment tests; (d) a scatterplot analysis; and (e) direct observations of his classroom performance. Based on results of these procedures, hypotheses related to the target behavior were formed and tested. Based on results of these tests, an intervention program was designed and implemented.

The record review process revealed that Lionel was, indeed, performing poorly in all his general education classes and that this pattern of behavior appears to have started approximately 2 years ago. Teachers consistently reported the same pattern: Lionel was unmotivated, frequently off-task, and inconsistently completing his assignments. Records also confirmed that Lionel had the diagnoses of Asperger disorder, ADD, and depression. He was being medically treated for ADD and depression. Educational records also indicated that Lionel had the skills to perform at or near grade level.

Interviews with two of Lionel's teachers, including his U.S. Government teacher, revealed a similar pattern of off-task behavior. Both teachers indicated that he was very reserved, albeit he appeared to get along with his peers, though with only minimal peer interactions. They also noted that he seemed to be invested in fitting into his class and with his classmates. He was thought to have a limited number of friends with whom he appeared to be most comfortable. However, the teachers were of the opinion that these individuals were tolerant of Lionel, but that they did not really spend much time in school or out of school doing things with him. Both teachers also noted he was an anxious individual who would become agitated and upset if he was confronted or made the center of attention. Both teachers were of the opinion that Lionel seemed to be willing to work on assignments that he fully understood but was reluctant to ask for assistance.

Lionel's mother indicated that her son was reserved and said little about school activities. She indicated that she and her husband were attempting to support their son and were willing to do what was needed; however, they had limited understanding of his day-to-day school activities and what might be responsible for his poor classroom performance. Lionel was unresponsive to attempts to interview him and requested that he not be required to talk about "his problems at school."

Functional assessment tests indicated that Lionel's off-task behavior was likely a function of an attempt to escape or avoid academic tasks. Escapism and avoidance of adult attention and difficult-to-understand curricula were consequentially noted as possible hypotheses.

Scatterplot analysis of Lionel's performance and off-task behavior revealed that he generally was off-task and minimally invested in classroom activities and assignments across various subjects, times of day, and days of the week. However, he performed better in his special education classes than he did in his general education classes, with the exception of physical education. His physical education teacher noted that Lionel was an "average student," who was quiet, albeit compliant and willing to participate in activities.

Direct observations (ABC/R analysis) confirmed that off-task behavior occurred across various classes, including U.S. Government. These observations also confirmed that Lionel was far less likely to be off-task in his special education learning center class than when he was in his U.S. Government class. These observations also confirmed that he became anxious and agitated when he was the center of attention or when confronted or urged to begin working. Finally, direct observation data strongly indicated that Lionel was highly prone to off-task behavior when faced with an independent paper-and-pencil task that he did not fully comprehend.

Based on the accumulated functional assessment data, the school personnel responsible for developing a behavior intervention plan for Lionel identified two primary hypotheses: First, Lionel engaged in off-task behavior to escape or avoid assignments that he did not completely understand. This was especially true for subjects that required comprehension of difficult reading materials, such as his U.S. Government text. Second, Lionel became anxious, agitated, and angry when he received reprimands for failing to work or when asked if he needed assistance.

The first hypothesis was tested by having Lionel's U.S. Government teacher provide additional information and explanations prior to giving independent assignments to her students. The teacher also provided Lionel and other students with examples of assignments they could use as models. Use of these methods significantly reduced Lionel's off-task behavior in U.S. Government.

The second hypothesis was tested by eliminating adult attention and prompts for off-task behavior. This process was introduced without also providing Lionel additional information and explanations for independent assignments. This testing procedure significantly reduced Lionel's agitation and anxiety. However, it also significantly increased his off-task behavior. Follow-up testing came in the forms of a written assignment rubric and a task analysis outline that described assignments. This phase of the hypothesis testing involved the teacher handing Lionel written assignment information without providing verbal explanations unless he requested an explanation. The results of that testing were significantly reduced off-task behavior and increased submission of written assignments.

Based on the results of the functional behavior analysis, a support plan was designed and implemented. The primary elements of that program involved giving Lionel and the other students additional information, assignment expectations, and work products prior to giving independent assignments and providing Lionel with written descriptions of assignments. Lionel also agreed to have one classmate in U.S. Government with whom he felt particularly comfortable be available for assistance if he encountered difficulties in understanding or completing assignments. These interventions significantly increased academic productivity and substantially reduced off-task behavior. Within his U.S. Government class, his off-task behavior dropped from an average of 65% during baseline to 28% during intervention.

Strategies for Behavioral Success

As previously outlined, the steps leading to selection, implementation, and evaluation of an appropriate intervention for individuals with AS/HFA are foundational and broad-based, albeit indispensable, steps. That is, it is unlikely that intervention will succeed without a clearly defined and measured target behavior; a thorough analysis of salient antecedent variables (e.g., curriculum or activity most associated with a target behavior, personnel connected to a problem, environments most likely to be associated with a target response, time of day when a targeted behavior is most and least apt to occur); and an understanding of functions that motivate a particular response (e.g., attention, failure to understand, communication, avoidance of an undesired activity). At the same time, the aforementioned information does not always easily reveal a clear and unitary management strategy or specific intervention. For instance, knowing that a child's out-of-seat classroom behavior typically occurs in math class during independent written work time and that it is likely motivated by an attempt to escape the activity does not automatically tell an intervention team the most effective and efficient strategy to use. Thus, in the present example, an intervention might involve one or more of the following strategies: modification of the task, including its level of difficulty, length, and so forth; social prompts and reinforcement for completing the task; use of a peer to prompt the student to work on the assigned task and to give the student social support; use of a self-monitoring or self-reinforcement program; and so on.

Selection of an appropriate intervention strategy involves consideration of a variety of options that fit a particular student and the circumstances. Children and youth with AS/HFA tend to be highly individualized in their responses, preferences, and tolerance for various strategies. Accordingly, there is no reliable formula that can be used to specify an exact intervention or support plan. Nevertheless, parents and professionals are able to craft supportive and efficacious support programs based on pre-intervention information and data in combination with consideration of the unique characteristics of individual students.

Because of the unique and individual characteristics of these students, intervention teams are advised to consider using a variety of effective practice methods. These methods include (a) environmental structuring and support, and (b) behavioral interventions. Because individuals with AS/HFA have a propensity for meltdowns when under stress, procedures for coping with such problems are also offered.

Environmental Structuring and Support

Children and youth with Asperger syndrome or high-functioning autism do not learn social behaviors in the same fashion or at the same rate as their nondisabled peers. They do not spontaneously and incidentally learn myriad and highly complex social responses, almost all of which vary at least slightly from situation to situation. For instance, beginning at a young age, children are expected to discriminate among situations in which it is appropriate to talk to and interact with other children (e.g., during recess as opposed to classroom "quiet time") and to select conversational topics that correspond to various situations, circumstances, and shared interests. Thus, a child waiting in line with peers for her turn in a game of kickball is more likely to experience a positive peer response to a conversation about the ball game or similar activity than to a conversation about an unrelated, narrowly defined topic in which other students have little or no interest.

Without assistance, most children and youth with AS/HFA can be expected to display a variety of socially incorrect, unaccepted, and nonreciprocal behaviors. Moreover, without support, these individuals are vulnerable to emotional stress and manipulation and apt to become agitated by social situations that they misinterpret or do not understand. Structure for children with autism-related disabilities also minimizes their being teased, bullied, or taken advantage of by peers.

There are no universally effective methods for structuring environments and situations for children with AS/HFA. Nevertheless, these children generally benefit from predictable environments and routines. The security that comes from being able to anticipate and understand activities, schedules, and expectations helps these children remain calm and enables them to appropriately meet various classroom, home, and community demands. Procedures that are helpful in creating such structure include (a) establishing clear expectations and rules for social behavior; (b) creating routines and schedules; and (c) offering physical, environmental, cognitive, and attitudinal support.

Expectations and Rules. Use of clear expectations for social and behavioral performance is one of the more effective and efficient means of establishing structure for children with Asperger syndrome or high-functioning autism. The importance of such expectations to these children's behavioral and social success is obvious: Children and youth with AS/HFA routinely experience difficulty understanding expectations and consequences. Accordingly, adults involved with these children must clearly and explicitly state, model, and illustrate rules—including desired behaviors. That is, these children should be instructed not only in what not to do, but also in acceptable behaviors. For example, students should not be told only that they are not permitted to play in the unfenced area next to the school where the teachers' cars are parked. Instead, they should also be instructed that they are permitted to play in the paved, fenced area around the school. Without such specificity, it cannot be assumed that children with AS/HFA will understand and be able to follow the rules.

Rules established for these learners should also be utilitarian. Although this suggestion has obvious relevance for all children and youth, it appears to be particularly important for children and youth with AS/HFA. *Rule-related functional value* is the result of establishing and enforcing rules that clearly and deliberately reinforce and facilitate students' social and cognitive development. Adults should not create rules that are designed either to develop children's compliance or to establish that the adults are "in charge" if such rules otherwise have no functional value.

Also, rules and expectations should be regularly reviewed, and children and adolescents should practice following rules by rehearsing desired classroom, home, and community behaviors and simulating potentially problematic situations. Finally, adults should closely monitor rules, maintain consistent expectations, and routinely apply consequences.

Expectations for behavior in the classroom and at home can be clarified by incorporating reviews of the expectations into daily routines. For example, an adult might briefly review "playground rules" prior to recess or "store behavior" prior to entering a store. Classroom and school rules and expectations should be presented visually, for example, on bulletin board posters that identify appropriate rules for an activity, as in the following:

During Free Reading Time:
- Choose a book or magazine to read.
- You may read anywhere in the room.
- You may read with a friend.
- You must read quietly.
- When the timer goes off, quietly return to your desk.

Expectations and rules may also be visually communicated without use of written words. Figure 4.3 illustrates a visually formatted method of structuring leisure-time choices for a youth who experienced difficulty choosing and staying with appropriate tasks during earned free time. The student was required to choose from the leisure-time choices shown and to remain engaged in the activity he selected for a minimum of 10 minutes.

Another means of helping individuals understand and follow rules is for adults to identify cues or use physical prompts that alert students to unacceptable behavior. For example, a teacher may indicate that he will hold up a clipboard when he observes a child failing to take her turn in a game during recess. In this scenario, the student would rehearse coming to the teacher for instruction on appropriate play behavior whenever she observed her teacher holding a clipboard above his head.

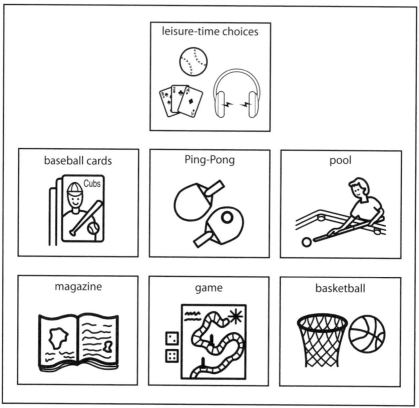

Figure 4.3. Example of visually structured leisure-time choices.

Routines and Schedules. Routines and schedules can also provide structure, building on the preference of children/youth with AS/HFA for predictability, order, and consistency. Most children and youth who are not disabled are able to effectively respond to environmental variables and variations and to adapt to their ever-changing world. In contrast, children/youth with AS/HFA tend to focus on only certain environmental variables and to have strong negative reactions to environmental changes. For example, an individual may fail to respond to information heard over the school intercom system. Other children with AS/HFA may become extremely upset when classroom schedules are adjusted to accommodate a schoolwide assembly or to respond to inclement weather.

Even though resistance to change is a common characteristic of these disorders, it is neither possible nor desirable to follow a routine without deviation. Nonetheless, it is important to recognize that many individuals with autism-related disabilities have a strong preference for routine and consistency. Thus, teachers, families, and others who are in regular contact with these individuals would be wise to establish and follow predictable routines and to prepare these individuals in advance of anticipated changes. For example, after discussing the situation, a parent may follow an alternate route to school. Although such a deviation may seem trivial, it may be significant for a child/youth with AS/HFA.

It is important to build on preferences for routine and consistency while introducing strategies to help children and youth deal with change, because learning to adjust to change has obvious implications for the well-being and development of individuals with AS/HFA. Group and individual schedules presented in written, pictorial, or a combination format, as shown in Figures 4.4 and 4.5, are useful in communicating the sequence of daily activities and in alerting children to new activities and schedule deviations.

Physical, Environmental, Cognitive, and Attitudinal Support. Physical, environmental, cognitive, and attitudinal support involves having adequate resources to effectively sustain, manage, and supervise children/youth with Asperger syndrome or high-functioning autism in various settings, including classrooms and other school settings (e.g., play areas and lunchrooms), home settings, and community settings (e.g., shopping centers, churches, and recreational sites).

Above and beyond all other resources, it is essential that children/youth with AS/HFA associate with adults and peers who are knowledgeable about the disorders, aware of individual needs, and capable of creating environments and situations to support these needs. It is essential that children with Asperger syndrome or high-functioning autism have the support of parents, family members, peers, teachers, and other support personnel (e.g., psychologists, speech–language pathologists, paraprofessionals) who are knowledgeable and skilled. In far too many instances, peers have bullied and provoked these children into engaging in inappropriate behaviors and have otherwise exploited their social disability. Accordingly, one major step in preparing supportive environments for these children/youth is to inform peers and teachers of the nature of the disorder, explain their role in supporting the children/youth, and enlist their help in ensuring appropriate protection of these individuals.

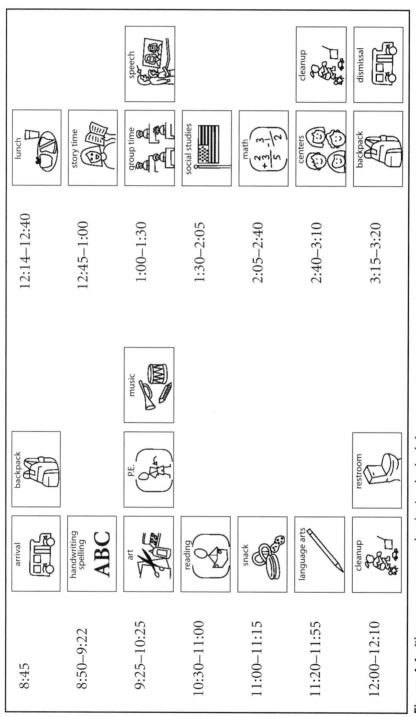

Figure 4.4. Elementary-age student's visual schedule.

THURSDAY, NOVEMBER 1		
Class	Room number	Target
Homeroom	8	Check to-do list assignment
Math	9	Write homework
Language arts	10	Bring keyboard and journal
P.E.	11	Hang with peer support guys
Lunch	12	Sit with Mac—use social scripts for conversation
Science	1	Check contract for focusing
History	2	Write homework
Resource room	3	Check with Ms. Taylor re: point system feedback
Computer club	4	Have fun!

Figure 4.5. Secondary-age student's written schedule.

Behavioral Interventions

Support for children/youth with AS/HFA can also come in the form of behavioral interventions that are compatible with these individuals' unique social characteristics. In this context, behavioral interventions refer to (a) manipulation of antecedent conditions (variables that precede a target behavior), such as changing a student's assignment to reduce stress and to prevent a problem from occurring; and (b) use of positive and negative consequences (stimuli presented contingent on a particular response, such as social praise for desired behavior). The uniqueness of these children and youth warrants particular attention when behavioral interventions are being considered. They require behavioral intervention strategies that do not rely heavily on a typical top–down approach. Strategies that work best include those in which students have an interest, an investment, and a choice. Accordingly, it is strongly recommended that, whenever possible and appropriate, students be involved in program development and implementation. Such participation increases the understanding of rules, expectations, and consequences and increases the chance that they will be proactive in program implementation and evaluation.

Cognitive Behavioral Interventions. Cognitive-based methods teach individuals to monitor and evaluate their own behavior, pace, or performance and to deliver self-reinforcement at established intervals. In this strategy, the locus of behavior control is shifted from an external source, such as a teacher or supervisor, to the individual. Cognitive behavioral interventions can be used to facilitate a variety of behavior changes, from task completion to on-task behavior in either school or work settings. The procedure is most appropriate for students who have the necessary skills and motivation to independently perform a particular task but are unable to complete it because of difficulties in understanding the elements of expected behaviors or performance, attention difficulties, and so forth.

For individuals diagnosed with AS/HFA, cognitive-based strategies often align well with these students' propensity for independence and self-directed activities. Cognitive methods also build on an individual's preference and aptitude for self-determination and self-management.

The basic steps required for implementing cognitive behavioral modification are detailed in Table 4.2. Figure 4.6 provides an example of one student's cognitive behavioral management data-collection sheet for the target behavior "follow teacher instructions."

Reinforcers. Related to the use of behaviorally based management programs, reinforcers refer to interventions that increase the occurrence of a desired behavior by following the wanted behavior with either a positive consequence or the removal of an unpleasant stimulus. For obvious reasons, the latter option is less preferred. Based on a thorough environmental and functional analysis of behavior, three forms of positive reinforcement have particular utility with children and youth with Asperger syndrome or high-functioning autism: (a) contingent activities, (b) social consequences, and (c) token economy systems (see Table 4.3).

Reinforcement programs may be best implemented through collaborative social contracts in which adults and the students with AS/HFA clearly define their goals, expectations, and consequences. Of course, reinforcers are not universally robust: They need to be selected based on individual preferences. For this reason, whenever possible, students need

Table 4.2
Steps for Implementing a Cognitive Behavioral Intervention Program

1. Pretraining Preparation

TARGET THE PROBLEM AREA. The first step in implementing a cognitive behavioral modification (CBM) training program is to identify the problem behavior. Initially, it is recommended that only one behavior be targeted at any one time. As students become familiar and comfortable with the program, multiple target behaviors may be simultaneously addressed. Target behaviors generally fall into two classes: (a) behaviors that need to be decreased (i.e., those that are disruptive, distracting, or annoying to others) and (b) behaviors that need to be increased.

Students should actively participate in evaluating and managing their own target behaviors. However, it is unlikely that most students will be motivated to initiate targeting a perceived response for change or to actively participate in the initial selection of a possible target for change. Accordingly, teachers, parents, and other adult stakeholders should assume leadership for selecting suitable behaviors for change. Subsequent to this initial selection, students should be invited and urged to participate in the process, including discussing with teachers and others the nature of the perceived problem behavior, defining the behavior, and leading a discussion of the importance of the behavior relative to the students' educational and social standing, and so forth. Of course, the teacher (and/or other adults involved in the program development process) should be prepared to define the behavior so that it is meaningful to the student.

IDENTIFY REINFORCERS. The CBM strategy is most successful when students are actively involved in the design and implementation of programs. In this connection, consideration of student preferences for reinforcers is strongly recommended. Obviously, adults need to be actively involved in this process and ultimately they must approve reinforcers that students may suggest. Nevertheless, CBM programs tend to be most effective when students and teachers (and other adult stakeholders) jointly decide which types of reinforcement will support the CBM, the frequency with which the reinforcement will occur, and so forth. Although three types of reinforcement can be used (social, contingent activities, tangible/edible), the primary use of contingent activity and social reinforcers is preferred.

PREPARE MATERIALS. Three items must be prepared: a timing device, a data-collection sheet, and self-management tools. The creation, organization, and use of the materials should be practical so that they will be easy to use for both the student and the teacher. Materials should also be selected based on student preference.

Timing devices, such as an audiotape or a wristwatch, can be used to designate time intervals. The length of the intervals should be commensurate with student attention. A timing signal will cue the student that it is time to document behavior. For example, if a student can stay on task for approximately 10 minutes, the signal should occur

(continues)

Table 4.2 *(continued)*

at 10-minute intervals. The student may require instruction on how to use the timing device.

A data-collection sheet is used to monitor student progress and to determine strategy effectiveness. The type of data-collection sheet used depends on the type of data collected. For example, frequency data allow teachers to measure the number of intervals the student was on task. Duration data can be used to measure the amount of time in minutes that a behavior occurs. The teacher may elect to synthesize student progress on a graph. This provides a visual representation of the student's progress based on the data collected. An example of a data-collection form is shown in Figure 4.6.

The type of self-management tool is also dependent on the student's functioning level and the task. The single most important consideration in choosing a self-recording and self-evaluation system is assurance that students understand what they are doing (so that they can consistently and accurately record selected target behaviors), why they are recording their behavior, and how the information will be used.

2. Discrimination Training

The discrimination training component assists students in becoming aware of their own behavior and how it affects learning and successful task completion. During this stage, the student is taught to specifically identify a target response and discriminate between examples and non-examples of the response. Instructional methods for use during discrimination training include videotaping, picture cues, direct teaching, modeling, verbal feedback, and physical guidance through the task. Because many students with Asperger syndrome or high-functioning autism may not be fully aware of a particular problem behavior and how their behavior affects them and others, it is important to provide them with a concrete representation.

Videotaping the student during the same classroom period that the CBM strategy will be used is an effective way to promote self-awareness. A 15-minute sample of a selected target behavior is generally sufficient for use during the discrimination training session. If data are being collected to document behavior change, a minimum of 3 to 5 days of videotape should be taken. This serves as baseline data. The videotape helps students realize relationships between their behavior and its effects. For example, clarifying the relationship between off-task behavior and failure to complete assigned work may appear obvious; however, some students may require a visual representation to fully understand the connection. The student is presented with concrete evidence of a target behavior and the impact it has, thereby helping him or her gain a clear perception of actual behavior without allowing denial mechanisms to cloud the issue. However, care should be taken to prevent this step from being viewed as punitive. The positive aspects of improved behavior and the student's ability to address the problem response should be emphasized.

The teacher then introduces CBM, explaining that this strategy will help the student address a particular behavior. The teacher and student view the videotape of the

Table 4.2 *(continued)*

student's performance, discussing the student's feelings about behaviors seen on the tape. The student then identifies specific elements of a target behavior. For instance, for the target behavior "on task," specific on-task and off-task behaviors seen on the tape could be discussed and recorded using a teacher-prepared behavior recording chart. Subsequently, the teacher and the student would jointly identify the criteria for understanding and recording the target behavior occurrence.

3. Self-Management Implementation

During self-management implementation, the teacher explains the CBM strategy, including the steps involved in implementing the program. The student learns through receiving a rationale, as well as through direct instruction, modeling, and guided practice. Self-management implementation depends on the method used, as well as on the student and his or her abilities, because each person learns at a different rate. Thus, what may take one person a few weeks to master may take another person a month.

The teacher instructs the student on the following steps:

a. *Self-monitoring*—The student listens to the timing signal. When the student hears the signal, he or she will self-evaluate relative to the identified steps for the target behavior. For example, for the target behavior "paying attention," a student will self-query on meeting the identified steps for the target (e.g., "Was I looking at my teacher?"; "Was I listening to my teacher's words?"; "Did I have the materials the teacher said I needed on my desk?"; and so forth.

b. *Self-recording*—The student quickly assesses whether he or she met the designated standard for each of the elements of the target behavior. For example, for the target behavior "on task," the student will self-evaluate whether he or she was attending by circling "yes" on the self-monitoring sheet. If the student was off task, he or she will circle "no" on the self-monitoring sheet.

c. *Self-rewarding*—The student rewards himself or herself for meeting the standard for a particular target behavior. For example, for a student who meets the criterion for "on-task behavior," he or she will be prompted to self-reinforce by saying, "Good job." The student's teacher will also reinforce the student. In instances where students fail to meet the standard for an evaluation period, they will be prompted to resume work and to self-prompt by quietly saying, "Get back to work."

The teacher models these three steps using the videotape that was prepared earlier. The teacher views the videotape with the student and models the self-monitoring process by listening for the timing signal; stopping the videotape when it is heard; and asking, for example, "Is [student's name] paying attention?" The teacher then verbalizes the answer and marks the appropriate answer on the self-monitoring sheet. Finally, the teacher models the use of the reward or prompting statement.

(continues)

Table 4.2 *(continued)*

After the teacher has modeled the strategy for several minutes, the student attempts to self-monitor while viewing the videotape. Initially, it will likely be necessary for the teacher to direct the process and give assistance to the student. During this step of the training, it is important that the student use overt speech, that is, vocalize the self-assessment, reward, and prompting statements aloud.

4. Self-Management Independence Training

The student practices the strategy under teacher direction, beginning with overt speech and fading to covert speech. The session begins with a review of elements of the target behavior. For example, for the target "on-task and off-task behaviors," a teacher or another program manager would review the purpose and rationale for selecting the target (to stay on task) and the goal of the support strategy (to complete assigned work during seatwork time and self-monitor behavior). The steps to be followed during the process (self-monitoring, self-recording, and self-rewarding) are also reviewed. Finally, the student discusses the strategy aloud using the selected timing signal and self-monitoring sheet. The student continues this process with overt speech until the process has become routine and the student is using it accurately. When the student follows the process correctly, he or she is instructed to fade overt speech to whispering, then to covert or silent speech. The teacher provides continual feedback on student progress.

At this point, the student begins using the self-monitoring and self-reinforcement program in actual situations. For instance, for on-task behavior, the strategy would be applied during seatwork time. The timing device and self-monitoring sheet are placed on the student's desk. It is recommended that the teacher closely monitor the student's program to ensure that the agreed upon protocol is being followed. In addition, the teacher will want to collect daily data on the student's behavior to establish strategy efficacy and to provide reliability on the student's self-assessment measurements. The teacher may choose to discontinue daily data collection when the strategy appears to be working. However, the teacher continues to monitor that the student is using the strategy correctly and maintaining on-task behavior.

5. Treatment Withdrawal

The ultimate goal of this strategy is to allow the student to independently engage in the targeted behavior at an acceptable rate. Thus, for this strategy to be deemed effective, the teacher's role in the program should be reduced. Fading should be done with the same careful consideration that went into the initial stages of discrimination training, self-management implementation, and self-management independence training. That is, the student should be able to initiate and complete the strategy without teacher assistance or with only minimal prompting. It is also important to remember that it is highly unlikely that teachers will be able to completely withdraw from participation

Table 4.2 *(continued)*

in the program. It is clear in the vast majority of cases that some teacher (or other adult) involvement in the program, including monitoring the targeted behavior and reinforcing and assisting the student in carrying out the procedures, is required for program maintenance and generalization.

6. Generalization Training

Generalization training allows the student to self-monitor the targeted behavior across different subject areas, activities, classrooms, or all three. In addition, it may help the student to target other, similar behaviors for which the strategy may be appropriate. Instruction at this stage assumes the same degree of importance as in the training phase. Unless the student is taught to use and modify the strategy as needed, lasting behavior change has not occurred.

Note. Adapted from "Implementing Cognitive Behavior Management Programs for Persons With Autism: Guidelines for Practitioners," by C. Quinn, B. L. Swaggart, and B. S. Myles, 1994, *Focus on Autistic Behavior, 9*(4), pp. 1–13. Copyright 1994 by PRO-ED, Inc. Adapted with permission.

to be actively involved in selecting reinforcers, including through use of menus that list various reinforcement options. Ideally, menus should be rotated frequently to ensure that students do not become sated on a particular reinforcer. These programs are frequently most effective and appealing when students are permitted to apply them through self-management and other cognitive-based methods.

Antecedent Intervention Programs. Antecedent intervention supports include myriad options that precede the occurrence of a target behavior. Thus, antecedent modifications do not rely on manipulation of consequences. Instead, they structure environmental conditions to reduce the probability of a behavior's occurring. For example, a child with AS/HFA who demonstrates her concern over hallway noises by becoming agitated and inattentive might best be dealt with by moving her desk away from the source of the noise, as opposed to designing consequences to modify the behavior. A student who regularly displays verbally inappropriate behavior and occasional aggression related to frustration associated with not understanding abstract algebra equations and geometry concepts might be successfully assigned to another math class. Thus, rather than applying consequences for unacceptable behavior,

Follow Teacher Instructions

Listen When Teacher Gives Directions

3   I listened carefully for my teacher's instructions.

2   I heard my teacher, but my listening could have been better.

1   I did not carefully listen for my teacher to give instructions.

0   My teacher did not give instructions during the recording period.

Raise Hand for Teacher Assistance

3   I did not understand and I raised my hand to get my teacher's assistance.

2   I asked for teacher assistance, but I forgot to raise my hand.

1   I did not understand, but I did not ask for teacher help.

0   I did not need teacher assistance during the recording period.

Follow Teacher's Instructions

3   I followed my teacher's instructions.

2   I did what my teacher told me to do, but I was slow in starting or finishing or I argued with my teacher.

1   I did not follow my teacher's instructions.

0   My teacher did not give me any instructions during the recording period.

Circle the number that describes how you followed your teacher's instructions.

9:00–9:15

I listened for my teacher to give instructions.

          0   1   2   3

If I did not understand, I raised my hand and asked the teacher for assistance.

          0   1   2   3

I followed my teacher's instructions.

          0   1   2   3

9:20–9:35

I listened for my teacher to give instructions.

          0   1   2   3

If I did not understand, I raised my hand and asked the teacher for assistance.

          0   1   2   3

I followed my teacher's instructions.

          0   1   2   3

Figure 4.6. Example of a student's cognitive behavioral management data-collection sheet for the target behavior "follow teacher instructions."

Table 4.3
Reinforcement Types and Descriptions

Reinforcer	Description
Contingent activities	This reinforcer makes certain preferred events (e.g., computer time) contingent on an individual's satisfactorily meeting some previously specified level of performance or behavior. For instance, after meeting a prescribed standard of academic work and behavior, a child might be permitted to work on a puzzle in the free-time area of his classroom. Children and youth with Asperger syndrome or high-functioning autism often have strong (albeit sometimes unusual) preferences for alone time and frequently benefit from the structure inherent in following adult-directed activities with preferred activities, which makes this a particularly effective tool.
Social consequences	Adults and peers offer contingent, supportive, and constructive verbal and nonverbal feedback, including praise, thanks, high-fives, and so forth. This tool is powerful if the student understands the social behavior being communicated and the reason it is being communicated. Social consequences, offered as overt social attention for desired behavior, can be one of the most effective ways of positively influencing the behavior and social development of individuals with Asperger syndrome or high-functioning autism.

antecedent manipulation measures involve modifying or mitigating those variables that are associated with the problem. Myriad variables can be used to create favorable antecedent conditions, including curricula, structuring methods, and various environmental supports (e.g., creating routines and priming students for transitions).

Behavior Contracts. A behavior or contingency contract presents an agreement among parties (e.g., teacher, student, parents) that specific behaviors will result in specific consequences. For example, a contract may be used to teach new behaviors, maintain existing behaviors, extinguish undesirable behaviors, or provide enrichment opportunities.

The contract focuses on positive outcomes, and skills and consequences (typically in the form of reinforcement menus) are stated in a manner that leads the student to success. Downing (1990) outlined the steps needed to develop, implement, and monitor a behavior contract. These guidelines are listed in Table 4.4.

Behavior Reduction Strategies. Behavior reduction strategies involve presenting undesired consequences or withdrawing reinforcement when individuals display specified undesired behaviors. Behavior reduction methods are appropriate only when it can be confirmed that students are able to perform a desired behavior. That is, it is inappropriate to present undesired consequences or withdraw reinforcement in instances where students are unable to perform the desired response. Parents and educators should carefully consider when or whether they should use behavior reduction approaches. Although these strategies can be effective for some of these students, they are often perceived as a form of top–down management and result in additional negative behavior and power struggles. Table 4.5 details different behavior reduction methods.

If behavior reduction strategies are used, positive alternatives should generally be implemented first. In addition, these guidelines should be followed:

- Implement behavior reduction programs through collaborative social contracts that clearly spell out goals, expectations, and consequences.
- Apply consequences in a firm, predictable, direct, and unemotional manner. Whenever possible, attempt to implement behavior reduction programs through self-management and other cognitive-based methods. For example, a child might be trained to quietly lay her head on her desk for 2 minutes when she displays a particular unacceptable behavior, as opposed to using a punishment method such as time-out.
- As much as possible, avoid communication and interactions that create opportunities for power struggles and confrontations.
- Be sensitive to conflicts related to behavior reduction strategies that may escalate into a crisis or physical confrontation.

Table 4.4
Steps for Developing, Implementing, and Monitoring a Behavior Contract

1. Meet with concerned parties.

The student, teacher(s), and parent(s) who will be supporting the contract meet to discuss one target behavior.

2. Determine conditions.

The parties determine when, where, and under what specific conditions the behavior occurs. The contract will be written to address these conditions.

3. Determine who will use the contract and where it will be used.

All persons who will be responsible for contract implementation must know their responsibilities.

4. Determine reinforcement.

Students should be allowed to participate in developing a menu of reinforcers. Reinforcers should be manageable but powerful enough to evoke the desired response. Menus should be rotated often to ensure that student motivation remains high.

5. Determine whether negative consequences will be used.

Contracts should be written in a positive way to increase behaviors. Negative reinforcers may not be necessary or even desirable if the positive reinforcers are motivating for the student.

6. Take baseline data.

The parties determine the frequency with which the behavior occurs. Data should be taken over at least 3 to 5 days to ensure that the behavior is typical for the student.

7. Determine reinforcement schedule.

The parties determine how often the student is to receive reinforcers. The contract should be structured so that the student has a successful experience; this will prompt the student to further work toward the contract goals.

8. Determine goals.

The parties determine the criteria for successful completion of the contract. Realistic and reasonable goals should be set, even if those goals do not represent the final level of expectation for the student. When the student consistently reaches the goals, the contract can be modified to target a higher goal.

9. Write the contract.

The contract should be written in terms that specify task and time demands, criteria for accuracy, and available reinforcers.

10. Discuss and sign the contract.

All concerned parties discuss the contract to ensure understanding. It might be necessary to supplement a discussion with drawings or icons for some students with Asperger syndrome. All concerned parties should receive a copy of the contract.

(continues)

Table 4.4 *(continued)*

11. Monitor the contract.

The parties set up a plan to evaluate and modify the contract if needed. All concerned parties should remain in regular contact with one another to ensure that student progress across settings is monitored. If the contract is unsuccessful, the parties need to address task appropriateness, time allotment, and student or environmental factors that could have impeded student progress.

Note. Adapted from "Contingency Contracts: A Step-by-Step Format," by J. A. Downing, 1990, *Intervention in School and Clinic, 26*(2), 111–113. Copyright 1990 by PRO-ED, Inc. Adapted with permission.

Table 4.5

Behavior Reduction Methods

Method	Description
Differential reinforcement of other behavior (DRO)	This method attends to and rewards behaviors that are not displayed for specified periods of time. That is, reinforcement is contingent on the nonoccurrence of a particular response.
Differential reinforcement of alternative behavior (DRA)	This method attends to and rewards behaviors that are more appropriate alternatives or forms of a behavior. This form of differential reinforcement may involve shaping and redirecting a student with AS/HFA.
Differential reinforcement of incompatible behavior (DRI)	This method attends to and rewards behaviors that are incompatible with the undesired behavior. Reinforcing students who experience difficulty in keeping their hands off other students when they are standing in line for keeping their hands in their pockets is a common DRI program, because having hands in pockets is incompatible with touching others.
Differential reinforcement of lower rates of behavior (DRL)	This form of differential reinforcement offers reinforcement for behaviors that occur less than or equal to a specified limit. Thus, DRL programs systematically lower acceptable rates of a target behavior. These programs are particularly effective with students who are interested in behavioral self-monitoring.

Behavior reduction strategies should generally be used only under the following conditions: (a) when positive reinforcement methods have not been successful, or when the nature or severity of a behavior necessitates a more immediate response; (b) if incompatible desired behaviors occur too infrequently (or cannot be sufficiently shaped) to serve as the focus of reinforcement; (c) if an undesired behavior is so intense as to be a danger to an individual; and (d) only when paired with positive reinforcement for desired behavior and systematically, promptly, and consistently carried out in accordance with an approved, written positive behavior support plan by well-trained professionals, staff, or parents or a combination thereof. The plan should include a clear, specific description of what is to be done, who will execute the plan, how long the procedures will be in force, and how the program will be evaluated.

Power Struggles and Aggression

It is common for adults who manage and interact with students with AS/HFA to become entrapped in power struggles, relatively frivolous inconsequential conflicts, and other nonproductive confrontations. Unfortunately, at least some of these situations may escalate into crises. For example, one teacher described her frustration in attempting to convince a youth of the necessity of regular bathing and personal hygiene. In an attempt to convince him of the advantages of good personal hygiene, she said that he would be unable to get a good job if he failed to follow accepted hygiene practices. His response was he intended to pursue a career as a home-based computer programmer. He argued that because he would not be around other people, there was no reason for him to bathe. The teacher then argued that his ability to find a date for the spring dance would be enhanced if he regularly showered and used deodorant. His response to this argument was that he had no interest in attending the school dance and intended to stay home and work on his computer. The teacher reported that this scenario was typical of her interactions with her student. He was highly skilled at entrapping her in power struggles and unproductive arguments that occasionally escalated into major confrontations and crises. The following list provides some suggestions for avoiding these common problems.

- Describe in direct terms the behaviors you want the student to display, behaviors about which you are concerned, or both. Inherent in this recommendation is the idea that the child or youth will be focused on the behavior of concern, rather than on the social consequences of the behavior.
- Avoid suggestive and indirect language. Such language not only is difficult for many students with AS/HFA to understand but also creates opportunities for power struggles and confrontations. For example, when a student says to a teacher, "Why do I need to do that?" the teacher should avoid making comments such as "You will understand when you are older—it's a maturity matter." Such vague statements often fuel the fire for argumentative behavior and lead to misunderstandings and misinterpretations of meaning and intent.
- Be sensitive to the fact that many individuals with AS/HFA may appear to lack emotion. Many of these children and youth are unable to easily understand and show their emotions. Thus, when under stress or when confronted with conflict, they may appear to be detached or calm. In these situations, teachers and parents may fail to recognize that the child is experiencing significant stress and emotion that he or she is unable to communicate or overtly manifest. Because of this misperception, an interaction may escalate into a bigger problem.
- Apply consistent, firm, and controlled interventions. Adults need to be able to apply resolved and predictable directives and consequences. Harsh, punitive, and unexpected directives and consequences often provoke power struggles and increased problems. Moreover, negative and confrontational responses may result in a crisis.

Children and youth diagnosed with Asperger syndrome or high-functioning autism are not inherently aggressive. Nevertheless, problems of aggression among these students are relatively common. The social deficits and excesses connected with AS/HFA, such as difficulties in engaging in age-appropriate reciprocal play and other social interactions, frequently create problems and frustrations that mushroom into aggressive and violent responses and counteractions. For instance, a student may experience difficulties interacting with peers as a result of not understanding commonly known and accepted social rules, thereby giving the appearance of being rude or unwilling to follow the rules of generally understood games. Problems may also arise when these students are unable to recognize or respond to subtle social cues (e.g., when a nondisabled peer tries to communicate that the student is standing too close).

Related difficulties, such as attending and responding to salient social cues; connecting these cues to previous social experiences; self-monitoring behavioral and social responses; rigidly attempting to apply social rules that are highly variable; and displaying poor empathy, social and emotional stiffness, and social awkwardness, may further exacerbate the behavioral and social problems and thereby increase the likelihood that these students will become involved in confrontational and aggressive situations. Furthermore, the emotional and social vulnerability and stress that are common among these individuals make them prone to aggressive outbursts, as well as to being targets for bullying and exploitation.

Because of their unique social and behavioral characteristics, students with AS/HFA may be responsive to therapeutic strategies that are different from those used with normally developing and achieving students and those with other types of disabilities. Strategies exclusively or primarily based on punitive measures typically do not work well with students who have AS/HFA. Such strategies almost always fail to address the underlying causes of these individuals' problems, including stress, poor problem-solving ability, poor organizational skills, and problems in predicting outcomes of social responses. Accordingly, students often manifest aggression because they have difficulty understanding and functioning in a world they perceive to be threatening, inconsistent, and unpredictable.

As previously suggested, students with AS/HFA require management programming that is uniquely crafted to meet their individual needs. Such programming should include (a) the support of structured environments, (b) opportunities to participate in cognitive-based management programs, and (c) the support of faculty and staff who are knowledgeable and skilled in dealing with power struggles and violence. These three salient elements of effective programming are detailed below.

Structured Environments

An essential element of an individualized management program that may curtail aggression is a structured environment. As suggested numerous times, children and youth with AS/HFA can be expected to have fewer episodes involving aggression and other behavioral problems and more positive social interactions and school experiences when they are provided with clear and consistent guidelines and support for appropriate behavior. Such guidelines and support are most effective when accompanied by clear models of acceptable behavior, opportunities to practice desired behavior, and feedback for acceptable and unacceptable performance. These students also tend to respond to programs that incorporate ongoing rule monitoring and maintenance of consistent behavioral expectations. Thus, routines and schedules can provide order, consistency, and structure for these students. Moreover, physical, environmental, cognitive, and attitudinal supports are essential in assisting these students in preventing and managing episodes of aggression. In this regard, students function best in settings where adults and peers understand their disability and where adequate resources exist to effectively manage and supervise them.

For example, a somewhat peculiarly acting student with AS/HFA is often teased for the way she dresses and talks and is generally made fun of in the hallways. In response to these situations, she sometimes screams and attempts to hit her harassers. These incidents often result in her being punished. In response to these problems, she and her teacher make a card for her to carry to remind her of appropriate choices of behaviors in response to teasing. This simple environmental support—applied in conjunction with other supports, including the education of her peers regarding AS/HFA and consequences for harassment—proves to be an effective intervention.

Cognitive-Based Management Programs

Opportunities to participate in cognitive-based management programs are important ways of managing the aggressive responses of many students with AS/HFA. These methods generally empower the students to self-evaluate and self-manage, so they can avoid the often poor outcomes associated with relying on top–down management programs, as well as the negative consequences of aggressive behaviors. Some students may respond positively to top–down strategies; however, there is strong evidence that many will resist or be unresponsive to them. Hence, as noted previously, it is generally recommended that, whenever possible, management programs be crafted to counter aggression by being cognitively based. In this connection, cognitive behavior modification programs, behavioral contracts, consequence maps, power cards, social stories, social scripts, cartoon analyses, social autopsies, and similar methods are recommended for consideration.

Knowledgeable and Skilled Faculty and Staff

Students with AS/HFA do best when supported by faculty and staff who are knowledgeable and skilled in dealing with power struggles and violence. Students with AS/HFA are particularly well known for being adept at creating power struggles with adults. Moreover, when trapped in power struggles and confrontations, they are more prone to acts of aggression. Accordingly, it is essential that school personnel design and implement programs so that they reduce opportunities for power struggles. Related to this notion, we suggest the following:

- Describe in specific terms the behaviors you want the student to display or about which you are concerned, rather than the social consequences of the behavior.
- Avoid emotion-loaded questions (e.g., "Why are you upset with me?"), and instead ask the student to describe the event of concern so that you can search for antecedents or triggers.
- Recognize that children and youth with AS/HFA may appear to be unable to understand and show their emotions. When under stress or when confronted with conflict, these students may appear to be emotionally detached or calm. In such situations, you may not recognize that these individuals are actually experiencing such significant stress and emotion that they may be unable to communicate.

In summary, in order to be effective in managing students prone to aggressive responses, educators and others must be able to consistently apply timely, firm, and predictable consequences. This process includes avoidance of punitive, harsh, and unanticipated consequences that are apt to provoke power struggles and to increase the likelihood of aggression.

Concluding Thoughts

Children and youth with Asperger syndrome or high-functioning autism are well known for their behavioral and social excesses and deficits. An essential aspect of planning and programming for these students involves development, implementation, and evaluation of effective management tools. Management tools for children and youth with AS/HFA clearly define and explain class rules, teacher expectations, and environmental constraints and structure. Also, supports help these individuals begin to recognize that they can request modifications or restructure their environment as needed. Therefore, self-monitoring and cognitive-based methods based on collaboratively developed social contracts, and used in combination with structured environments and related supports, are highly recommended.

chapter five

Social-Skills and Social Interaction Planning, Instruction, and Management

There is agreement among professionals, parents, and other stakeholders that individuals with AS/HFA often face significant social challenges. Accordingly, there is universal agreement among various stakeholders that social interaction opportunities and social-skills development and support are essential for children and youth with AS/HFA. Researchers and practitioners have clearly demonstrated both the advantages and social validity of improved social-skill capacity among individuals with these disorders, as well as those with other forms of autism-related disabilities. The negative effects and outcomes associated with failure to develop and support appropriate social skills are also clear. To be sure, social skills impact friendships and social interactions, employment, independent living, quality of life, and myriad other facets of human behavior throughout the life cycle.

Social skills comprise a complex area of human behavior. Although they are broadly rule governed, these rules and their associated protocol vary across location, situations, people, age, and culture, making it difficult (if not impossible) to teach social skills that will be appropriate for

---

Note. Portions of this chapter are from "Understanding the Hidden Curriculum: An Essential Social Skill for Children and Youth With Asperger Syndrome," by B. S. Myles and R. L. Simpson, 2001b, *Intervention in School and Clinic, 36*(5), pp. 279–286. Copyright 2001 by PRO-ED, Inc. Reprinted with permission.

every situation. There are myriad simple examples of this claim, such as differences in how one might interact with a friend in a church or synagogue in contrast to interactions that might occur at a party. Even basic and relatively simplistic social behaviors (e.g., initiating and responding to a social greeting) are in practice quite complex, variable, and highly nuanced. Consider, for example, that the means used by a child to greet a friend in the classroom differs from how he or she greets a friend at the local mall. The greeting used the first time that the child sees a friend will also differ from the greeting exchange when they see each other a few minutes later. Furthermore, the words and actions used in greetings differ depending on whether the child is greeting a teacher or a peer. Greetings are thus complex, as are most social skills.

It is also evident that when planning a student's support and intervention program, considering social skill and social interaction quality and situation suitability is more important than merely increasing the quantity of social initiations or responses. Using again the example of "social greetings," students who greet each peer in their classroom in the same fashion over and over throughout the day, even if the greeting is contextually appropriate for some situations (e.g., the first time a friend is seen upon entering a school), would be problematic. Thus, effective and productive social-skill and social interaction planning for children and youth with AS/HFA requires careful preparation and individualized engineering. In this regard, basic social enhancement principles can serve as foundation elements for a program to develop social skills.

General Principles of Social-Skills Development and Social Interaction Planning and Support Programming

Principle 1

Although social interaction problems of individuals with Asperger syndrome or high-functioning autism are often described as mild social norm deviations, this perception should in no way diminish the significance of these problems—Individuals with AS/HFA are not known for extremely deviant behavior, such as self-injury, highly aberrant self-stimulatory behaviors, or bizarre responses. Rather, they tend to be socially different or quirky in their behavior. The social problems evidenced in this characteristic pattern are often incorrectly perceived to be relatively unimportant or easily corrected. However, there is overwhelming evidence that there are severe social consequences for individuals with AS/HFA. Although it is true that the behavior of such individuals appears to be less atypical than the extreme responses of some children with autism spectrum disorders, especially those with more classic and severe forms of the disorder, this in no way should be perceived to attenuate the impact of these difficulties.

Principle 2

Social interaction skills must be explicitly taught to students with AS/HFA, and the students' peers must also be taught social interaction support behaviors—Communicating to a student that his behavior is unacceptable without explicitly providing a more appropriate alternative behavior, or otherwise failing to instruct the individual in making a desired response, is clearly ineffective. Children and youth with AS/HFA can acquire desired social skills only when adults and peers with whom they interact offer appropriate direct instruction, including strategies for skill generalization and maintenance. Furthermore, peers and adults who have opportunities to interact with persons with these disabilities must be instructed in how to support and maintain these desired responses, including serving as age-appropriate behavior models, providing feedback related to acceptable and unacceptable behavior, and using contingent social reinforcement. Finally, it is painfully apparent that without education and training many peers of students with AS/HFA can be expected to ignore, bully, and discriminate against their classmates with special needs. That students with AS/HFA are able to demonstrate significant progress when suitable instruction, models, and related supports are provided by peers makes it clear that an effective social interaction program must include a substantial measure of peer training and support.

Principle 3

Parents, professionals, and peers must be assisted in developing and maintaining reasonable social-skills expectations for individuals with AS/HFA—High-functioning autism and Asperger syndrome are conditions that come with severe and lifelong social challenges. Accordingly, even under optimal conditions, it is unreasonable to expect that children diagnosed with these disorders will completely overcome their disability or that social skills will somehow become a relative strength subsequent to training and intervention. Acceptance of this circumstance should in no way diminish high expectations for these students or detract from expected outcomes. It does, however, remind educators and parents involved in the lives of children and youth with AS/HFA that education and training are tools that are used to support individuals with these exceptionalities, rather than strategies that can be used to "cure" them of their social difficulties. Just as it would be unrealistic to expect that a child with a severe form of spina bifida would become a National Basketball Association professional basketball player, it would be equally unrealistic to expect that a child could achieve goals that require outstanding social skills. Nonetheless, such children can be taught social skills that will allow them to achieve fulfilling social outcomes and a high-quality social life.

Principle 4

High-quality reciprocal social interactions are most apt to occur in the absence of aggression and grossly unacceptable behaviors—Peers of students with AS/HFA, as well as other people in the community, are fundamental to these students' engaging in quality social interactions and developing needed social skills. Indeed, without the participation of peers, there are severe limitations on the development of social skills by students with AS/HFA. Many peers of individuals with these disabilities are interested and willing to participate in social support programs. Even in the most positive of environments, however, these peers will generally be intolerant of aggression and overtly atypical behaviors. For example, students who chronically spit, hit, or kick others; display sexual behaviors in public; and so forth will create significant barriers to social interaction. Accordingly, adults who coordinate social interaction support and training programs must be mindful of the need to mitigate these interfering behaviors as a part of an effective social support program.

Principle 5

Curricula and skill development programs should be geared to differentially address the nature and makeup of a social problem—Various researchers and practitioners have observed that children, youth, and adults vary in the manner in which they demonstrate social excesses and deficits. Gresham (1998) identified three unique types of social-skill problems: social-skill acquisition deficits, social performance deficits, and social fluency deficits. Each of these problem types represents a unique form of a social problem and the intervention and supports connected to each form will be different. *Social-skill acquisition problems* refers to those in which an individual lacks the knowledge needed to perform a social skill or wherein there is an inability on the part of an individual to understand and differentiate the relative appropriateness of particular social behaviors in specified settings. An example of such a deficit would be a child who lacks the knowledge and skills required to play a particular game with peers at recess. *Social performance problems,* in contrast, refers to an individual's failure to demonstrate a particular social skill in a required social situation, in spite of possessing the social skill. An example is the child who can perform a needed social skill in a classroom social-skill training situation (e.g., following the rules of a board game with peers) but who fails to perform appropriately in a real-life game situation with peers in a play group. *Social fluency difficulties* refers to not having comfort and ease in demonstrating and performing a social skill at appropriate times. This type of deficit is recognition that making a new social skill an integrated element of one's repertoire requires practice and confidence. The diverse nature of these social problems requires different types of social instruction and supports. For example, the type of training that would be offered to a student who does not understand the rules of a game would be different from the training provided to a student who understands the rules and who can demonstrate them in a training setting, but who fails to follow the rules when playing the game with general education peers at recess. Successful social-skills training and support outcomes are dependent on designing individualized intervention programs that fit the nature of the problem.

Principle 6

Design and shape programs to instill confidence and a positive attitude about social relationships—In the final analysis, social-skills training and social interaction programming is all about assisting persons with AS/HFA to participate in and enjoy living, working, playing, and being with others.

An undeniable component of social contact success is instilling a positive and confident attitude about relationships. In large measure, good results are most apt to occur when persons accept who they are, including their unique personalities and characteristics, and the individuality of every other person on the planet. Such understanding extends to helping these students accept that they will not necessarily always understand the nuances of every social situation; however, this does not necessarily and automatically create problems. One of the most important elements of social-skills training and social interaction engineering is to help trainees develop positive attitudes about the outcomes of social interactions; the fundamentally positive outcomes of being a part of the human community; and the capacity to engage others in a confident manner reflective of one's individuality and unique human features.

Selecting Socially Valid Social Targets for Support and Intervention

There is no question those individuals who are involved in educating or parenting children and youth with AS/HFA—and individuals with these conditions, themselves—have myriad social targets for intervention from which to choose. Individuals experience excesses and deficits within various social domains. Yet helping persons with these challenges understand and appropriately use social skills in a variety of settings is no easy matter. Significant time and effort costs associated with such instruction and support are almost universally present. Consequently, it is imperative that social-skills targets have clear and practical social validity. For that reason, any social skill taught to a student should have the potential to yield clear social benefit.

Skills that are particularly noteworthy are those that are fundamental and pivotal to a number of domains. As noted below, these skills can be used in school, home, and community settings and in individual and group situations. Socially oriented targets offered for consideration are grouped within three general classes of social behavior: (a) peer and adult social interaction, relationship, and cooperation skills; (b) self-management, personal responsibility, and self-realization skills; and (c) school-related and academically related social skills. Based on individual needs and on stakeholders' and students' vetting decisions, social targets within these three classification areas are identified for intervention.

The listed targets are conceptual illustrations of salient elements falling within the three broad social behavior classes. Hence, the specific targets are not intended to be an exhaustive list but rather representative behaviors within the major areas of classification. Furthermore, these groupings are overlapping; behaviors within each classification may also apply to another area. It is also important to note that social proficiency requires that children and youth have relative strength in each of these areas. Thus, while priority decisions of stakeholders are a necessity, so, too, is the realization that social competence cannot be achieved unless individuals manifest basic social capability within each area.

Peer and Adult Social Interaction Skills, Relationship Skills, and Cooperation Skills

Social targets within this area focus on pro-social interaction and social participation skills. Targets within this area are broadly scripted, foundational in nature, and serve as the underpinning and supporting framework for building and using a variety of more advanced and specialized social skills that are correlated with social interaction success.

- participating in cooperative play activities
- participating in organized play, including following established rules and protocol
- initiating social bids; responding to social bids
- requesting and giving information appropriately
- sharing
- giving and asking for assistance appropriately
- giving compliments and encouragement
- engaging in age-appropriate conversations
- engaging in productive problem solving within group settings
- showing age-appropriate affection
- maintaining a conversation with peers and adults
- recognizing and appropriately responding to authority and rules

- appropriately coping with conflict
- giving and accepting age- and socially appropriate consequences and feedback

Self-Management Skills, Personal Responsibility Skills, and Self-Realization Skills

Skills within this frame focus on behaviors that permit individuals to monitor and self-manage their manners and actions, particularly those needed to participate in a dyad or larger group. These skills also recognize that an important element of social competence is awareness of the needs, motivations, and preferences of others. Finally, this area spotlights the need for individuals to be appropriately assertive and socially proper in communicating their needs, wants, and predilections.

- being aware and appropriately communicating social interaction preferences (e.g., group size, activity, familiarity with group members)
- being aware and appropriately communicating and demonstrating peer relationship preferences (e.g., familiarity, age, gender)
- being aware and appropriately communicating and demonstrating adult relationship preferences
- appropriately voicing and using avoidance strategies (e.g., exiting an uncomfortable social situation)
- communicating and demonstrating appropriate attention-seeking strategies
- being aware and appropriately communicating and dealing with stress and anxiety
- being aware and appropriately communicating preferences for eye contact and eye gaze
- being aware of personal preferences for physical orientation and distance within groups and assertively and appropriately communicating these preferences
- recognizing and appropriately responding to authority and rules
- recognizing and appropriately respecting the property and boundaries of self and others

- demonstrating age-appropriate self-care and hygiene skills
- recognizing and demonstrating age-appropriate ethical and socially responsible behavior
- demonstrating age-appropriate positive attitude toward self and others
- demonstrating awareness of personal interests and appropriately indicating that others may not share the interest
- demonstrating appropriate self-control and self-regulation within a variety of social situations

School-Related and Academically Related Social Skills

These social skills directly correlate with social competence and building social capacity within school settings. Included are skills that show a positive relationship with academic success and social acceptance and capability.

- following rules, classroom conventional protocol, and rule compliance, including asking and answering questions, participating in classroom discussions, and so forth
- demonstrating appropriate classroom attending behavior
- completing teacher-assigned tasks and submitting on-time and completed assignments
- following directions
- demonstrating accepted social behavior and academic participation skills within small-group and cooperative-group activities

That this group of social behaviors falls within an independent category is recognition of the monumentally important experiences and opportunities that learners with AS/HFA have in school settings.

Supports and Interventions for Achieving Preferred Social Outcomes

Developing desired social skills and facilitating positive, constructive, and affirmative social interactions between children and youth diagnosed with

AS/HFA and others is no easy task. Effective methods do exist, however, and use of these strategies bodes well for training that yields meaningful benefit. These methods are discussed in the following sections, under four basic types: (a) explicit instruction of identified social targets, (b) social understanding and social problem solving, (c) social interpretation interventions, and (d) peer-mediated programs.

Explicit Instruction of Identified Social Targets

A variety of social skills and social behaviors can be taught to individuals with AS/HFA via use of explicit instructional strategies. In this context, *explicit instruction* refers to using a structured approach to identify and teach specific behaviors associated with social competence. That is, subsequent to identifying one or more skills needed for improved social performance, an instructor directly teaches an individual the skill. Commonly employed instructional methods include coaching students to correctly perform particular social behaviors; offering models of desired social behavior; providing opportunities for students to role-play, practice, and rehearse identified skills; providing feedback and reinforcement to students relative to demonstrating specific skills; and providing opportunities for using and practicing skills in natural settings. Skills of various types and characteristics can be directly taught, including social acquisition, performance, and fluency skills (Gresham, 1998).

Basic steps are used to explicitly increase the quantity and quality of peer interactions and teach social skills. First, specific socially valid social targets with clear and precise operational definitions are selected for instruction. Targets with multiple elements include task-analyzed steps. For example, for the target skill "playing a board game with a peer during classroom free time," the steps associated with the behavior are identified. Second, methods for measuring the defined behavior and a student's progress in learning it are identified. Third, the methods or strategies for directly teaching the skill are identified, including use of (a) adult prompting and coaching, (b) commercial and teacher-made social-skills programs, and/or (c) one or more social enhancement strategies. Fourth, students are instructed in the identified skills, using best-practice methods. Such methods include modeling (e.g., demonstrating the desired social behavior related to the board game); providing multiple opportunities to practice desired behaviors (e.g., allowing the child to practice playing the board game with teachers and others before playing the game with peers); providing instructional prompts (e.g., prompting the child to drop dice on the board and move her game piece the correct number of spaces); reinforcing desired behaviors (e.g., praising the child for cooperatively playing the game with a peer); and providing multiple opportunities to engage in the desired behavior, including in natural settings (e.g., giving the child opportunities to play board games with different peers at different times of the day). Finally, stakeholders are continuously given opportunities to evaluate and modify the training programs.

Direct instruction of identified social behaviors requires careful examination of related skills, including understanding the developmental scope and sequence of social targets. It is not unusual for children and youth with AS/HFA to evidence an uneven profile of social skills. For that reason, it is essential that program engineers and stakeholders understand the sequence in which these skills develop. Without an understanding of scope and sequence, one may fail to realize that a child is missing an important prerequisite skill that might make the child learn a more advanced skill by rote, thereby precluding it from becoming a functional and generalized asset. For example, if a student does not understand that tone of voice communicates a message, then teaching the more advanced skill of using a respectful tone of voice to teachers may have little or no meaning. That is, if the student learns by rote to use that tone of voice, it most likely will not be generalized to other settings.

Adult Social-Skill Prompting and Coaching

Teachers, parents, and other adults, in cooperation with children and youth, can prompt and coach by identifying situations and settings in which learners with AS/HFA are able to demonstrate particular social behaviors in natural or contrived venues. Thus, adults directly guide students in desired responses. Students are first primed and coached in making appropriate social responses for a situation. For instance, if the social activity under consideration involves a child playing a ball game with classmates at recess, the first step would be to ensure that the student understands the rules and activities of the game and has the necessary prerequisite skills to participate in the activity. Subsequent to this preparation, the adult coach would lead the student to the site of the activity and then prompt the individual to engage in behaviors associated with the target objective. For example, in the case of the child playing a board game with classmates during classroom free time, the adult coach would prompt the student in the steps connected to joining and participating in the activity (e.g., approach a peer with an invitation to play, obtain the game from its designated storage space, ask the peers to choose a color for game pieces, and so forth).

Following are examples of adult social-skill prompting and coaching programs to teach children to participate in group leisure activities.

Alex

In an effort to develop a social activity in which Alex could participate during recess, Mr. Goldberg selected four square, an activity Alex and his classmates enjoyed and commonly participated in. Mr. Goldberg analyzed the skills needed by Alex to participate in this activity: (a) identify one or more partners, (b) request that they join in playing four square, (c) follow rules of the game (e.g., play fair, take turns), and (d) put away materials when directed by a teacher or at the conclusion of recess. Mr. Goldberg then taught the skills to Alex, first by modeling them and then by asking Alex to role-play the steps with him. Next, he gave Alex opportunities to practice the new skills with different peers and teachers. During this time, Mr. Goldberg provided prompts and reinforcement to Alex as needed, thus ensuring that he had multiple opportunities to use these new skills during various recess periods.

Angela

Ms. Rodriguez, a third-grade teacher, noticed that during free periods, Angela was not engaged in an activity. Ms. Rodriguez prompted Angela to ask another student to participate in an activity such as playing a computer game. Following this prompt, Angela approached a peer and asked if she would like to play Family Feud on the computer. The peer agreed to play a computer game; however, she indicated a desire to play a different game. In response, Ms. Rodriguez prompted Angela to offer a list of choices to her peer. When the students mutually agreed on a computer game and began to play, the teacher stayed close by. Ms. Rodriguez praised Angela for her playing techniques and prompted her as needed.

Advantages of adult social prompting and coaching are numerous. The system is geared to ensure an increased level of positive and semistructured social interactions with peers. This type of training also guarantees a strong instructional component and feedback. Adult social prompting and coaching also sets the stage for fading support, thus making students more independent. Disadvantages of this type of instruction are that it may disrupt ongoing social interactions and exchanges between peers. That is, the mere presence of an adult may interfere with naturally occurring and maximally normal peer relationships and interactions. This type of training may also promote prompt dependency if steps are not taken to ensure that children do not become overreliant on an adult coach. Finally, adult coaching and prompting programs may fail to generalize skills to other settings and situations. For instance, a child who is taught to play a particular board game with a limited number of students in her classroom may show little interest in playing similar games or engaging in alternative peer activities, playing with new children, or engaging in the desired behavior outside her classroom. Thus, social-skills training based on adult social prompting and coaching must be geared to respond to these potential problems.

Commercial and Teacher-Made Social-Skills Curricula and Programs

These curricula and programs are commonly used to teach various social behaviors to children and youth with AS/HFA. There are numerous commercial programs and incalculable informal and teacher-made options for instructing students in social skills. These programs have unique features—such as the age group they address, diagnostic groups they emphasize, and type of skills they emphasize (e.g., classroom vs. community skills)—yet they tend to share basic instructional elements. These types of programs also share common training elements: modeling, role playing and rehearsal opportunities, and performance feedback. It is also important to note that these types of programs can have limited benefit unless accompanied by plans for transferring training to a variety of settings and situations and opportunities to practice new skills in natural settings. Evidence for this claim is the ubiquitous presence of students who can perform various skills associated with particular social instruction training packages in classroom settings, but are unable to make functional use of these skills in natural settings.

Social-skills curricula are available to cover a wide variety of skills. For example, *Do-Watch-Listen-Say: Social and Communication Intervention for Children With Autism* (Quill, 2000), offers instructors a core social-skills curriculum that includes steps for teaching nonverbal social interaction, social imitation, and organization. McGinnis and Goldstein (1997) developed a curriculum that addresses (a) basic and foundational social skills, (b) school-related skills, (c) friendship-making skills, (d) dealing with feelings, (e) alternatives to aggression, and (f) dealing with stress. Duke, Nowicki, and Martin (1996) provided a school-based curriculum to teach nonverbal language in the areas of (a) paralanguage, (b) facial expression, (c) space and touch, (d) gestures and postures, (e) rhythm and time, and (f) personal hygiene. Shure (1992) approached social skills from a problem-solving view, providing direct instruction on (a) pre–problem-solving skills, (b) alternative solutions, (c) consequences, (d) solution–consequence pairs, and (e) means–end thinking.

Instruction Based on One or More Social Enhancement Strategies

A variety of methods and strategies are available to directly and explicitly teach social skills and support social interaction programs. These tools may be used independently or in combination with other explicit instructional methods. For example, a teacher may introduce a particular skill set using a commercial program; follow that program with an adult coaching program to move the skill into natural settings; and support, expand, and strengthen the program using video modeling in combination with a social story.

Several explicit instructional support methods are described below, including (a) social stories, (b) social scripts, (c) acting lessons, (d) the Power Card, (e) video modeling, and (f) teaching the "hidden curriculum."

Social Stories. Because of their relatively strong cognitive and language skills, children and adolescents with AS/HFA often benefit from the structure imposed by self-instructional and self-control problem-solving procedures. That is, they are often able to profit from strategies based on directives and guidance for responding to various situations. One of the most promising of these options is social stories (Gray & Garand, 1993; Norris & Dattilo, 1999; Simpson & Myles, 2008; Swaggart et al., 1995). A social story describes social situations specific to individuals and circumstances. For instance, a social story might be developed for a youth who attends a general education English class. The story includes a description of the youth, the setting, peers and adults associated with the setting, and the youth's feelings and perceptions related to the setting (e.g., the youth likes to read and write in his class journal). There are also directive statements that describe appropriate behaviors for the setting (e.g., upon entering the classroom, the youth should sit at his desk and take out his textbook, and until the bell rings he may quietly talk to people seated near him). Thus, this method involves structuring an individual's behavior and social responses by offering individualized, specific response cues. Although the empirical efficacy of social stories has not been definitively established, preliminary indications are that it may be a beneficial method of offering structure for many children and youth with AS/HFA.

Following are two examples of social stories. The first was developed for a child to assist him with problems he experienced during lunch. The second was developed for a youth who was of concern to parents and classmates because of poor personal hygiene.

Lunch Behavior

Every day I look forward to lunch. Lunch is a time I get to eat and to be with other children in Ms. Zenith's class. At noon Ms. Zenith announces that it is time to get ready for lunch. When she tells me, I get my lunch from my locker and walk to the cafeteria. Sometimes the cafeteria is noisy. I can sit at any table during lunchtime. I like to sit with my friends. When I am finished with my lunch, I throw away my trash. When the bell rings, I go back to my locker and get ready for my next class.

The Science of Sweat—Why I Need to Take a Shower and Use Deodorant Every Day

When boys and girls reach puberty they begin to *sweat* more than when they were younger. Sometimes they sweat a lot. Sometimes they sweat a little. Most people sweat even when they don't feel hot.

Another name for sweat is *perspiration*. When perspiration comes out of our pores, it is clean. This sweat doesn't smell. Within seconds, however, *bacteria* will appear and begin to live and grow in our perspiration.

These bacteria smell bad. *It is best to wash these bacteria off every day.* If we don't wash the bacteria off every day, more bacteria will come each day. Most people don't like the smell of other people's perspiration with bacteria in it. Most people think it smells really awful.

It is important to bathe and wash our armpits and genitals every day. If we cannot take a shower or a bath, we can wash our armpits and genitals with a wet washcloth and soap. *Then we can put deodorant on our armpits. If we are clean and wear deodorant, other people usually cannot smell the bacteria on our skin.* Our friends usually like it better when they cannot smell the bacteria on our skin.

If we put deodorant on our armpits without having washed off the bacteria we will glue the bacteria from days before to ourselves. This will smell REALLY bad!

It is also important to wear clean clothes. The sweat from our bodies gets onto our clothes, especially the armpits of our shirts and in the crotch of our underwear. Sometimes clothes we have worn for several hours or more may look clean but they usually smell like bacteria that are in sweat. *Most people don't like the smell of bacteria in sweat.* In fact, most people think it smells really yucky!

So, after we shower or bathe it is usually a good idea to put on clean clothes, especially a clean shirt and clean underwear. That way we will not get bacteria back onto our bodies and *others will not be able to smell yesterday's perspiration on our clothes.*

Most people want to smell clean and fresh. We usually want others to think we smell clean and fresh, too. *If we bathe or shower or wash carefully and wear clean clothes every day, we will feel more confident because we will smell clean and fresh.*

Note. "The Science of Sweat" adapted from an intervention program written by Edna Smith, PhD. Adapted with permission.

Table 5.1 provides guidelines for social story construction for students with Asperger syndrome or high-functioning autism.

Social Scripts. Children and youth with AS/HFA may benefit from having adults structure their behaviors through the use of scripts. For instance, a child and his teacher may practice a script for joining in a group game at recess. This option minimizes problems these children may experience

Table 5.1

Guidelines for Social Story Construction

1. Identify a target behavior or problem situation for social story intervention.

The social story author should select a social behavior to be changed, preferably one in which improvement can result in increased positive social interactions, a safer environment, additional social learning opportunities, or all three. The behavior should be broken down into its component parts and based on the student's ability level. For example, during lunch, Bob grabs food from his peers' plates and eats it. He exhibits this behavior at school, home, and restaurants. People who do not know Bob often react in a hostile manner. Accordingly, grabbing food from other people's plates is targeted for modification because it is socially unacceptable and interferes with development of more acceptable social contacts.

2. Define target behavior for data collection.

For several reasons, it is imperative to clearly define the behavior on which data will be collected. Data collection is important for several reasons. First, all data collectors need an identical understanding of the targeted behavior to ensure reliability in measuring change. In addition, the behavior should be defined in such a way that the student understands the behavior to be exhibited. For example, Bob's current eating behavior consists of eating and grabbing. *Eating* is defined as sitting and consuming food only from the plate that is in front of him. *Grabbing* is defined as removing food from a plate other than his own.

3. Collect baseline data on the target behavior.

Collecting data over an extended period allows the educator to determine a trend. Baseline data collection can last from 3 to 5 days or longer. To measure Bob's food-grabbing behavior, the observer can place a tally mark on a sheet of paper each time Bob grabs food from a peer's plate during lunch. The observer then logs the total number of tally marks onto a separate sheet of paper with the corresponding date.

4. Write a short social story using descriptive, directive, and perspective sentences.

A good rule of thumb for writing social stories is to use descriptive and perspective sentences for every directive sentence in the story (Gray, 1994). Stories should be written in accordance with the student's comprehension skills, with vocabulary and print size individualized for each student. The stories should be written in the first person and in present or future tense (to describe a situation as it occurs or to anticipate an upcoming event, respectively). Students, themselves, may be involved in these activities.

(continues)

Table 5.1 *(continued)*

5. Choose the number of sentences per page according to the student's functioning level.

Presentation of the social story is dependent on the student's functioning level. For some students, one to three sentences per page is adequate. Each sentence allows the student to focus on and process a specific concept. Depending on the student's skill level, more than one sentence per page may result in an overload of information such that the student does not comprehend the information.

6. Use photographs, hand-drawn pictures, or pictorial icons.

Pictures may enhance student understanding of appropriate behavior, especially with students who lack reading skills. For example, icons have been shown to be effective learning tools for children and youth. Gray (1994), however, cautioned that illustrations may too narrowly define a situation, resulting in limited generalization. Thus, decisions about whether to use pictures with social stories should be made on an individual basis. A picture on Bob's social story might depict him eating appropriately.

7. Read the social story to the student, and model the desired behavior.

Reading the social story and modeling related behaviors as needed should become a consistent part of the student's daily schedule. For example, the story may be read just prior to the activity targeted by the story. Accordingly, Bob's story might be read to him right before lunch or at the beginning of the day to help him anticipate the situation and appropriate behavior. Depending on the student's functioning level, the teacher or the student may read the story. The student who is able to read independently may read the social story to peers so that all have a similar perspective of the targeted situation and appropriate behaviors.

8. Collect intervention data.

The educator should collect data throughout the social story program, using the procedures described for collecting and analyzing baseline data.

9. Review the findings and related social story procedures.

If the student does not respond with the desired behavior after approximately 2 weeks of the social story program, the person coordinating the intervention program should review the social story and its implementation procedures. It is recommended that if program alterations are made, only one variable be changed at a time (e.g., change only the content of the story, rather than simultaneously changing the time the story is read and the person who reads it). By changing only one factor at a time, the educator can determine the factor or factors that best facilitate a student's learning. For example, changing the time that Bob's food-grabbing social story is

Table 5.1 *(continued)*

presented, from just before lunch to earlier in the morning, may allow him to reflect on appropriate behaviors and thus improve the program. On the other hand, if the time and the story content were changed at the same time, the teacher would be unsure of which factor was responsible for Bob's behavior change.

10. Program for maintenance and generalization.

After a behavior change has become consistent, the educator may want to fade use of the social story. Fading may be accomplished by extending the time between readings or having students responsible for reading the story themselves. By their very nature, social stories permit generalization across environments. Thus, teachers should assist students in applying social story content to various situations. For example, the teacher could assist Bob in using his appropriate eating skills during snack time, at parties, and in restaurants. In addition, the teacher should ensure that the student continues the appropriate behavior. Finally, students with sufficient independent skills may be assisted in identifying social goals for which they may develop their own social stories.

Note. Adapted from "Using Social Stories to Teach Social and Behavioral Skills to Children With Autism," by B. L. Swaggart et al., 1995, *Focus on Autistic Behavior, 10*(1), 1–16. Copyright 1995 by PRO-ED, Inc.; and from "Implementing Cognitive Behavior Management Programs for Persons With Autism: Guidelines for Practitioners," by C. Quinn, B. L. Swaggart, and B. S. Myles, 1994, *Focus on Autistic Behavior, 9*(4), 1–13. Copyright 1994 by PRO-ED, Inc. Adapted with permission.

in spontaneously generating language and dealing with the complexity of deciding how to approach peers and the anxiety that may accompany making these initiations. Moreover, when paired with peer interaction training (i.e., direct instruction and adult- and peer-mediated strategies), it provides a structured interactive routine that facilitates predictable responses.

There is no question that scripting social interactions has severe limitations in producing high-quality, naturalistic interactions. That is, it is difficult to script interactions, and when scripts are used, they tend to result in somewhat stilted, pedantic, and clumsy responses. Clearly, it is impossible to script the responses that come from scripted social statements. Hence, it is virtually impossible to prepare students who use scripts to know the responses of others unless they, too, are using scripts. Nevertheless, social scripts can be effectively used to structure initial appropriate initiations (e.g., statements for engaging or connecting with other students) by learners with social deficits. Furthermore, this strategy tends to be most effective in combination with peer training. That is, peers who are engaged in interactions based on social scripting require information regarding how to respond and strategies for moving conversations and interactions beyond initial social scripts.

Acting Lessons. Citing their personal experience, some adults with AS/HFA suggest that acting lessons are an appropriate means of teaching children and youth about social and emotional issues to aid in self-awareness, self-calming, and self-management. During acting lessons, children and youth learn to express, verbally and nonverbally, emotions in specific situations. They also learn to interpret others' emotions, feelings, and voices. Perhaps more important, acting class participants engage in simulations and receive feedback from an instructor and peers regarding their performance. There is little empirical support for using acting lessons; hence, this method cannot be viewed as an evidence-based method. Nevertheless, when used in conjunction with other methods and with particular learners who appear suitable and motivated for this type of training, it may prove beneficial.

The Power Card. The Power Card is a visual aid and social support mechanism that builds on a child's special interest, fascination, or narrowly focused area of concentration to teach appropriate social interactions, behavior expectations, and related codes of social behavior. A scenario is created around an individual associated with the child's special interest and the behavior or situation that needs to be addressed. Written at the individual's comprehension level, the scenario may contain pictures or graphics related to the special interest. The individual associated with the special interest then attempts a solution to the problem. The child is then encouraged to try out the appropriate behavior, which is written in a series of short steps. A Power Card, the size of a bookmark, business card, or trading card, is then designed for the child to carry. The Power Card contains the short series of steps and a picture of the special interest (Gagnon, 2001).

For example, Mark is a highly intelligent sixth-grade student with AS/HFA. He hopes to attend Harvard and speaks of this often to anyone willing to listen. He begins many sentences with, "When I go to Harvard. . . ." Even though Mark is an excellent student, he struggles socially and finds that he has little in common with other children his age. Despite a desire to have friends, he is not quite sure what to do in social situations. His interactions typically consist of bragging about his academic skills and referring to those who are not quite as bright as he is as "peasants." He also has difficulty understanding humor and tends to laugh inappropriately and loudly. The following scenario and the Power Card example shown in Figure 5.1 were introduced to Mark to address his tendency to brag and laugh loudly and inappropriately.

 ## Dave

Dave is proud to be a student at Harvard. He spent many hours studying in middle school and high school so that he could achieve his dream. He spent so much time studying that he had little time for other things. When he found out that he was accepted to Harvard, he spent a lot of time bragging to others in his high school class and laughing loudly about his accomplishment. No one wanted to talk to him about Harvard, but Dave just told himself that they were jealous of his accomplishments.

When Dave got to Harvard, he realized that he wanted to have friends, but he continued his bragging behavior. He also continued to laugh too loudly and at inappropriate times. Dave scheduled a meeting with his English professor and explained his problems to him. The professor gave him the following advice:

- Don't brag about yourself. Others will like you more if they have a chance to discover how wonderful you are on their own.
- You can tell when to laugh by laughing when others laugh. If you are unsure about laughing, it is better to just smile.
- If everyone in a group is laughing, try to blend your laughter with theirs.

Mark, you do not have to wait to get to Harvard to practice these three things. Dave now knows that he would have enjoyed middle and high school much more if he had tried these things when he was younger.

Video Modeling. There is considerable anecdotal support for the contention that many children and adolescents with AS/HFA positively

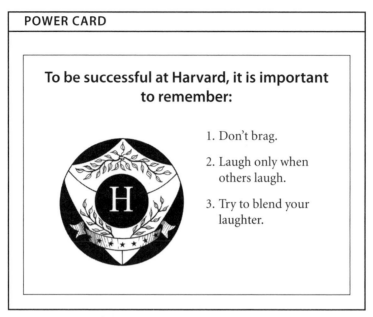

Figure 5.1. Sample Power Card. (The card should be about the size of a trading card.)

respond to instruction that uses video models. Charlop-Christy and Freeman (2000) and others (Apple, Billingsley, & Schwartz, 2005; Bellini & Akullian, 2007) suggest that this positive response is a function of removing many of the traditional social requirements associated with studying face-to-face social interactions and permitting learners to decrease the number of stimuli and images they are required to monitor and respond. Videos also permit individuals to observe and learn without the social anxiety and discomfort that often accompanies social interactions between individuals with AS/HFA and others and to permit them to fully concentrate on the skills presented in the video. A variety of social and communication behaviors can be taught via use of video modeling, including conversation skills, social initiations and responses to initiations, and play behavior. Videotapes of desired social models can be efficient in terms of time and student–staff scheduling and can be economically cost efficient by allowing use of the same taped materials with multiple children and youth.

Video programs can use children and youth with AS/HFA as their own models or peers, or other models can be used to illustrate designated skills. Videotapes are especially beneficial because they allow these learners to observe or have pointed out to them elements of effective social and social-communication skills such as facial expressions, eye contact, and so forth in a socially safe and direct manner. To be sure, many individuals have reported discomfort when asked to look at or study individuals' faces and eyes during real-life interactions. Videos can also be used to depict the point of view of other individuals. That is, an instructor can insert thoughts or words related to a tape scenario that an individual is watching.

There is insufficient research literature to declare video modeling an evidence-based method. Yet, sufficient information is available to strongly suggest that it is a promising method and that when used appropriately and with fidelity, it may contribute to students' acquiring a variety of valuable and functional social skills.

Sigafoos, O'Reilly, and de la Cruz (2007) identified 10 basic steps in using video modeling and prompting. These elements are outlined below.

1. Select a socially valid target behavior for video model instruction.

2. Get the right equipment (i.e., camera, videotape player, monitor).

3. Write a script connected to the skill you are teaching and/or develop a task analysis based on the steps of the skill.

4. Collect baseline data on the skill that is being taught.

5. Make the instructional video of the skill that is being taught (i.e., crucial steps for instruction, video models, spectator vs. participant perspective, and sounds and speech associated with the tape).

6. Arrange the teaching environment (i.e., time, setting, and materials used in the video instruction).

7. Present the video models and/or video prompts to the individual being taught.

8. Monitor the progress of the student relative to the target behavior.

9. Troubleshoot problems that may arise in the course of training (e.g., lack of improvement, reinforcement).

10. Fade the video models and video prompts to support independent performance and guard against video program dependency.

Teaching the "Hidden Curriculum." One important social-skills area that has long been neglected is the "hidden curriculum": the dos and don'ts for everyday behavior that are not spelled out but that everyone somehow knows (Bieber, 1994)—except for children and youth with AS/HFA. The hidden curriculum includes skills, actions, modes of dress, and so on that most people know and take for granted. Every society and every school has a hidden curriculum. This unspoken curriculum is the one that causes challenges—and, indeed, grief—for those with AS/HFA.

Hidden Curriculum: Example 1

In the halls at school, the hidden curriculum is in operation. Before school, Jacob saunters up to Sam, a third-grade student with AS/HFA, and says, "How's it hangin', dog?" Sam gets extremely upset and yells, "I am not a dog!" Jacob, who was merely using the latest "in" greeting, shrugs his shoulders and comments to a friend walking with him, "Man, he's weird. I'm just gonna stay out of his way." Sam, on the other hand, remains unsettled until he has an opportunity to meet with his resource teacher, Mrs. Miller, at 10:30. During a 15-minute discussion, his teacher interprets the situation for him and helps him understand that Jacob was just saying a friendly hello. When Sam asks Mrs. Miller how she and the other kids have learned that greeting, Mrs. Miller shrugs her shoulders, unable to come up with a response.

Hidden Curriculum: Example 2

Everyone knows that Mrs. Robbins allows students to whisper in class as long as they get their work done, whereas Mrs. Cook does not tolerate any level of noise in her class. Similarly, everyone knows that Mr. Johnson, the assistant principal, is a stickler for following the rules, so no one curses or even slouches in his presence. Everyone also knows that the really tough guys (the ones who sometimes bully unsuspecting kids) hang out behind the slide, just out of teacher view. Everyone knows these things—everyone, that is, except the student with AS/HFA.

Outside of school, the hidden curriculum is an even bigger issue. What is the hidden curriculum for talking to or taking rides from strangers? The bus driver is a stranger, but it is permissible to accept a ride from her. It is not okay to ride with the stranger who pulls up to the curb and stops. The cashier at the grocery store is a stranger, but it is acceptable to make small talk with her. It is not okay, however, to divulge personal information to someone who is standing in the produce section. It is okay to accept candy from the distributor who is giving free samples at Toys "R" Us, yet it is not prudent to take candy from a stranger standing on the street corner.

Individuals with AS/HFA need to know not to argue with a police officer, what different teachers' expectations are, how to behave in each teacher's class, which students to interact with and which to stay away from, and which behaviors attract positive attention as well as which attract negative attention. Understanding the hidden curriculum can make all the difference to students—it can keep them out of detention or worse trouble, and it can help them make friends. In this regard, teachers and parents are in a strategically advantageous position to teach the hidden curriculum via use of explicit direct instruction.

The hidden curriculum covers a multitude of areas. For some of these, a generous investment of time is required to ensure that the student understands; other "rules" can be learned in a matter of minutes. As previously stated, the hidden curriculum varies across location, situations, people, age, and culture. Therefore, it is impossible to generate a comprehensive list that applies to all students with AS/HFA in all situations. There is no universally set way to instruct students on the hidden curriculum. A variety of methods can be used; the important matter is to communicate and teach individuals with social difficulties those elements of the accepted social protocol that they may have failed to grasp. Table 5.2 provides some examples of hidden curriculum items that can serve as a starting point for helping individuals with this exceptionality understand this very complex topic.

Social Understanding and Social Problem Solving

Individuals with AS/HFA regularly show significant interest in social relationships and connecting and interacting with others. Yet, in spite of this motivation, and for reasons such as limited social problem-solving skills and social cognitive awareness, they, by definition, experience difficulty in developing and maintaining high-quality and mutually acceptable social relationships.

Table 5.2
Examples of Hidden Curriculum Items

1. Do not tell the principal that if she were a better listener kids would like her.
2. You should not have to pay students to be your friends.
3. Do not talk to other kids in the classroom when the teacher is giving a lesson.
4. When the teacher is scolding another student, it is not an appropriate time to ask the teacher a question.
5. When you are with classmates you don't know very well and you are the center of attention, do not pass gas, pick your nose, or scratch a private body part.
6. During a fire drill, go with your class to the nearest exit. This is not the time to go to the bathroom or to ask to go to the bathroom.
7. Do not tell classmates about family secrets.
8. Do not draw violent scenes in school.
9. During a conversation, face the speaker and position your body in that direction.
10. Speak to teachers in a pleasant tone of voice, because they will respond to you in a more positive manner.
11. When your teacher gives you a warning about behavior and you continue the behavior, you are probably going to get into trouble. If you stop the behavior immediately after the first warning, you will probably not get into trouble.
12. If one of your classmates tells you to do something you think might get you into trouble, you should always stop and think before acting. Friends do not ask other friends to do things that will get them into trouble.
13. Not all teachers have the same rules for their class. Some teachers do not allow any talking unless you raise your hand. Others may allow talking if you are not disruptive or annoying other students. It is important to know the rules different teachers have for their class.

Note. Adapted from "Understanding the Hidden Curriculum: An Essential Social Skill for Children and Youth With Asperger Syndrome," by B. S. Myles and R. L. Simpson, 2001b, *Intervention in School and Clinic, 36*(5), p. 282. Copyright 2001 by PRO-ED, Inc. Adapted with permission.

Social understanding and social problem-solving interventions are based on the premise that social difficulties and weaknesses of individuals diagnosed with AS/HFA are primarily a result of deficient social cognitive awareness and inadequate social problem-solving skills. This approach to improving social communication and relationships involves teaching and coaching individuals foundational social cognition skills. In contrast to teaching discrete social skills, these methods concentrate on helping individuals (a) identify and interpret emotions (their own and those of others); (b) understand the perspectives of others; (c) expand and improve their theory of mind capacity; (d) become more sensitive and aware of the verbal and nonverbal emotional cues that accompany social situations; (e) develop their social executive capabilities and resources; and (f) become more skilled in using social problem-solving strategies to deal with day-to-day challenges. This approach to social-skills instruction focuses on giving individuals the skills to deal with a multitude of challenges and to enable them to generalize their social assets across settings, people, and related situations. For instance, Garcia Winner (2008) promotes the *I Laugh* framework for social thinking. *I Laugh* is a reference to the social thinking process strategy steps: **I** (*initiation*, i.e., teach students effective initiation responses for interacting with other), **L** (*listening with eyes and brain*, i.e., teach students to interpret others' thoughts and intentions), **A** (*abstract/inferential meaning*, i.e., teach students to infer about what is going on), **U** (*understand perspective*, i.e., train perspective taking for interacting with others), **G** (*Gestalt/get the big picture*, i.e., teach students to understand the main ideas or gist of situations), and **H** (*humor*, i.e., teach students to understand the nature, meaning, and appropriate circumstances for humor).

A variety of curricula and related programs designed to teach social thinking and social understanding and to improve and expand social problem-solving skills are commercially available. These programs, such as the *Social Thinking* curriculum (Garcia Winner, 2007), *Building Social Relationships* (Bellini, 2008), and *Do-Watch-Listen-Say* (Quill, 2000) have been used to teach perspective taking, social reciprocity, and social problem solving to students with AS/HFA. Crooke, Hendrix, and Rachman (2008) used a social behavior mapping approach to teach individuals to identify expected and unexpected behaviors and actions that may occur in social settings, along with suitable and less suitable responses and outcomes and consequences based on those actions. These social thinking and social problem-solving resources all rely on the dissemination of information and related activities that permit students to discuss real-life and significant socially focused topics; role-play interactions and skills under discussion; view differences of perception among different communication participants; consider proper and improper ways of communicating and the outcomes of these variable ways of responding; and apply, discuss, and evaluate social thinking and problem-solving strategies that relate to real-life experiences and situations.

Social understanding and social problem-solving interventions and training programs are often effectively applied through use of established social thinking and social problem-solving curricula. As noted above, consumers can choose from among several options. These curricula and programs can be augmented and supported by incorporating a variety of informal program activities, including the ones listed below.

- Discuss with students the behaviors and feelings associated with individuals displaying different facial expressions and body language. For each facial expression (e.g., excitement and anticipation, anger, lack of interest), a teacher or another adult discusses with a student what this person's face and body seem to be saying, as well as appropriate strategies for interacting with that individual. Photos, TV, and other stimuli—as well as displays that occur during role playing—can all be used for these activities. Subsequent to basic skill development in this area, it is important to help learners undertake this activity in real situations in natural settings.
- Discuss with students issues related to verbal and nonverbal language and the manner in which words, phrases, and actions/behaviors can have different meanings. This conversation should also address matters related to needing to understand what another person is communicating in order to build positive relationships and interactions. A variety of activities can be used to achieve goals in this area, including role playing and real-life interactions in natural settings.
- Help students understand that the way they respond to and interact with others affects interactions and relationships. Identify and discuss personal and other behaviors that lead to pleasant feelings and unpleasant feelings. Role playing and other simulation activities are good strategies for building skills in this area.
- Role-play conversations with adults and classmates using examples and non-examples of various social target skills (e.g., listening and not interpreting). For each role-playing example, discuss the consequences of effectively and ineffectively using the skill.

For instance, role-play the use of comments that support and fail to support continuation of a conversation. Videotaping the conversations for feedback and reviewing taped target behaviors allows students an opportunity to view their interactions and then reflect on and discuss what worked and what needs improvement.

- Create social problem and social challenge scenarios that students can use for discussion. These scenarios describe problems that require students to apply social understanding and social problem-solving skills. Examples of possible problems are listed below.

Social Scenario: Example 1

You and several other students are marooned on an island for several days. You have food, water, and shelter while on the island. You also are permitted to choose from among 20 other items and materials for use on the island (e.g., rope, shovel, writing materials). However, you are only able to select 10 of the 20 items. Your task is to agree on which of the 10 items you and your group would want to have with you and why you would want those particular items.

Social Scenario: Example 2

You are riding your bicycle with some other kids when one of the riders has a flat tire. You are a couple of miles from home, it is beginning to rain, and you have about 30 minutes before dark. What should you do?

Social Interpretation Interventions

Social interpretation strategies are designed to help individuals understand and profit in the future from social events that occur. The focus of social interpretation methods is on events and situations that individuals with AS/HFA failed to understand in the past or that resulted in a problem or a less than satisfactory outcome.

Social interpretations recognize that even after receiving high-quality social instruction based on effective methods, persons with AS/

HFA require further interpretation of social events. Among the interpretive strategies that may have merit with some individuals, albeit without the designation of being "scientifically based," are (a) cartooning, (b) the Situation-Options-Consequences-Choices-Strategies-Simulation strategy, and (c) social autopsies.

Cartooning

Visual symbols such as cartooning have been used to enhance the processing abilities of persons in the autism spectrum and to enhance their understanding of the environment (Earles-Vollrath, Cook, & Ganz, 2007). The cartooning technique has been successfully implemented with both children and adolescents by a variety of professionals, including educators, counselors, mental health professionals, and related service personnel (Arwood, 1991; Gray, 1995; Howlin, Baron-Cohen, & Hadwin, 1999).

Comic strip conversations, a particular form of cartooning, were introduced by Gray (1995) to illustrate and interpret social situations and provide support to "students who struggle to comprehend the quick exchange of information which occurs in a conversation" (p. 2). Comic strip conversations promote social understanding by incorporating simple figures and other symbols in a comic strip format. Speech, thought-bubble symbols, and color are used to help the individual see and analyze a conversation. According to Attwood (1998), "comic strip conversations permit children to better understand the social meaning of exchanges that are inherent in play and conversation. Many children with AS/HFA are confused and upset by teasing or sarcasm. The speech and thought bubble as well as choice of colors can illustrate the hidden messages" (p. 72). Educators can draw a cartoon that is representative of events that transpired in a social situation to facilitate understanding or assist the student in doing his or her own illustrations.

Effectiveness of cartooning has limited scientific verification (Simpson et al., 2005). Nonetheless, there is mounting clinical and anecdotal evidence that some students with AS/HFA may potentially be good candidates for social learning based on adults' use of a comic format to dissect, break down, analyze, and interpret social situations and interactions. That is, in a fashion similar to the way in which comic strips are designed, a social situation can be analyzed in step-by-step fashion with an individual, including an attempt to speculate about the motives, interpretations, and social responses of others.

Tom

Tom, an eighth-grade student with AS/HFA, often had difficulty under-standing the intentions of others. He was particularly concerned about what girls said about him, reporting that they "made fun of him." Tom's teacher used a cartoon format to illustrate an incident that caused Tom a great deal of anxiety. Specifically, Tom was troubled because a girl told him he had a "cute butt." The girl was attempting to tell Tom that she liked him, but Tom perceived the comment as sexual harassment and told the girl that she was a sexist pig. Figure 5.2 contains a comic strip that Tom's teacher used with him to interpret the situation.

Situation-Options-Consequences-Choices-Strategies-Simulation (SOCCSS) Strategy

The Situation-Options-Consequences-Choices-Strategies-Simulation strat-egy is intended to assist students who experience social interaction prob-lems to sequentially understand social situations and interactions and to plan for more effective responses under similar circumstances in the fu-ture. Thus, SOCCSS helps students understand problematic social events and situations and lets them see that they have to make choices about a given situation, with each choice having a consequence. The SOCCSS strategy works as follows:

1. *Situation*—When a social problem arises, the teacher works with the student to identify the situation. Specifically, they identify (a) who was involved; (b) what happened; (c) the date, day, and time of occurrence; and (d) reasons for the present situation. To-gether, they define the problem and state a goal through discus-sion, writing, and drawings.

2. *Options*—The student and teacher brainstorm several options for the identified behavior. At this point, the teacher accepts all student responses and does not evaluate them. Typically, the options are listed in written or pictorial format. According to Spivack, Platt, and Shure (1976), this step is critical to problem solving. The ability to generate multiple solutions diminishes student frustration, encourages the student to see more than one perspective, and results in student resiliency.

Figure 5.2. Sample comic strip conversation. *Note.* From "Using Social Stories and Comic Strip Conversations to Interpret Social Situations for an Adolescent with Asperger Syndrome," by M. F. Rogers and B. S. Myles, 2001, *Intervention in School and Clinic, 36,* p. 312. Copyright 2001 by PRO-ED, Inc. Reprinted with permission.

3. *Consequences*—Together, the student and teacher evaluate each of the options generated. Kaplan and Carter (1995) suggested that the options be evaluated for efficacy (Will the solution get me what I want?) and feasibility (Will I be able to do it?). Each

of the consequences is labeled with an E for efficacy or F for feasibility. For younger children, the options can be labeled as plus (+) for acceptable or minus (−) for unacceptable, ordered on a rating scale, or identified by happy or sad faces. The teacher works as a facilitator, helping the student develop consequences for each option without dictating the consequences. The teacher uses pointed questions to help the student develop his or her own consequences.

4. *Choices*—During this stage, with the assistance of an adult, the student selects the option or options that will have the most desirable consequences.

5. *Strategies*—A planned action is developed by the student and teacher/facilitator. The plan should be generated by the student to facilitate ownership. The teacher should ask questions that lead the student into developing an effective plan.

6. *Simulation*—The student is given an opportunity to role-play the solution. In the simulation phase, the student might do the following: (a) find a quiet place to imagine how the strategy will work, (b) talk with a peer about the plan of action, (c) write down on paper what might occur when the strategy is implemented, and (d) practice or role-play with one or more people the strategy developed to address the problem.

Figure 5.3 provides an example of a worksheet that can be used to facilitate use of the SOCCSS method.

Social Autopsies

Social autopsies were developed by Richard LaVoie (Bieber, 1994) to help students with learning and social problems develop an understanding of social mistakes. An autopsy, in the traditional sense, is the examination and inspection of a dead body to discover the cause of death, determine damage, and prevent occurrence of the cause of death in others. A social autopsy is an examination and inspection of a social error to discover the cause of the error, determine the damage, and prevent it from occurring again. When a social mistake occurs, the student meets with an educator, a counselor, or another qualified professional to discuss it. Together, in a

SOCCSS WORKSHEET

Situation	
Who	What
When	Why

Options	Consequences	Choices

Strategies

Simulation Type	Simulation Outcomes

Follow-up

Figure 5.3. Situation-Options-Consequences-Choices-Strategies-Simulation (SOCCSS) worksheet. *Note.* Adapted from "Understanding the Hidden Curriculum: An Essential Social Skill for Children and Youth With Asperger Syndrome," by B. S. Myles and R. L. Simpson, 2001b, *Intervention in School and Clinic, 36*(5), p. 284. Copyright 2001 by PRO-ED, Inc. Adapted with permission. Originally adapted from *Men on the Move: Competence and Cooperation "Conflict Resolution and Beyond,"* by J. B. Roosa, 1995, Kansas City, MO: Author.

nonpunitive and reasoned manner, they identify the mistake. They then discuss who was harmed by the error. The third step of the autopsy is to develop a plan to ensure that the error does not occur again. Because of the visual strengths, problem-solving deficits, and language-processing problems of children with AS/HFA, social autopsies may be enhanced by using written words or phrases or pictures to illustrate each of the steps.

Peer-Mediated Programs

Peer-mediated strategies involve socially competent peers who are taught to initiate, respond to, and support social interactions with children and youth who have AS/HFA. Following training, these individuals are placed in social situations where they participate in social activities with children and youth with social excesses and deficits. Unlike adult-mediated strategies, peer-mediated strategies use few, if any, social interaction prompts and cues initiated by adults. Rather, children with AS/HFA or their peers participate in social activities independent of direct adult involvement. As a result, the natural interactions of peers, albeit supported by peer training and adult oversight, are used to develop social skills, facilitate peer interactions, and support development of peer relationships.

This strategy has been associated with an increase in positive, appropriate behaviors by individuals with disabilities, which in turn promotes peer acceptance. There is some indication that peer-mediated strategies are most effective when individuals volunteer to participate in peer-mediated activities, as compared to when students are nominated by a teacher or other adult to participate. Use of groups composed of two peers and one child with AS/HFA has also been advocated by some researchers as a means of obtaining higher levels of social interaction and promoting more normal social interaction patterns. There is also some indication that popular, high-status peers, especially those who volunteer and are naturally motivated to positively interact with students with AS/HFA are particularly effective in these roles. In spite of that, it is important to note that a variety of individuals has been trained to participate in peer-supported social and related activities, and teachers and parents are often surprised to find that classmates who were not initially identified turn out to be the best peer-support candidates.

An example of a peer-mediated strategy follows.

Latanya

Ms. Simmons decides to adopt a peer-mediated strategy to increase social interactions between Latanya and her classmates. This decision is based on Ms. Simmons's observation that Latanya is consistently isolated from her peers during recess, free time, and lunch periods. Prior to selecting an appropriate peer, Ms. Simmons identifies a classmate who occasionally talks to and plays with Latanya. Ms. Simmons invites the peer to participate in a social-interaction enhancement program. Upon the peer's acceptance, Ms. Simmons trains Latanya and the peer to interact during a variety of activities, including responding to play invitations, prompting procedures, and reinforcement methods. Subsequent to peer training, Ms. Simmons observes the students, makes suggestions, and offers feedback as needed. However, during the social activity itself, she allows Latanya and her peer to interact independently. Later, Ms. Simmons invites other students to consider volunteering to participate in the program.

There are a number of advantages to using peer-mediated strategies. This approach is the most natural means of promoting socialization because it relies on naturally occurring interactions between peers. After initial training, adults permit children to socialize, thus ensuring that activities are based on normally occurring social interactions and on behaviors of socially competent peers rather than on artificial or simulated scenarios. Following recruitment, orientation, and training, peer-mediated strategies are relatively easy to implement and typically offer the best results in terms of quantity and quality of social interaction.

Challenges associated with the use of peer-mediated strategies include the time and effort required to recruit, train, and supervise student volunteers who are involved in social interaction programs. Anyone who has ever run such an operation can attest that it takes time and sustained effort. At the same time, it is also important to note that the same individuals who acknowledge the effort required to operate these programs will also declare that they are typically unmatched in terms of the social outcomes they deliver. Additional challenges and questions regarding peer-mediated programs include the question of whether social interaction skills will generalize to other peers, environments, and situations, because the learners with AS/HFA are trained to work with designated peers in their classroom on certain activities. There is also a question of whether skills developed by children through peer-mediated strategies will be maintained over time. In this connection, just as with other forms of social interaction programming, it is essential that generalization and maintenance programs be planned.

Steps involved in organizing and operating a peer-mediated social support program are described below.

- *Identify and arrange for appropriate social interaction opportunities*—Because children and youth diagnosed with AS/HFA are often members of general education classes, these activities will typically be incorporated as a part of naturally occurring classroom and school activities, including lunch, free time, recess, and so forth. Related to identifying situations that offer social interaction and social relation opportunities it is important to consider factors that will enhance social interactions and motivate students to participate in program activities. Teachers and other program engineers need to assess the social assets, interests, and motivation of each student with AS/HFA to determine the social activities for which he or she is best suited. Consideration of a student's ability to respond to various levels and intensity of social demands is also imperative. For example, understanding that a student finds competitive group games very stressful or that he or she doesn't have the motor skills and game knowledge to do well in certain playground activities will have obvious utility. Strategically using contextual and setting variables can also significantly increase the chances of successful social outcomes. Knowing, for example, that a student with AS/HFA prefers and excels in certain game or leisure activities or likes to use certain types of materials (e.g., felt pens to do art) can be beneficially used to create and engineer activities. Other setting and contextual considerations are students' preferences for familiar vs. unfamiliar peers, preferences for interactions with same vs. different gender classmates, and penchants for interacting with a single classmate vs. different size social groups.
- *Recruit volunteers for peer-mediated activities*—It is recommended that educators solicit volunteers for these activities, especially from among groups of peers who seem to have naturally occurring and

ongoing relationships with students with special needs, including those diagnosed with autism-related disorders. It is important to recognize and emphasize to recruits that they are being asked to support and be involved in peer-to-peer activities with classmates and that the role is not one of supervisor, behavior manager, or surrogate teacher.

- *Train volunteers for peer-mediated activities and roles*—In this step, one or more educators help students with AS/HFA identify and appropriately use the knowledge and skills required to take advantage of social interaction opportunities. That is, it is important that students with AS/HFA have at least the rudimentary skills and knowledge to participate in designated social activities. Adult-mediated explicit instruction, social thinking and social problem solving, and social interpretation interventions are all used in this phase of instruction. This step will also involve instructing peer participants about the nature and characteristics of AS/HFA and their role in supporting their classmates with the disorder. Also within this step is dissemination of basic information on how to participate with, interact with, and respond to a classmate with AS/HFA. Some role-specific and specific-response information is essential, such as what to do if the student requires behavior management intervention. However, much of the information given to student volunteers involves instructing them to do those things that are naturally a part of interacting and having mutually beneficial relationships with peers. Overscripting student volunteers or excessively structuring students in their activities and relationships can interfere with achievement of goals and objectives inherent in participation in age-appropriate peer activities and mutually beneficial relationships.

- *Ensure that students with AS/HFA and their peers receive benefit and reinforcement for their social interaction efforts*—Ultimately, the success of peer-mediated programs will be dependent on whether participants, including those with special needs and their nondisabled classmates, find the activities, interactions, and relationships beneficial, enjoyable, and satisfying. Accordingly, educators involved in structuring these programs are urged to look for ways to ensure positive experiences for the participants.

- *Provide ongoing support for student participants*—Primary benefits from peer-mediated social activities are the naturally occurring interactions and relationships that take place. Nonetheless, it is essential that teachers and other designated adults closely monitor the programs and provide supports as needed. Stepping in to intervene with a potential behavior problem, clarifying game rules and requirements, and coaching or prompting a child with AS/HFA and the designated peer are all examples of basic responsibilities of educators and thus are not counterproductive to developing and maintaining naturally occurring peer-to-peer relationships.
- *Evaluate program components, personnel, and outcomes and make modifications as needed*—Peer-mediated program monitoring and evaluation is essential. Only through such an ongoing process can needed program amendments be made, including changing or modifying the program activities, recruiting new peer volunteers, implementing maintenance and generalization plans, and so forth. As a part of this process, subjective feedback of student participants and consideration of their recommendations for improving programs is strongly recommended

Concluding Thoughts

By definition, children and youth with AS/HFA experience social-skill and social interaction problems and deficits. Accordingly, it is prudent to assume that all individuals with these disorders require some form of social training and support. The type and nature of this training will vary in accordance with differing needs, situations, and circumstances. There is no single method that will universally be most suitable and effective. Explicit instruction of identified social targets, social thinking and social problem solving, social interpretation interventions, and peer-mediated programs will be appropriate under certain conditions and with particular individuals.

The challenges associated with instructing learners with AS/HFA to effectively use social skills and to engage in functional and positive social interactions with peers and adults are noteworthy. There is every reason to believe that the process is difficult and that returns on efforts to teach social behaviors to learners with special needs have often been less than satisfactory (Bellini, Peters, Benner, & Hopf, 2007). Nevertheless, the nature of AS/HFA demands that significant attention be given to the development of improved social skills among individuals with these disorders. Without question, suitable individualized planning in conjunction with strategic application of support, structure, and correct use of social-skill and social interaction methods bodes positively for children and youth learning and using functional social skills and making social interaction progress. Positive outcomes are most apt to occur when specific and clearly defined social behaviors are taught in naturalistic settings and situations; when there is planning for acquisition, performance, and fluency deficits; when learners have access to realistic and positive models, realistic rehearsal opportunities, performance feedback, and appropriate reinforcement; and when generalization and maintenance plans are identified and implemented during all stages of training and support.

chapter six

Evidence-Based and Effective Methods for Learners

chapter author:
Lisa Barrett Mann

There is significant pressure on schools today to provide "evidence-based" interventions for students with special needs, including those with Asperger syndrome or high-functioning autism. Parents are becoming increasingly aware of the importance of early intervention in autism spectrum disorders (ASDs) and are, rightfully, demanding that their children be provided appropriate services as early as possible. Meanwhile, the federal No Child Left Behind Act of 2001 (NCLB) and many federal educational programs call on schools to implement instructional strategies and educational practices that have been proven effective through scientifically based research.

The question schools struggle with, though, is "Which interventions for children with Asperger syndrome and high-functioning autism *are* based on scientific research?" The terms *evidence-based* and *research-based* are now being routinely used in the advertising and packaging of educational materials. Sadly, these labels are often marketing ploys and provide no guarantee that the materials are, indeed, based on high-quality research (Simpson et al., 2005). Meanwhile, professionals tend to advocate ASD interventions that conform to their own philosophy and professional training; for example, a specialist in applied behavior analysis (ABA) is more likely to recommend a behavioral intervention to address a child's challenging behavior, while an occupational therapist is more likely to endorse sensory integration therapy (Tincani, 2007).

In theory, parents and schools are supposed to be able to turn to the Department of Education's What Works Clearinghouse (WWC) as a central, reliable source of scientific evidence on effective educational practices. In 2002, the WWC was awarded $18.5 million to assess and report on effective programs. However, as of late 2008, it had yet to report on any practices specific to special education or ASDs, much less Asperger syndrome and high-functioning autism. In an effort to help fill that void, this chapter provides a systematic review of the literature to identify and analyze the evidence base for various interventions used with children who have high-functioning autism or Asperger syndrome.

The Need for Intervention Data Specific to Asperger Syndrome and High-Functioning Autism

A primary goal of intervention research is to determine the most effective practices for children *with specific characteristics* (National Research Council [NRC], 2001). Given that children with Asperger syndrome and high-functioning autism (AS/HFA) generally have at least average—and often advanced—cognitive and verbal abilities, we cannot assume that the same interventions are appropriate for them as for children with severe impairments in these areas. Yet, most treatment and outcome research in autism spectrum disorders actually has been focused on children with "classic autism" (i.e., those who also have significant challenges in cognition and language).

When Simpson (2005) evaluated 33 commonly used interventions and treatments for children with ASDs, only 4 (applied behavior analysis, discrete trial training, pivotal response training, and *Learning Experiences: An Alterative Program for Preschoolers and Parents* [LEAP; Strain & Cordisco, 1994]) showed significant and convincing efficacy and support. None of these interventions, however, were backed by any studies showing their efficacy specifically for children with Asperger syndrome or high-functioning autism.

There is, in fact, a dearth of intervention research focused on children at the high end of the autism spectrum—and the studies that *have* been done have shown that no intervention strategy has been equally successful for all participants or for all areas assessed (Tsatsanis, Foley, & Donehower, 2004). Regardless of the many claims one can find on the Internet, there is no such thing as a one-size-fits-all intervention for Asperger disorder and high-functioning autism. Indeed, one of the most frustrating aspects of the disorder—for both parents and professionals— is the difficulty in predicting which intervention(s) will be effective for which child and for which aspects of his or her behavior.

The Importance of Experimental Design

High-quality scientific intervention research is vital because it protects us from making false assumptions about an intervention's effectiveness. Despite their lack of empirical evidence, parents and professionals alike have often been convinced by some programs' claims of dramatic, all-encompassing improvements and even returns to normalcy among participants (Simpson, 2005). When that has happened, unrealistic expectations have been nurtured and, with limited time and funds available, caring adults have passed over proven strategies in favor of "miracle cures" that were neither miraculous nor curative.

It is not hard to jump to an incorrect conclusion about an intervention—even the most well-meaning, intelligent people have done it. If you implement an intervention and the child shows subsequent improvement, it is natural to assume that the intervention was the cause of that improvement. Yet one of the most basic, underlying tenets of experimental design is that "correlation does not equal causation." In other words, just because B occurred after A, you cannot assume that A caused B.

Suppose, for example, that Wonderbar University piloted its new Better Behavior intervention curriculum at Wilson Middle School. Every lunch period for 2 months, six boys with Asperger syndrome went to the counselor's office and worked on the curriculum with Mr. Dean, a special graduate student from Wonderbar. Over those 8 weeks, the boys' mean number of problem behaviors (meltdowns, acts of physical or verbal aggression) decreased from four per day to less than one per week. Does that mean the Better Behavior program caused the improvement? Maybe, but not necessarily. Perhaps the reduction in problem behaviors was actually the result of one or more of the following:

- the boys not having to eat in the cafeteria every day, where the smells and noises overloaded their sensory systems
- the boys spending 30 minutes a day focusing on appropriate social behavior—and their behavior would have improved just as much with any social-skills curriculum
- the boys spending 30 minutes a day with Mr. Dean, whom they all liked and wanted to please
- two class bullies being expelled during that period—so the boys were no longer being taunted in the hallways between classes (and the fact that it happened during the intervention period was just coincidence)

Wonderbar's study employed a simple pretest/posttest format, a form of pre-experimental design. Because pre-experimental research, which also includes case studies, cannot rule out extraneous factors, it cannot be used as evidence of an intervention's effectiveness. (Although promising results in a pre-experimental study might indicate that it would be useful to do further research.)

Controlled Designs

To avoid making spurious assumptions about cause and effect, scientific research design requires that controls be used to neutralize the effects of other factors as much as possible. How controls are implemented depends on the research design. Three common controlled designs include (a) randomized controlled trials, (b) quasi-experimental design, and (c) single-subject design.

Randomized Controlled Trials

In a randomized controlled trial, a large pool of similar participants is randomly assigned to an intervention group or a control (no intervention or different intervention) group. This is generally considered the "gold standard" for evaluating an intervention's effectiveness (Institute of Education Sciences, U.S. Department of Education, What Works Clearinghouse, 2009). However, given the difficulty of recruiting a large number of children with ASDs who are similar in behavior, intelligence, verbal skills, living circumstances, educational settings, and so forth, it can be very difficult to evaluate special educational interventions using this model, according to the NRC (2001). It can also pose an ethical dilemma, unless two treatments are being tested and are believed to be equally promising. Even then, the researcher must closely monitor every child's family, as many will seek additional outside treatments for the children that would compromise the study's results. Another issue with randomized group design is that the smaller the size of the group, the larger the outcomes must be in order to show statistical significance.

When experimental group design has been used in ASD intervention research, the NRC found that it has generally been for evaluating comprehensive treatment programs (e.g., applied behavior analysis), while single-subject designs are more common for documenting response to individual practices.

Quasi-Experimental Design

Because of the difficulty in recruiting appropriate subjects and the expense and labor intensity of treatment, most ASD intervention studies have been conducted with small sample sizes (NRC, 2001). However, when the number of subjects is smaller and they vary significantly in their characteristics, random assignment is unlikely to result in equivalent groups. Therefore, researchers will often employ a quasi-experimental design in which they assign children to the experimental and control groups by matching on (hopefully) relevant characteristics. Of course, it is impossible to predict exactly which characteristics might be ones that would affect intervention efficacy. A researcher might try to create equivalent groups by matching on age and performance IQ, when, say, it might really be children's sensory sensitivities or verbal IQ that most affect their response to the intervention.

Single-Subject Design

Single-subject designs are more common than experimental or quasi-experimental designs in ASD intervention research, according to the NRC. While group designs are more sensitive to average changes across groups, single-subject designs are sensitive to changes within individuals' behaviors. Experimental control in single-subject design is usually shown by documenting three demonstrations of the experimental effect at three different points in time with a single participant or across three different participants (Horner et al., 2005). Unlike case studies, which don't employ rigorous controls, single-subject studies may be used to establish evidence-based practices (Horner et al., 2005). Two common single-subject approaches are reversal design and multiple baseline design.

In a typical reversal, or ABAB design, after baseline condition data (A) are established, the intervention condition (B) is introduced, then withdrawn (A), and then introduced again. This systematic process permits researchers to determine that the intervention (B) co-varies with the manipulation of the intervention. In multiple baseline designs, the intervention is not withdrawn, but its introduction is staggered across participants, settings, activities, and so forth, to demonstrate that change in behavior co-varies with the introduction of the intervention. Although single-subject research can be interpreted through statistical analysis, it is traditionally demonstrated using line graphs that illustrate the change in behavior within and across conditions of the study.

Horner et al. (2005) proposed that an intervention can be documented as "evidence based" by single-subject research only if (a) the practice is operationally defined; (b) the practice is implemented with fidelity; (c) the context in which the intervention is used is defined; (d) results document a functional relationship between the intervention and the change in behavior; and (e) the experimental effects have been replicated across at least five acceptable studies, done in three different locations, with a combined total of 20 or more participants.

Review of Evidence-Based and Effective Interventions

The information in this section reports research on interventions for individuals diagnosed with Asperger disorder or high-functioning autism. The information is (a) a systematic review of peer-reviewed experimental, quasi-experimental, and single-subject (with at least three changes in condition) studies related to the effectiveness of interventions for individuals with Asperger disorder or related disabilities published prior to 2009 and (b) an analysis of the evidence base for each identified intervention. Studies that included individuals with high-functioning autism, pervasive developmental disorder–not otherwise specified are included in the review. Studies that combined results for ASDs with and without co-morbid mental retardation were excluded, as were studies that employed pre-experimental designs (e.g., case studies or open trials) and studies that employed medical or pharmaceutical treatments.

To locate articles, a computerized search was conducted of the PsychINFO, Educational Resources Information Center (ERIC), and Wilson Web databases, using combinations and variations of the following search terms: *Asperger, intervention, treatment,* and *outcome.* In addition, an individual computerized search for the keyword *Asperger* or *Asperger's* was conducted of the *Journal of Autism and Developmental Disorders* and of *Behavior Modification,* and article titles and abstracts were reviewed for possible fit. After identifying initial studies fitting the above criteria, additional studies were located by conducting an ancestral search of their references.

In all, 78 intervention studies related to Asperger syndrome or high-functioning autism were initially identified for review, of which 44 were subsequently excluded based on their pre-experimental design. In total, 34 studies fit criteria for inclusion in this review. The review process led to classification of intervention methods into eight categories: (a) cognitive behavior therapy, (b) social stories, (c) social-skills training, (d) video modeling, (e) errorless learning techniques, (f) parent training programs, (g) emotion recognition software, and (h) other interventions.

Space limitations of this chapter allow only a brief review of the most salient facts from each study. In the larger research project, each selected study was systematically reviewed and analyzed across multiple factors, including *Target Behavior(s), Subject(s), Study Design, Setting, Intensity of Intervention, Measurement Method, Findings, Generalization Probes, Maintenance Probes, Limitations, Treatment Integrity, Inter-observer Agreement, Sufficiency of Information Provided to Replicate Study,* and *Implications for Future Research.*

Cognitive Behavior Therapy (CBT)

Cognitive behavior therapy emphasizes the important role a person's thought processes have on his or her feelings. CBT typically involves six steps: (a) assessment, (b) affective education (recognizing and understanding emotions), (c) cognitive restructuring (correcting distorted or dysfunctional beliefs), (d) stress management, (e) self-reflection, and (f) scheduling of activities to practice new cognitive skills in real-life situations (Attwood, 2007).

Evidence of Effectiveness

Of the interventions reviewed, CBT had the largest body of evidence, with 163 subjects across three group studies.

- Chalfant, Rapee, and Carroll (2006) used a CBT intervention with 47 children ages 8 to 13 years who had both Asperger syndrome or high-functioning autism and co-morbid anxiety disorders. Following 12 weekly (2-hour) group sessions, 71% of the children in the intervention group no longer fulfilled DSM-IV-TR (2000) diagnostic criteria for an anxiety disorder, while all children in a wait-list control group still did. Significant reductions in anxiety symptoms were seen in the intervention group as measured by self-report, parent report, and teacher report.
- Sofronoff, Attwood, and Hinton (2005) used a randomized, controlled trial to compare reduction in anxiety symptoms among 71 ten- to twelve-year-olds with Asperger syndrome divided into three groups: a child-only CBT intervention, a child plus parent intervention, and a wait-list control group. Both intervention groups demonstrated significant reduction in parent-reported anxiety symptoms at follow-up, and a significant increase in the children's ability to generate positive strategies in a hypothetical anxiety-provoking situation. Interestingly, although the child-only intervention group showed slightly more improvement at the end of the 6-week (12 hours total) program, the group in which parents had been trained as co-therapists showed significantly more improvement at the 6-week follow-up.
- After their success with the anxiety management trials, Sofronoff, Attwood, Hinton, and Levin (2007) used a similar CBT intervention to address anger management difficulties in 45 ten- to fourteen-year-olds with Asperger syndrome. However, in this case, all parents of children in the intervention group received training. Compared to the wait-list control group, parent reports indicated a significant decrease in episodes of children's anger, both at the end of the intervention program and at the 6-week follow-up.

Analysis

Neither anxiety nor anger management problems are primary features of Asperger syndrome or high-functioning autism, although they are frequently reported by parents and teachers. In fact, anxiety disorders may co-occur in as many as 47% to 84% of children with Asperger syndrome (Chalfant et al., 2006). Numerous randomized controlled trials have shown CBT to be an effective treatment for typically developing children with anxiety disorders (Cartwright-Hatton, Roberts, Chitsabesan, Fothergill, & Harrington, 2004) and, to a lesser extent, anger (Sukhodolsky, Kassinove, & Gorman, 2003).

The three cited group studies—all conducted in Australia—support the use of CBT as an appropriate intervention for anxiety or anger management problems in children with AS/HFA. However, it is important to note that all three studies used programs that were created or adapted specifically to meet the needs of children with AS/HFA. Chalfant's group adapted Macquarie University's Cool Kids program to make it more visual and concrete, with more emphasis on relaxation and exposure and simplified cognitive activities (e.g., picking "helpful and unhelpful thoughts" from a list, rather than having to spontaneously generate them). In both of Sofronoff's groups, the program was designed specifically for children with Asperger disorder by clinician Tony Attwood. Interestingly, while CBT is usually the domain of psychologists, Attwood's programs were designed so that a teacher, a speech pathologist, an occupational therapist, or a parent could implement the program (Attwood, 2007).

Recommendations

The studies reviewed here suggest that CBT is an evidence-based intervention for children with high-functioning autism. The method may also be useful in reducing anxiety and dealing with anger management problems. However, professionals implementing such programs should have experience with children who have high-functioning autism or Asperger disorder and an understanding of their cognitive, social, and communicative differences.

Social Stories

A social story is a short, individualized narrative written to help an individual with an ASD understand an activity and its associated behavioral expectations (Crozier & Tincani, 2007). Although *social story* is a term often used generically, Carol Gray (2004) has trademarked Social Story to indicate a specific style and format, including a specified ratio of descriptive, directive, perspective, control, cooperative, and affirmative sentences. Using a constructive approach, Social Stories give the child positive examples of what to do in a given situation, rather than what not to do (Attwood, 2007).

Evidence of Effectiveness

Two strong single-subject studies were identified that showed evidence of the effectiveness of social stories in decreasing undesirable behaviors in children with AS/HFA. Both studies used reversal (ABAB) designs:

- Crozier and Tincani (2007) used a social story to decrease inappropriate play behaviors (e.g., hitting, grabbing, and kicking) and increase appropriate ones (e.g., asking to use materials, offering materials to others, using materials cooperatively, and making appropriate comments) in three preschoolers with ASDs, including one whose characteristics were consistent with Asperger disorder.
- Bledsoe, Myles, and Simpson (2003) used a social story to help a 13-year-old boy with Asperger syndrome and attention-deficit/hyperactivity disorder (ADHD) improve his table manners (e.g., fewer food spills and more wiping mouth with a napkin).

Five other studies paired social stories with other interventions, using multiple baseline designs, to evaluate effective results:

- Two studies by Bock (2007a, 2007b) used social stories to teach SODA (Stop-Observe-Deliberate-Act), a cognitive strategy for recognizing relevant social cues and, in turn, choosing appropriate social behaviors. Four boys, ages 6 to 12 years, increased their percentage of time engaged in social behavior during cooperative learning, lunch, and activity/recess.
- Scattone (2007) used three videotaped social stories plus video modeling to enhance conversation skills in a 9-year-old boy. The multiple-baseline across-behaviors study demonstrated an increase in eye contact; social initiations; and, to a lesser extent, smiling.

- Sansosti and Powell-Smith (2008) used computer-presented social stories plus video models to increase joining-in behaviors (e.g., initiating or participating in a preferred play activity or conversation with other children) for three children with high-functioning autism or Asperger syndrome. It was interesting to note that for two of the three children in this study, appropriate behaviors increased at first and then fell off when their peers failed to respond to their social initiations. Once an additional phase was added to the study, in which a teacher prompted other students to play with the boys when asked, the boys' joining-in behaviors increased again and were maintained at follow-up. (This is an important factor to keep in mind when implementing any social intervention: If a child's newly taught behavior is supposed to be reinforced by others' responses [be they peers, parents, or school staff], you had better be sure those others are going to respond appropriately!)
- Social stories were also used as components of two cognitive behavior therapy programs that were successful in decreasing anxiety and anger management problems in children with Asperger disorder (Sofronoff et al., 2005; Sofronoff et al., 2007).

However, not all studies showed such effective results. Two studies do not support social stories as an effective intervention:

- In a multiple-baseline across-participants study by Sansosti and Powell-Smith (2006), social stories were implemented to improve social behavior during recess for three boys (ages 9 to 11 years). While improvements were seen in one boy's sportsmanship and another's maintenance of conversation, the third did not show an increase in joining-in behaviors.
- Adams, Gouvousis, VanLue, and Waldron (2004) used a single social story to attempt to reduce problem behaviors during homework for a 7-year-old boy with Asperger disorder. An ABAB design was employed to look at four different behaviors: crying, screaming, falling, and hitting. However, data did not co-vary with introduction and removal of the independent variable (the social story). In fact, three out of four targeted behaviors (crying, screaming, and hitting) actually increased during the first

intervention phase. While the behaviors showed a decrease during the second intervention phase, the child's father had changed his own behavior during the second baseline phase: Instead of trying to verbally cajole the child, he had begun assertively redirecting the child's frustration behaviors.

Analysis

Social stories have become increasingly popular in recent years (Myles & Simpson, 2001a), and there is a growing body of single-subject research that suggests some effectiveness for use with individuals with ASDs. However, the studies discussed illustrate that results of social story research are not uniformly positive.

Social stories are a deceptively "easy" intervention. However, not all social stories are created equally—in fact, their quality can vary tremendously. Poorly written social stories may be far less effective than well-written ones. Gray (1995, 2004) has attempted to address that issue by giving very specific guidance on the structure and format of social stories, but those instructions can be cumbersome and difficult to follow. Moreover, many studies that have shown positive results did not conform to Gray's guidelines (Kuoch & Mirenda, 2003).

Because there is so much variation among social stories, it is much harder to compare their effects. When a researcher uses different social stories for different children (e.g., Sansosti & Powell-Smith, 2006) and/or different target behaviors (Sansosti & Powell-Smith, 2006; Scattone, 2007), one can no longer assume he or she is comparing "apples to apples"—two variables are being manipulated, instead of one. If every child in the study responds well in every situation, effectiveness can be assumed. But if the study does not produce a consistently positive response, it becomes difficult to sort out whether the social story was ineffective because (a) it wasn't the right intervention for the circumstances or (b) the particular social story used was not effective—while one written differently might have been.

On the flip side, there may be social story research studies that do not get published because the story was too effective. If a researcher has planned an ABAB design, but the social story works for a child immediately, his behavior may not deteriorate again during the second baseline phase, because he has already learned the lesson taught. If that happens, the researcher could publish a case study—but it would not be considered evidence of effectiveness (a bit of a catch-22 effect in intervention research).

Recommendations

Because social stories are a low- or no-cost intervention, and there is limited and low risk involved in using them, the body of evidence is sufficient to recommend them for use with children who have AS/HFA. However, particular attention needs to be paid to the content and quality of the story. In addition, those implementing the story need to ensure that the results that the story predicts for desirable behavior (e.g., "If I ask nicely, the other kids will play with me") truly come to fruition.

Social-Skills Training

Social-skills training is not a single, specific intervention. Rather, it is a broad term used to describe interventions that are designed to teach individuals the skills necessary to navigate their social environments, assimilate into their peer groups, and interact with both familiar and unfamiliar people (Rao, Beidel, & Murray, 2007). Typically, social-skills instruction is done through small-group programs that facilitate interaction among members. As discussed in Chapter 5, the curricula and procedures used can vary tremendously, and may focus on specific skill areas, such as nonverbal communication, or attempt to address fundamental deficits, such as theory of mind (Howlin & Yates, 1999). All the programs identified in this review utilized multiple techniques in different combinations. Social-skills training techniques can include the following:

- direct skill instruction (explanation, demonstration, practice, and/or feedback)
- role playing (practicing and improvising socially appropriate behaviors)
- group discussion
- peer initiation (typically developing peers initiate and encourage social interactions in natural settings)
- peer tutoring (typically developing peers perform direct skill instruction and give positive feedback)
- adult prompting and coaching in actual social situations
- cognitive interpretation (training in theory of mind, facial affect, body language, idioms, etc.)

- cognitive strategies (using specific strategies for interpreting social situations or emotions and then responding appropriately)
- cognitive scripts (practicing rote dialogue to use in specific social situations)
- behavioral reinforcement (immediate or delayed consequences paired to specific social behaviors)
- computer programs
- games and recreational activities
- peer support networks and peer training

Evidence of Effectiveness

Eight controlled group studies were reviewed relative to evaluating social-skills training for students with Asperger disorder or high-functioning autism. The combined total of participants for the studies was 378.

- Solomon, Goodlin-Jones, and Anders (2004) conducted 20-week groups (1.5 hours per week) for boys ages 8 to 12 years ($n = 17$). Training techniques included direct skill instruction, group discussion, cognitive interpretation, cognitive strategies, role play, and parent training. Children in the intervention groups improved significantly in facial expression recognition and problem solving, compared to children in the wait-list control group. No significant improvements were seen on theory of mind tasks.
- Bauminger (2007) used a cognitive-behavioral-ecological (CB-E) intervention with two groups of elementary-school-aged boys and girls with high-functioning ASDs—the original group of 11, who had participated in an individual CB-E program the previous year, and a newly recruited, matched group of 15. For seven months, each child received twice weekly, small-group social-skills instruction (direct skill instruction, cognitive interpretation, and cognitive strategies) in their own school (along with two typical peers and 0 to 2 classmates with high-functioning ASDs), as well as weekly individual sessions with a teacher to practice skills and to clarify issues from the group session. Following the intervention, children in both groups demonstrated a significant improvement in emotion recognition and in their cooperative capabilities within the intervention groups. However,

they did not exhibit an increase in spontaneous social interactions during recess.

- Lopata, Thomeer, Volker, and Nida (2006) and Lopata, Thomeer, Volker, Nida, and Lee (2008) evaluated an intensive 6-week (30 hours per week) cognitive behavior treatment program for 6- to 13-year-olds with Asperger syndrome, which was evaluated over the course of four summers. The curriculum included select lessons from the commercially available *Skillstreaming* program (Goldstein & McGinnis, 1997), as well as lessons related to interpreting abstract language and facial expression, and therapeutic activities designed to foster cooperation and social interaction. Children were assigned to one of two testing conditions: one with a behavioral reinforcement system (a "token economy," in which they could earn and lose points toward edible treats and field trips) or one in which they received general, naturalist feedback (e.g., "Good job!") throughout the day. Both studies (which evaluated the first 2 years and second 2 years of the project, respectively) found significant improvements in social skills and reduction of problem behaviors, with neither feedback condition proving superior over the other.

- Three studies examined the effects of a less traditional approach to social-skills intervention—LEGO therapy. This program combines aspects of behavior therapy, peer modeling, and naturalistic communication strategies, while using LEGO building blocks as a therapy medium. Children worked cooperatively to build projects, with an "engineer" who gave verbal instructions, a "supplier" who searched for the necessary pieces, and a "builder" who put them together. In the original study detailing the intervention, LeGoff (2004) found that 47 children, ages 6 to 16 years, who received weekly group and individual sessions, showed significant improvements in frequency of self-initiated social contact, duration of social interactions, and reduction in social aloofness after 12 and 24 weeks of intervention, compared to wait-list controls. That was followed by a retrospective study (LeGoff & Sherman, 2006) that compared 60 children with ASDs who had participated in LEGO therapy for at least 36 months with a matched control sample of 57 children who had received other continuous mental health and educational services during the same period from other providers. Although children in both groups improved, those in the long-term LEGO intervention improved significantly more in social competence and reduction of autistic-type social behaviors. (However, there was more variability in outcomes among the comparison group, likely because of different therapists and different treatments used—suggesting this was not a good control group.) Most recently, Owens, Granader, Humphrey, and Baron-Cohen (2008) compared use of LEGO therapy (group sessions only) to the Social Use of Language Programme (SULP; Rinaldi, 2004; a direct teaching approach based around stories, group activities, and games) in 6- to 11-year-olds with high-functioning ASDs over the course of 18 weeks. Both intervention groups showed significant reduction in maladaptive behaviors compared to a no-intervention control group, while only the LEGO group improved significantly on autism-specific social interaction scores.

• Beaumont and Sofronoff (2008) investigated the effectiveness of the *Junior Detective Training Program,* a 7-week (2 hours per week) program that combined small-group sessions, parent training sessions, teacher handouts, and a computer game about a futuristic secret agent who specializes in decoding suspects' thoughts and feelings. Forty-nine children with Asperger syndrome, ages 7 to 11 years, were randomly assigned to either the intervention or wait-list control group. The intervention group demonstrated significant improvements in social skills, based on parent and teacher ratings, as well as improvements in emotion management strategies. However, there was no significant improvement in ability to recognize emotions.

Analysis

Academia is only just beginning to scientifically evaluate social-skills programs for children with Asperger disorder or high-functioning autism. (The oldest of the studies reviewed above were published in 2004, and four of the eight were published in 2007 or 2008). The six programs identified above all demonstrated some effectiveness in improving social skills and/or decreasing problem behaviors. Yet, all used a different combination of multiple intervention techniques, ranging from direct skill instruction to a video game.

Of all the programs identified, LEGO therapy demonstrated the strongest results. It was the only program that had been evaluated by two completely different sets of researchers (including Owens et al., 2008, from the prestigious Autism Research Centre at University of Cambridge) and was the only one with direct evidence of generalization (i.e., increased duration of social interactions on the playground).

Facilitating generalization—getting children to use their newly acquired social skills outside the clinic setting—has been a known challenge in social-skills programs (Rao et al., 2007). In addition to the LEGO program, measurements completed by parents and teachers also suggested that the *Junior Detective Training Program* and Lopata's (Lopata et al., 2008) summer social treatment program led to positive outcomes that generalized to other settings. While these three programs may, on the surface, vary tremendously, there were some commonalities:

- small group size (3 to 7 children)
- low teacher–child ratio (at least 1 adult for every 3 children)
- curriculum developed or adapted specifically for children with high-functioning ASDs
- a program that included the following: (a) games and/or fun, cooperative activities; (b) role play or rehearsals (in LEGO, during one-on-one group time); (c) cognitive strategies (in LEGO, discussed during one-on-one time)

Lopata et al. (2008) and Beaumont and Sofronoff's (2008) groups also included direct skill instruction, modeling, and affective education.

Recommendations

Although no single best practice curriculum or methodology has emerged for social-skills training, recent studies have shown that some programs can be effective in increasing pro-social behaviors and decreasing problem behaviors. When evaluating a potential social-skills program for a child with Asperger syndrome or a high-functioning autism, one should look for the same characteristics as those listed in the most successful programs above. In addition, the teacher/facilitator should have training and experience in working with children with high-functioning autism.

Video Modeling and Video Self-Modeling

Video modeling is an intervention wherein a subject views a video representation of a desired behavior and then attempts to imitate that behavior. The person demonstrating the behavior can be an adult, another child, or a peer. When the person attempting to learn the behavior views video of himself or herself successfully performing it, the technique is referred to as *video self-modeling* (Bellini & Akullian, 2007). Typically, video modeling is packaged with other intervention elements (e.g., prompting or rehearsal), rather than used as a stand-alone intervention (Apple, Billingsley, & Schwartz, 2005).

Evidence of Effectiveness

Four multiple-baseline studies that used video modeling or video self-modeling as an intervention for children with AS/HFA were examined. Two of them incorporated social stories as well.

- In a two-part study with 5-year-olds, Apple et al. (2005) used video modeling to significantly increase receptive compliments (e.g., when someone says, "Look!" you say, "Cool!"). It took the addition of a self-management phase (with tangible reinforcement), however, to increase self-initiated compliments.
- Delano (2007) used video self-modeling to improve the essay-writing performance of three adolescent boys with Asperger syndrome. After working with individual scripted self-modeling videos on self-monitoring strategies and a mnemonic strategy for composing a persuasive essay, the multiple-baseline across-responses and across-participants study showed increases in mean number of words written, number of functional essay elements, and duration of essay-writing time.
- Scattone (2007) used a combination of video modeling and videotaped social stories to enhance conversation skills in a 9-year-old boy. The multiple-baseline across-behaviors study demonstrated an increase in eye contact and social initiations, but had minimal success in increasing smiling.
- Sansosti and Powell-Smith (2008) used a combination of video modeling, prompts, and computer-presented social stories to increase joining-in behaviors (initiating or participating in a preferred play activity or conversation with other children) for three

children with high-functioning autism or Asperger syndrome (see discussion in the Intervention: Social Stories section of this chapter).

Analysis and Recommendations

Video modeling and video self-modeling have been used successfully across various disciplines and populations (including neurotypical learners) to teach a variety of skills (Sigafoos, O'Reilly, & de la Cruz, 2007). A meta-analysis of 23 single-subject design studies by Bellini and Akullian (2007) showed that video modeling was effective in teaching a wide variety of functional, behavioral, and social-communication skills to children with ASDs and that the skills were maintained over time and generalized across people and settings. Based on existing literature, including the aforementioned studies identified in this review, there is efficacy support for video modeling/self-modeling, including when the method is used in combination with other techniques (i.e., prompting, self-management strategies, social stories, and so forth). In summary, there is evidence to support video modeling as an evidence-based intervention appropriate for use with children who have Asperger syndrome or high-functioning autism.

Errorless Learning Techniques

Errorless learning (also referred to as *errorless teaching*) is a technique mainly associated with discrete trial training that involves presenting a discriminative stimulus (e.g., an instruction from a teacher) in a manner that maximizes the likelihood of a correct response (Simpson, 2005). In essence, it is the opposite of trial-and-error learning. In errorless learning, a desired behavior is taught and reinforced in a manner that ensures a learner's success and mastery of each step in the learning process.

Evidence of Effectiveness

Two single-subject studies used errorless learning techniques effectively with children with Asperger syndrome or high-functioning autism:

- Cameron, Shapiro, and Ainsleigh (2005) used a changing criterion design in an errorless learning approach to teach a 9-year-old boy with Asperger syndrome to ride a bicycle. Previous attempts to teach the child to ride a bicycle had been unsuccessful, and because he had fallen in the past, he was intolerant of instruction. After doing an eight-step task analysis that took into account the child's specific needs, a very gradual, sequential program was implemented over the course of 64 sessions. During that period, for every minute the child spent on the bike, he earned a minute of video games (his most preferred activity). By the end of the program, the child was able to ride his bicycle and continued doing so after the video game reinforcement was discontinued.

- Ducharme, Sanjuan, and Drain (2007) used a multiple-baseline across-subjects design to evaluate an Errorless Compliance Training approach with three boys with Asperger syndrome (ages 4, 6, and 10) who were extremely noncompliant with daily parental requests. Mothers first delivered a range of requests to their children and recorded their responses, after which the researchers calculated the "compliance probability" for each request with each child. They then categorized the requests into four probability levels, from those that children almost always complied with (Level 1) to those that commonly led to opposition (Level 4). Mothers were trained in how to deliver the requests and record their children's responses and were instructed to reinforce compliance, ignore noncompliance, and avoid making requests from more difficult probability levels than the current stage at which they were working. During the first phase of treatment, mothers only made Level 1 requests of their children. Requests from Levels 2 through 4 were phased in sequentially over several weeks. Children's compliance with Level 4 requests increased from a mean of 26% at baseline to 80% at the end of the study, and to 85% at a 2-month follow-up.

Analysis and Recommendations

Errorless learning is a technique that has proven successful in animal studies and in experiments with humans with normal development, mental retardation, ASDs, and other conditions (Mueller, Palkovic, & Maynard, 2007). It can be, however, a slow, labor-intensive approach to implement. The two single-subject studies are promising but are not sufficient evidence to declare errorless learning an evidence-based intervention for individuals with AS/HFA. At the same time, many of these children are perfectionists, and fear of making an error can frequently lead them to refuse to even try an activity unless they can be sure of doing it perfectly (Attwood, 2007). For these children, errorless learning could be an avenue worth exploring. Moreover, while studies on errorless learning documented long-term, extensive interventions, errorless learning does not have to be perceived as an all-or-nothing approach. For a child with a low threshold for frustration, breaking lessons down into smaller, easier chunks is a relatively simple, risk-free strategy that can easily be employed by parents or educators with minimal training.

Parent Training Programs

Parent training programs are generally designed to help mothers and fathers understand some of the underlying reasons for their child's behavior problems and to train them in how to better manage these behaviors at home and at school. Parent training can be either a stand-alone intervention or one component of a multimodal intervention.

In a typical parent management training (PMT) session, a therapist will (a) explain a social learning principle, (b) model a technique for dealing with a behavioral issue, and then (c) coach parents on implementing the technique (Feldman & Kazdin, 1995).

Evidence of Effectiveness

Three studies identified in this review used wait-list control group designs to evaluate stand-alone parent training programs:

- Sofronoff and Farbotko (2002) looked at a PMT program for parents of children (ages 6 to 12 years) recently diagnosed with Asperger disorder. Forty-five mothers and 44 fathers were randomly assigned to workshop, individual sessions, or wait-list conditions. Both intervention groups received the same training, which consisted of education about Asperger syndrome and characteristic behaviors; instruction on using comic strip conversations and social stories; and lessons in managing behavior problems, anxiety, rigid behaviors, routines, and special interests. The workshop group received the entire intervention training in one day, while the individualized session group received the training over the course of six weeks. Parents in both intervention groups reported their children were exhibiting significantly fewer problem behaviors at both 4-week and 3-month follow-up. Mothers in both intervention groups reported significant improvement in self-efficacy, but fathers did not.

- In a follow-up study by Sofronoff, Leslie, and Brown (2004), 51 parents received the same PMT training as detailed above. Both intervention groups reported that their children demonstrated improved social skills and significantly fewer and less intense behavior problems at the 4-week and 3-month follow-ups, with parents in the individual intervention sessions reporting the best outcomes.

- Solomon, Ono, Timmer, and Goodlin-Jones (2008) explored the use of a slightly modified version of Parent–Child Interaction Therapy (PCIT) with 19 parents of boys (ages 5 to 12 years) with high-functioning ASDs plus significant behavior problems. PCIT—a parent-coaching program originally developed for children ages 2 to 7 years with behavioral disorders—takes a unique approach to parent training in that it includes real-time coaching through a "bug-in-the-ear" microphone while a coach watches from behind a one-way mirror. The study was divided into two 6-session phases. During the child-directed interaction phase, parents were taught to be "attuned" to their children by giving positive attention and praise and by ignoring negative behavior while refraining from criticizing, disciplining, making requests, giving commands, or asking questions. During the subsequent parent-directed interaction phase, parents were coached to give simple, concise, age-appropriate commands and to consistently reinforce child compliance. Results of the study showed that PCIT did not result in a significant reduction in problem behaviors or parental stress levels. However, parents did report that they saw significant improvements in their children's flexibility (e.g., willingness to try new things or to share) and that they found their children's problem behaviors to be less distressing than prior to intervention.

Parent training was a major component of six other programs in this chapter, including studies exploring cognitive behavior therapy (Chalfant et al., 2006; Sofronoff et al., 2005; Sofronoff et al., 2007), errorless compliance training (Ducharme et al., 2007), and social-skills training (Beaumont & Sofronoff, 2008; Solomon et al., 2004).

Analysis

According to the American Psychological Association (2007), PMT has been proven a beneficial treatment for oppositional behavior in children and has shown promising effects for children with autism and other conditions. Moreover, training parents of children with ASDs to implement intervention techniques has been shown to decrease inappropriate behavior, increase communication skills, and improve the quality of family life by reducing parental stress (Ingersoll & Dvortcsak, 2006).

It is important to note that the programs identified in this review differed from the traditional PMT model, which is heavily grounded in operant (behavioral) conditioning techniques (Feldman & Kazdin, 1995). Except for PCIT (Solomon et al., 2008) and errorless compliance training (Ducharme et al., 2007), all the parent training programs identified in this review employed cognitive behavior techniques and emphasized educating parents on the characteristics of Asperger syndrome or high-functioning autism and their relation to behaviors.

Studies in this review supported parent training specific to AS/HFA as a technique that, either as a stand-alone program or as part of a multimodal approach, may play a role in improving social skills and/or decreasing problem behaviors, anxiety symptoms, or anger management problems. On the other hand, PCIT, a parent training program that has shown evidence of efficacy with children with behavioral disorders (Herschell, Calzada, Eyberg, & McNeil, 2002), appeared to be less effective for children with Asperger syndrome or high-functioning autism spectrum disorders except in improving flexibility.

Recommendations

There is evidence of effectiveness for parent training programs that educate parents on the characteristics of high-functioning autism or Asperger syndrome and teach them basic cognitive behavior techniques for dealing with their children's behaviors and challenges. However, that evidence does not generalize to the wide variety of other parent training programs on the market today—some developed specifically for ASDs, some more generic.

Emotion Recognition Software

Many individuals with Asperger syndrome or high-functioning autism have difficulty recognizing cues that indicate the thoughts or feelings of others (Baron-Cohen, Jolliffe, Mortimore, & Robertson, 1997). This deficit is sometimes referred to as *poor theory of mind* or *mind-blindness* (Baron-Cohen, 1995). Emotion recognition software is designed to teach recognition of emotions through photos, audio clips, and/or video. The computer programs may include libraries of emotions, lessons, quizzes, and games. Software to date has focused on facial expression and voice cues.

Evidence of Effectiveness

Three controlled group studies have assessed the use of emotion recognition software for individuals with Asperger disorder or high-functioning autism:

- In Bölte et al. (2002), five adolescent or adult males trained 2 hours per week for 5 weeks on a computer program that included 500 photographs of faces displaying various emotions. Subjects in the intervention group improved significantly on the computer-based test for reading emotions in the face and the eyes, while a matched control group demonstrated no improvement. However, there was no evidence of the improvements generalizing beyond the computer-based test.
- Golan and Baron-Cohen (2006) published two studies of Mind Reading software, an interactive guide to 412 complex emotions and mental states. In the first study, 19 adults with Asperger syndrome used the Mind Reading software at home for an average of 17.5 hours (range = 10 to 36 hours) over 10 to 15 weeks. The intervention group improved significantly more than did a control group on a test of reading emotions in the same faces and voices as the Mind Reading software, but not on any more generalized tests. In the second study, one intervention group used the software at home and met weekly in a group with a tutor, who worked with them on recognizing facial and vocal expressions of emotion. The control group attended social-skills lessons that focused on conversation rules, emotional expressions, body language, job interviews, and friendship. After 10 weeks, the intervention group (software + tutor) improved significantly more than the control group (social skills) did on tests using voices and faces from the software program, but there was no significant difference between the two groups on any more generalized tests.

- In addition, Beaumont and Sofronoff's (2008) *Junior Detective Training Program* to teach social skills included a computer game with lessons on emotion recognition. While the intervention group showed improved social skills, the numbers did not demonstrate significant improvement in ability to recognize emotions (see the Intervention: Social-Skills Training section of this chapter for further discussion).

Analysis and Recommendations

Emotion recognition software is an intriguing concept, as many individuals with AS/HFA seem to have a special interest in computers (Attwood, 2007). Moreover, the concept intuitively makes sense—using software with videos, pictures, and/or voices, individuals can study emotional cues, review them, work at their own pace, and test themselves on their learning. However, to date, there is a paucity of objective scientific studies that show evidence of this software leading to improved recognition of emotions in real life. In fact, data to date suggest that improvement in emotional recognition does not necessarily generalize beyond the material in the software itself—not even to other facial photos or movies. While research is ongoing, at this time there are no software programs that can be considered evidence-based interventions for learners with AS/HFA.

Other Interventions

Four other studies were identified that met the criteria for inclusion in this review. However, because only one single-subject study was published for each intervention, there is not sufficient evidence to make any generalized conclusions about their usefulness for individuals with Asperger syndrome or high-functioning autism.

- Clarke, Dunlap, and Vaughn (1999) used strategies that would typically be associated with Structured Teaching and the TEACCH (Treatment and Education of Autistic and related Communication-handicapped Children) program to improve a child's behavior during morning routine.
- Mruzek, Cohen, and Smith (2007) used contingency contracts and self-monitoring to decrease tantrums, antisocial vocalizations, and physical aggression in a 10-year-old with high-functioning

autism and a 9-year-old with ADHD and probable Asperger syndrome.

- Tiger, Bouxsein, and Fisher (2007) used differential reinforcement of short response latencies to decrease a 19-year-old's latency in answering questions and solving math problems.
- Myles, Ferguson, and Hagiwara (2007) employed a personal digital assistant (PDA) to help an adolescent with Asperger syndrome improve his recording of homework.

Patterns in Reviews of Interventions

In this systematic review of the literature, 34 scientific studies (i.e., utilizing experimental, quasi-experimental, or single-subject designs) were identified that examined intervention effects on individuals with Asperger syndrome or high-functioning autism. Of the studies that were reviewed, 29 showed evidence of effectiveness. Those studies demonstrating efficacy included the following:

- Eight controlled group studies of social-skills interventions (three of these used LEGO therapy, while the rest used a variety of curricula)
- Three controlled group studies of parent training programs and six other studies that employed parent training as part of a multi-component intervention
- Three controlled group studies of cognitive behavior therapy (two of which included social stories)
- Five single-subject studies that employed social stories (three of them in combination with other interventions)
- Four single-subject studies that used video modeling in combination with other techniques (e.g., social stories, prompting)
- Two single-subject studies that used errorless learning techniques
- One single-subject study that used structured teaching techniques
- One single-subject study that used contingency contract and self-monitoring

- One single-subject study that used differential reinforcement of short response latencies
- One single-subject study that used a PDA

It is interesting to note that, while three of the four interventions that Simpson (2005) had found to be evidence-based interventions for autism were behavioral interventions (applied behavior analysis, discrete trial training, and pivotal response training), 20 of the 29 studies identified here that demonstrated effectiveness with Asperger disorder or high-functioning autism were primarily grounded in cognitive or cognitive behavior theory. Behavior theory (the basis of applied behavioral analysis and discrete trial training) is concerned primarily with an individual's *overt* response to a stimulus and how to change that response through reinforcement, prompting, fading, shaping, errorless learning, punishment, and extinction (Simpson, 2005). Cognitive theory, on the other hand, is concerned with a person's *underlying beliefs and perceptions* and how those influence his or her emotional, behavioral, and even physical responses to events (Ellis, Abrams, & Abrams, 2008). Cognitive behavior interventions draw from both theories. While it is seen as necessary to change a child's thought processes and beliefs if change is to occur, elements of behavioral intervention are used as well (e.g., modeling, shaping, fading, and rehearsal). However, there is more of a focus on an internal locus of control (e.g., self-monitoring and self-reinforcement) in cognitive behavior interventions than in behavioral ones (Simpson, 2005). Cognitive and cognitive behavior methods require that an individual have the capacity for self-understanding and be motivated to behave within accepted norms (Simpson, 2005). Therefore, these strategies are considered more appropriate for children with higher cognitive and language skills (Simpson, 2005).

Eight of the interventions identified in this review relied heavily on technology, which is not surprising. Not only do many individuals with Asperger syndrome or high-functioning autism seem to have an affinity for technology, but society in general is becoming more technology dependent. Technology alone, however, is not enough to ensure an effective intervention. While video modeling appears to be effective in improving a range of behaviors, from giving compliments to writing essays, emotion recognition software has yet to be shown effective in improving any real-world skills for individuals with Asperger syndrome.

Concluding Thoughts

In order to make informed programming decisions, parents and professionals need empirically supported evidence regarding the different intervention options. To date, no intervention strategy has been equally successful for all participants with Asperger syndrome or high-functioning autism, or for all areas assessed (Tsatsanis et al., 2004). This systematic review of the literature confirmed that while several interventions have showed evidence of effectiveness in helping children with AS/HFA achieve behavioral or social goals, no single "best practice" has emerged.

It is vital, therefore, to design individualized programming for each child that will be most likely to foster success for him or her. Accordingly, when choosing an intervention for a child with AS/HFA, one should ask several questions:

- What behavioral or social goal is the intervention supposed to address? (No intervention, after all, has been shown effective in "curing" high-functioning autism spectrum disorders.)
- What interventions have the best evidence, to date, of effectiveness with similar goals in children with AS/HFA?
- What are the relative costs (in both time and money) of attempting the interventions?
- What risks, if any, are inherent in the interventions?

Weighing the answers to these questions should help in making an informed decision. Of course, it is important for readers to keep in mind that lack of scientific evidence for any given intervention does not necessarily mean that the intervention is ineffective for students with AS/HFA. Rather, it means that there is no proof that it is effective. Some of the interventions currently recommended by national and international experts with extensive clinical or classroom experience—for example, organizational supports (Myles & Adreon, 2001), comic strip conversations (Gray, 1994), antiseptic bouncing (Myles & Southwick, 1999), and Power Cards (Gagnon, 2001), to name just a few—do not have multiple published scientific studies supporting their use with Asperger disorder or high-functioning autism. However, the field of AS/HFA intervention is very young. The oldest study identified in this review was published in

1999, and the majority of the identified studies (22 out of 34) were published between 2006 and 2008.

Again, no single intervention has been established as yet as a definitive best practice for AS/HFA, although cognitive behavior interventions have, to date, the most evidence of effectiveness. So if, after a reasonable trial, one intervention is not successful, it makes sense to move on and try another approach.

A lack of evidence-based interventions may be perceived as a discouraging sign, yet it is hoped that readers will recognize the enormous opportunity for new research. Not only university-based researchers, but also teachers and clinicians have a great chance in the coming years to contribute to the knowledge base and, ultimately, to positive outcomes not just for their own students or patients, but for individuals with Asperger syndrome or high-functioning autism around the world.

chapter seven

Understanding the Impact of Asperger Syndrome and High-Functioning Autism

Parents and families of children and youth with Asperger syndrome or high-functioning autism—as well as the individuals with these disabilities, themselves—contend with a variety of challenges for which they routinely have little or no training. They may experience anger, disappointment, frustration, and a variety of other emotions related directly or indirectly to the disorder. The same is true of individuals with any disability and their parents and families. At the same time, however, they are expected to understand, advocate, and support themselves or their family members with these challenges, often without the benefit of information about the condition and with little public understanding of it. Hence, in addition to having to deal with significant personal challenges with little or no support, these individuals and families often must educate others about the mysteries, characteristics, and challenges associated with Asperger syndrome or high-functioning autism.

For these reasons, the voices and reflections of individuals with AS/HFA and their parents and families comprise this chapter. Our hope, and the hope of those who have contributed, is that their experiences will benefit other parents, families, and professionals who live and work with individuals with AS/HFA.

Zachary

Zachary is a 32-year-old graduate student diagnosed with Asperger syndrome. With the assistance of his mother, he reflects on the challenges of his disability.

Ever since I was a little boy, I knew that I was different from other "typical" children: I was shaky, nervous, slow, and pokey. I was sensitive to some loud noises. I was very anxious when it came to dealing with animals, especially big ones. Looking back, I see that some of these fears were unreasonable. For example, late one evening about 50 big, black-and-white cows got out of our meadow and were in the yard around our house. I hid in the house, crying. Not only was I afraid of the cows and of their size, but I thought that in a group they could knock down our three-story brick farmhouse.

I was scared of my father, a big man with a beard and mustache and a very loud voice. I could not take jokes or kidding. I took everything literally and, therefore, did not understand jokes, especially those of my uncle, whom I thought was making fun of me.

I went to a preschool and day-care center from the ages of 3 to 5 years. There were many students, and it was a very long day. I hated it. I loved the year that I spent with five other kids and a babysitter and felt very comfortable there. Prior to kindergarten, I had gone once a week for services with the local intermediate unit, where they worked with me on large and small motor skill development. During kindergarten and first grade, I spent some time in the special education resource room, particularly for help with writing. While there, I looked after a boy who had ADD (attention-deficit disorder). I felt like his friend and helper.

In school, I often needed repetition of directions because I usually did not understand things on the first request or explanation. I had handwriting difficulty. With a shaky hand, putting the pencil on the line was hard enough. Being anxious, I would press too hard on my #2 pencil, and the point would break. Even though I got perfect scores on spelling and vocabulary quizzes, I always had trouble with nouns. I would refer to things as "thingies," and try to demonstrate the form or function of the item with my hands. Time limits and constraints would heighten my tenseness. During "Mad Minutes," I could not finish the work-page. However, I knew all the answers. Although I got frustrated, I did not cry, nor did I act out; instead, I kept my feelings to myself.

I think that I have always been anxious—although perhaps my family didn't always recognize it. When I was upset, my body would get rigid and tight, even as a little baby. Fear of animals and scary things would make me tense and I would cry. Whenever I had to do something "solo," I would experience "performance anxiety" for the first 2 or 3 minutes, and then I would be OK.

I often felt awkward. I was the last swimmer to finish and the kid who seldom got a hit in baseball, but I had fun and tried hard. I remember going to a dance in junior high school and feeling really awkward.

My family remembers some particularities in my growth and development (as an infant and small child):

- I teethed early (at 5 weeks old), cut three teeth in one weekend (early experience with pain).
- I was colicky and cried a lot every night from 9 to 11 P.M. from ages 6 weeks to 3 months (immature nervous system).
- I had sensitive ears and hated the wind blowing in the car.
- I liked to dig at my ears and other people's ears and face parts and explore them.
- I wouldn't walk on grass in my bare feet as a toddler.
- I hated sand and was afraid of the ocean; however, I enjoyed swimming in a pool.
- I had finicky eating habits, and textures of foods mattered a lot.
- I walked late (18 months), talked late (3½ years), cried a lot, was weaned late, began sleeping through the night late (17 months), and ran late (6 or 7 years of age).
- I always had shaky hands and small tremors.
- I was very cooperative and obedient.
- I pouted easily.
- I didn't care a lot about friends.
- I did things with my family.

Even though I was different from other kids, looking back, there were many times when my reactions were normal and well controlled. In junior high, I remember going down the hall to health class when tears of loss (caused by a fire that had destroyed my maternal grandparents' home that we called "the Ridge") began to flow. After talking with the guidance counselor for about an hour, I went back to my classes. Once, when I had to memorize and recite the Gettysburg Address, I was not ready on time. When I cried, the teacher allowed me to reschedule for the next day, when I was well prepared. In elementary school, I was one of two spellers in a spelling bee with a spell-off that lasted 20 minutes between myself and a student by the name of Nick. There was a huge crowd of parents and fans gathered; people still talk about it. I was very focused. In senior high, I would hurry down the halls, afraid I'd be late for class. However, I would be sure to get passes after math classes on testing days. In 12th grade, I was able to help other students in the special education resource room. So I learned to accommodate.

Throughout my development, I learned to find alternative methods to compensate for my poor motor skills. When I was little, I would sit on the floor and move in a way so that I wouldn't knock toys (especially building blocks) over. I would focus on a task and prepare well for it. In elementary school, I learned to ask for help, ask for more time, and/or stay in at recess to finish work. In high school, I discovered BIC Matic Grip mechanical pencils and always had three or four of them with me; they were very helpful. In college, when I got frustrated and asked for help, I would be told that I was too smart to receive assistance. In spite of frustration, I would find places that had a calming atmosphere so that I could review and rewrite notes. I would allow plenty of time for tasks to be completed. At my present university, I prefer studying upstairs near the office windows. I live at a group home for adults with special needs. There I study and read at the dining room couch—not in the bedroom or in the TV room.

In spite of frequent discomfort, looking back, I remember that there were places that I did feel comfortable. I enjoyed the children's tree house at the town library. I liked our parlor—blue and peaceful and off-the-beaten track in our farmhouse. I also enjoyed resting on couches. I liked studying in the college laundry room because it was quiet. I also studied well at the residence hall desk—in contrast to the college library, which was too big.

I always loved numbers (in contrast to nouns) and activities connected with them. My interests still include music (vocal and instrumental) and sports. I especially like to remember scores and statistics. Even as a very small boy, I had an affinity with numbers. I had excellent arithmetic skills. I could add up the grocery bills without a calculator. I enjoyed being a top seller for scouts, band, and choir.

Currently, I am a second-year graduate student at a major research university. I am pursuing a master's degree in autism spectrum disorders. I am a part-time student; I take six credits per semester. In the future, I hope to continue my schooling and try to complete a doctorate in special education. I would like to continue to work in a college and/or university setting as a professor, counselor, and/or residence advisor. I hope to write some books about how I deal with my Asperger syndrome on a daily basis. Finally, I hope to become a motivational speaker and advocate for all children with special needs.

 ## Michelle

Michelle is a teenager with Asperger syndrome. Her diagnosis was made when she was 12 years old. Before then, Michelle's odd, stubborn, and detached nature was a mystery, as were the means to help her.

Michelle was always a "difficult" child whose dogged adherence to her own unique way of doing things made life difficult for her and those around her. Even her birth was difficult and unique: She was delivered faceup (the reverse of the norm). This might have been endearing, but as with so much of Michelle's subsequent "uniqueness," the effect was unnecessary travail. In this case, faceup meant 23 hours of painful labor for Mom.

Michelle was not an easy infant to love. She showed displeasure regularly and effectively by uncontrolled, unrelenting screaming. This was especially so on occasions marked by change. A car trip at 3 months, for example, meant ceaseless wailing on the road. The only peace came with sleep, and that was unpredictable and scarce. Hotel rooms, relatives' homes—any strange environment—were met in a similar way. Eventually, Mom and Dad resigned themselves to the idea that this was just colic, even though it didn't always fit what the book said, especially the part about "gone in 3 months" (6 or 8 was more like it!).

As an infant, Michelle was always a bit stiff and squirmy when held. She never cuddled, and she resisted physical closeness and affection. Although she could be engaged socially in play and enjoyed silliness, she was not inclined to interact with others and preferred playing alone. Near the end of the first year, she began to demonstrate a faraway look when in the company of other children. A photo of her first birthday party is typical—four other little girls are all focused on some minor event, while Michelle has a trancelike expression, her thoughts focused elsewhere. Then, as now, Michelle was rarely "in the moment." She is barely aware of people, objects, or events happening now. Her mind is elsewhere—actively thinking—but not here, not now.

Socially, Michelle the toddler was much the same. Her mom made repeated efforts to foster friendships by inviting little girls to play, but things seldom clicked. Usually, Michelle seemed disinterested. Even when Michelle tried to interact with others, her efforts were awkward and ineffective. At about this same time, though, Michelle did find a friend, a neighbor girl named Tamika. Tamika was quite slow and almost as unusual in her behavior as Michelle (e.g., Tamika, who was supremely self-assured, unselfconsciously kept a pacifier in her mouth most of the time, well into her 5th year!).

The two girls were almost constant companions from the age of 1 until 6 years, when Tamika and her family moved. Each seemed oblivious to the oddities of the other. Although their personalities did not mesh, they succeeded as friends by adopting a parallel style of play, each doing her own thing, but "together." This style persisted until Tamika moved, well past the age when parallel play is considered normal.

At age 2, Michelle got a baby brother. Although Michelle's brother assumed secondary importance to her friend Tamika, he was nonetheless a close companion, whose acceptance of Michelle was total. Michelle, for her part, took a protective role toward her baby brother.

At age 4, Michelle was enrolled in preschool 3 days per week. Her parents, convinced that she was very bright, were shocked at the negative reports from her teachers. They were very concerned that Michelle did not interact well with the other children. About the same time, Michelle developed an odd attachment to a tree by the house. An old scrub oak in the backyard inexplicably became "her" tree, a fond attachment that was mentioned several times a year and lasted almost a decade. Her affection was demonstrated by long periods spent at the base of the tree and by excited, animated remarks about the tree, Michelle's "old friend."

Grade school was an interesting time. Standard IQ testing conducted with all of the kindergarten students indicated that Michelle had a full-scale IQ of 130. Nevertheless, her teacher, an older woman with a definite authoritarian bent, was unhappy with Michelle's work and behavior. She seldom made appreciative remarks about Michelle to her parents. Instead, she often seemed disgusted with Michelle, and Michelle often appeared sad and frustrated. Not surprisingly, the teacher recommended that Michelle repeat kindergarten.

Michelle was lucky to get a new and very different kindergarten teacher the second time around. The teacher obviously liked Michelle and had an appreciation for her unique ways. This teacher, in fact, appeared to like all children, seemed happy and secure, and was not hung up on authority. This was a perfect recipe for Michelle, and it produced a happier, more contented student.

Over the years, this teacher model worked well for Michelle on many occasions. Stern, authoritarian teachers, even though beneficial for many students, were bad for Michelle. Michelle was never able to please the "regimentarian," whose emphasis on order and punctuality was largely beyond Michelle's grasp. Teachers like this could be counted on to have a negative effect on her performance and on her behavior, and especially on how she felt about herself.

It was fortunate that the ensuing 4 years of school brought a succession of reasonably accepting, supportive teachers who allowed Michelle to be herself. They usually found her interesting and engaging, in her own unique way. They were realistic about her progress but nonetheless were careful not to be overcritical of her spotty schoolwork and inattentiveness in class. Although Michelle was by no means an ideal student, she was compliant and never disruptive.

Michelle's behavior around other children continued to be unusual in grade school. Described as aloof, unattached, and a lone wolf, Michelle rarely interacted with other kids at school unless as part of a group game directed by the teacher. During free times at recess, Michelle would typically wander about by herself, happily engrossed in her own thoughts. The main exception to this pattern—and it happened regularly—was that she would often seek out adults for conversation. The conversation was usually one-sided, with Michelle rambling on in a somewhat pedantic fashion about some topic of her choosing. Out of politeness and a certain degree of interest, teachers allowed this but would eventually break it off to discourage monopolizing by Michelle and to encourage her to mix with other kids.

Home life for Michelle during most of grade school followed the pattern set earlier. Friendship with Tamika remained the same as before until Tamika moved. Despite the central and important role that Tamika had played, her parting, although duly noted on many occasions, was not met with any overt sadness or sense of loss. Attempts to foster interaction with "normal" girls continued to be unsuccessful but were seemingly more painful for Michelle's parents than for Michelle.

A move to a different neighborhood around age 8 brought a new selection of potential playmates for Michelle, but there was no improvement. One interesting relationship did develop out of the move, however. Michelle came to revere a pretty and rather snobbish little girl next door and made overtures of friendship. A relationship did develop, because of Michelle's obvious high regard for the neighbor and the neighbor's esteem for anyone who recognized how wonderful she was. After several months, however, the relationship grew tiresome for the neighbor, who abruptly ended it.

Michelle, unfazed and unashamed, made repeated, earnest, although awkward, efforts to regain the friend. After several failures, she hit on something that worked—she became the neighbor's servant, performing all sorts of tasks in return for the attentions of her "friend." Even when this unusual arrangement lost its appeal for the neighbor, Michelle accepted this second loss of the friend without remorse or humiliation. Unfortunately, this detached attitude toward humiliation was not to last forever.

At home, grade-schooler Michelle spent a great deal of her time alone in her room. With the exception of a brief interest in stamp collecting, she had difficulty maintaining attention to any particular activity and thus would rapidly pass from one activity to another, never completing anything. Dad made a fairly regular habit of reading to Michelle in her room, especially *Highlights* magazine, which gave mutual delight. Michelle liked doing homework with Dad at this stage, especially when Dad presented the material verbally. It was also at this stage that Michelle's extreme inherent messiness became apparent in her room; at the table; and particularly at school, where her disorganization was always duly noted by the teacher.

Michelle obviously did not want to be messy and disorganized, and she was never hostile at attempts by others to help her "shape up." She simply was incapable of sustaining organization. It is likely that her inattention to the here and now made neatness seem unimportant. Organization may also have demanded too dear a price, requiring as it does a sustained marshaling of attention, which for Michelle was very tedious, tiring, and even exhausting.

Grade 5 marked a significant change at school. Not only did the difficulty of the work increase at this time, but the teacher also departed from his predecessors' laissez-faire attitude. He demanded conformity in schoolwork and was unwilling to be flexible about this. Despite her native intelligence, Michelle was generally unable to cope with the demands of finishing work and turning it in of her own accord, not to mention keeping track of homework assignments and so on. Efforts on the part of her parents to modify teacher demands in light of Michelle's shortcomings were not successful. It was the teacher's belief that developing organizational ability and responsibility came first. Any child could do it, if he or she would only will it. This remained the predominant refrain of Michelle's teachers for the next 4 years, resulting in Michelle's not improving noticeably in responsibility or organization and in her learning very little.

The rigidity of the fifth-grade teacher was repeated by the sixth-grade teacher, only much more so. Although dynamic and effective with most of her class, this teacher was unable to accept nonconformity in a student, or messiness, or disorganization, or any of the many traits that flow out of these three. This teacher could make the trains run on time, but she was unconcerned about those who were left at the station, usually Michelle. In fact, Michelle's nonconformity eventually made the teacher dislike her.

At the same time that Michelle's teachers were becoming convinced of her unworthiness, Michelle was reaching the same conclusion on her own. In early adolescence, Michelle was experiencing the same growth of self-awareness that most kids do. Although for most kids this process is positive, in Michelle's case it was not. Up until then, the fact that Michelle was a loner who was unable to connect with other children and be part of the group had been of little concern to her. She was content to spend recess and lunch virtually alone and was unconcerned about her lack of friends.

Once self-awareness developed, however, Michelle's realization that she did not fit in was very painful. As a result, she became depressed, and her cheerful demeanor changed to one of sadness, frustration, and even anger. At home, she stayed in her room almost exclusively. To relieve stress, she began the distressing habit of cutting on herself with a pin or small knife. Although the cuts were superficial and not dangerous, they were obvious enough to send shockwaves throughout the school and family. It was clear to those who knew her well that the cutting was not intended to produce harm, but to relieve stress; however, caring adults at school and elsewhere were anxious about it. Questions about suicide naturally followed. Yes, she sometimes thought about dying. Yes, she had thought about suicide. As you might imagine, this was all it took to unleash a flood of attention. Michelle, who was suffering from an inability to connect and to engage others in conversation, had found a means to be important, to avoid being ignored.

What followed was not good. Michelle not only received endless attention from adults and kids alike for disquieting remarks, but also quickly learned the game and became very good at it. Manipulation did not enter into Michelle's intentions, though. To Michelle she was simply getting what she needed in the best way she knew. Of course, any child could be seduced by this sort of instant attention. Whereas most early adolescents sense the cost and avoid talking about suicide entirely, or else give it up fairly rapidly, Michelle did not understand, and so she persisted. Once this suicide material lost its impact, it was replaced with other shocking things. Unfortunately, Michelle could not comprehend the negative impact it was having on peers, for whom the sense of her oddness and undesirability was only strengthened.

This behavior eventually led Michelle to the psychologist's office, where the downward spiral continued. In an effort to uncover any underlying psychopathology, the psychologist encouraged Michelle to express any morbid or horrible thoughts that might be lurking in the dark recesses of her mind. Michelle, for her part, was most willing to oblige. In time, she produced loads of shocking fantasies for the doctor, who, in exchange, provided Michelle with lots of high-quality, satisfying attention.

Both doctor and patient were duped. For the psychologist, the result was a wildly mistaken diagnosis of extremely morbid personality. For Michelle, the attention merely reinforced the notion that shocking remarks work. Michelle's remarks about cutting and suicide became even more common, supplanted in time by fictitious musings about her lesbianism, multiple personalities, and criminal friends.

Brent

Brent is a child who carries a diagnosis of Asperger disorder. His father describes the challenges, mysteries, issues, and joys associated with raising him.

Santa Claus was preparing to visit the preschool our son attended. It was time to question the children singly about the Christmas presents they hoped to get. Suddenly, our boy pulled Santa's chair away, and jolly old St. Nick went down in a heap. The other children and their parents didn't know what to make of it. Neither did my wife or I.

More than 8 years were to pass before we received a diagnosis of Asperger syndrome, often called *high-functioning autism,* for Brent. The diagnosis helped us understand the embarrassing preschool incident with Santa and over a dozen other examples of our son's quirkiness over the years.

Although Santa reportedly has recovered, my wife and I are worn sick dealing with pediatricians, psychiatrists, psychologists, allergists, pharmacologists, therapists, educational consultants, and counselors—not to leave out medical insurers, public and private school personnel, and homeschoolers. Oh, yes—we also moved 900 miles to a presumably allergy-friendly environment (where new allergies replaced old ones) and within a couple of months moved right back to accommodate our homesickness. We were prepared to go to any length.

The Asperger diagnosis, however late, now helps lessen what must be called "parental panic." We're sharper about what to expect, about how we should deal with it, and about being ready to cope with the unexpected. One might reasonably ask whether such a diagnosis also brings apprehensions about our son's future—about his prospects for navigating successfully the maze of social rituals, the most stressful of all the dark places that people with Asperger syndrome must enter. Yes, the diagnosis has brought new worries, particularly about his impending adolescent dating and whether he will understand fully the commitment required for marriage, for child rearing, and for productive work relationships. There's also the worry about which Asperger traits he might pass on to his children.

And yet—even with all the day-to-day adjustments for us, as well as those future uncertainties—there's an unexpected upside. More on that in a moment.

The Asperger syndrome diagnosis and our subsequent examination of the literature has helped us understand much that has haunted us for years, questions such as these:

- Why, when he was a toddler and able to speak clearly, did our son respond with only a vacant stare to our cheery greetings?
- Why did he resist hugs, yet during naps with me or my wife, he seemed to glue the full length of his body to our backs?
- Why did he throw himself to the floor and scream when anyone turned on a vacuum cleaner?
- Why were his questions becoming more and more repetitious, as though he'd never heard our answers?
- Why, through most of his boyhood, couldn't our son catch a ball playing one to one with his dad or learn to throw it accurately?
- When a classmate's dog died and our son learned of it, why did our boy react by laughing in the bereaved youngster's face?
- Why after play experiences that brought resentful howls from teammates did our son insist that he'd only wished to help the other side?
- Why in his earlier school years did he become terribly disoriented when having to shift to new tasks?
- Where did all those on-again, off-again tics come from—and the odd hand and arm movements, incessant coughing, stuttering, and loud nose blowing?

- What triggers those periodic and frightening anxiety attacks, at times marked by vigorous self-biting and hand banging?
- Why do "friends" abandon him with such heartbreaking consistency?
- Why for so long was he uncomfortable in pants snug at the waist and intent on wearing inappropriate but softer sweat clothes?
- When our son is being introduced to individuals, why does his body stiffen and his face assume a startled expression, even though he can address a roomful of people with relative ease?
- How is it possible for him to play the piano with near perfection for an audience when the performance follows unsteady practice sessions that frequently end in emotional breakdowns?
- Why are his reading comprehension scores declining alarmingly?
- When furnished with a wide range of reading material at an early age, why did he immerse himself instead in promotional books from automobile showrooms?
- What accounts for the near-zero motivation and low energy level in a youngster of such high intelligence?
- What makes our son convert a simple apology into a kind of persevering self-flagellation—to a point that used to drive us to distraction?

Where there were only guesses before there are now answers—though of limited satisfaction—to all of these questions in the context of Asperger syndrome. Notice also from the varying tenses that there's been a movement forward in our son's ability to shift tasks, catch a ball, and dress more appropriately. There's also been progress in terms of our increased understanding and our growing conviction that some Asperger traits can be short-circuited, if not overcome.

Although doctors can judge where the combinations of behavior might place a child on the continuum of autism, they're far from knowing why children with Asperger syndrome manifest these behaviors. There is also little consensus on whether the most distressing Asperger symptoms can truly be changed, be it by behavior modification or through biochemistry.

We parents, on whom medical practitioners depend for answers to a greater extent than we might have expected, are pretty much at the same stage as those who first tried to invent the wheel. Parents must first examine every clue as to what might benefit or in some way comfort their children; try it; try it again; and, failing in that approach, back off and try something else.

For example, my 12-year-old son and I attended a conference of the organization More Advanced Autistic People (MAAP). Among the many things I learned was that Asperger children like to be "wrapped" or "cocooned" at times (which helped explain his early-childhood napping position). For months before the conference, my son had developed a nightly habit of coughing and twitching 30 to 90 minutes before falling asleep. When he asked (in the motel room on the way back from the conference) whether he could lie down with me, I said, "Sure!" and proceeded to stroke his head slowly, rhythmically, and very gently. He coughed maybe 9 or 10 times and fell asleep within 5 minutes. On subsequent tries of this same method at home, I got it down to less than 2 minutes. At the time of this writing, such stroking doesn't seem necessary at all, though we might expect that tic to return. The lesson? He may be growing up and almost as tall as Dad, but there's still a little boy in there—my little boy with special needs.

Those needs now oblige us to know the effects of loud noises on our son and to do everything to avoid them. (Remember the vacuum cleaner?) For instance, unproductive yelling at our younger son, who vexingly has attention-deficit/hyperactivity disorder, has been cut way down. The sensory problems of our son with Asperger syndrome also involve touch and the way in which various articles of clothing affect or discomfort him.

Conversations and social experiences are being given new attention so that my wife and I might discover how to clear the path through what is a terrifying jungle for people with Asperger syndrome. We now know more about the way our older boy thinks and about the neurologically based differences between how he sees the world and how we do.

We've discovered a few Asperger traits in ourselves, which has helped explain past and present quirks to ourselves and to one another. It's given us clues as to how we may help our boy outgrow similar traits that we know served us poorly.

We still find it hard to believe that it took so many professionals so many years of sifting through our son's symptoms before two of them working in concert came up with the diagnosis of Asperger syndrome. Had we known sooner what we know now, we could have averted a number of school crises that have begun to grow more severe in recent years, particularly the way our son's addressing and questioning teachers is customarily perceived by them. He's flippant with teachers—because he has a sense of humor that doesn't take social conventions into account. He may be saying to himself, "I'll try this and see what happens." And when teachers hand out assignments involving six or seven steps and deadlines far in the future, such as a term paper or research project, our boy is overwhelmed. As a sign of wanting to do the right thing about such assignments, he may particularize point by point in order to understand everything expected of him. But it's that questioning that drives teachers up the wall. Seeing that reaction, he decides to run from the task mentally and emotionally. The night before the assignment is due, he may or may not tell us about it and seek help.

Because the label of high-functioning autism now places our son as a public school student under the protection of the Americans With Disabilities Act (1990), that law is being applied helpfully now. Unlike the experiences of the past, not all teachers are dismissing our boy's quirks by saying things like, "I know when he's pulling my chain." Thanks to the in-house presence of middle-school special education professionals, something resembling a coping network is now on alert. We're not saying there's intervention before a crisis, such as an anxiety attack. But there is certainly new school staff energy being applied to emergencies involving our son so that those situations don't get worse. We've even noticed a growing preference by the special staff to work through the problem at school rather than sending him home. We'd always given him that alternative to ensure he knows there's a safe haven, but maybe their way will be better for him.

Because children with Asperger syndrome tend to be couch potatoes, given their difficulties in sports, our son was becoming obese. My wife came up with the idea of hiring a personal trainer, who now visits frequently to work out with Brent. Within a very short time, our son started looking better. He seemed also to be feeling better, physically and emotionally. We don't care what this may cost if it works to make our boy healthier and happier.

Earlier I indicated an upside to our sudden immersion in the world of Asperger syndrome and to our learning that our son has this now identifiable, though complicated, disability. We draw optimism from such positives as his abilities in art, music, computers, and math and in memorization, analysis, and special reasoning skills. Where will they lead him? In her book *Thinking in Pictures and Other Reports From My Life With Autism* (1995), Temple Grandin (whom we heard speak at the MAAP conference) makes a good case for the possibility that Albert Einstein may have had what we now call Asperger syndrome. She names other notables with these traits. Dr. Grandin has high-functioning autism and is a remarkable achiever in animal science. She has designed one third of all livestock-handling facilities currently used in the United States. Just knowing that such a productive life as hers is possible has brightened the outlook for our child.

As parents, we're now beyond asking "Why us?" Because children with Asperger syndrome show nearly as many differences from one another in symptoms as they do similarities, support group help is limited. Our main focus now is to guide him toward doing his best in every way while he's still at an age when we can be of maximum influence.

Whenever we look at or listen to this beautiful, talented, heart-of-gold youngster and realize we're lucky enough to be able to say, "He's ours!" we have no doubt about our abilities to meet whatever challenges Asperger syndrome presents.

Edward

Edward's mother describes the journey and challenges of understanding and accommodating the unique needs of a child with Asperger disorder. Issues relating to siblings are also described.

Living with a child with Asperger syndrome means truly living life one day at a time—frequently 1 minute at a time. Even when the correct diagnosis has finally been reached and you begin to understand where your child's problems come from, living with Asperger syndrome causes a tremendous amount of frustration and stress for everyone in the family. It affects every aspect of our lives and at times threatens to overwhelm us. But this is our son, so we continue to struggle to make it through one more day.

Each day we are on guard because we never know what situation we may have to deal with. It might be just one of the many misunderstandings that occur so often when Edward is with other people in which we need to intervene to mediate, interpret, or guide him through. It is just as likely that we may have to deal with a situation that is potentially dangerous to him or others because he doesn't understand cause and effect. As Edward has gotten older, his drastically inappropriate behaviors that occur when he is overstressed have become less frequent but more dangerous. Since there are no warnings to let us know that Edward is becoming stressed, and since he is unable to recognize this himself, we all live with at least a slight "fight-or-flight" response whenever he's around. We must be prepared to take quick, decisive action in situations we would never even have thought of having to deal with. Even though we know that his aggressive and dangerous actions are a stress reaction and not usually related to what is currently going on around him, or aimed at "the victim" personally, it is impossible not to get upset when they occur.

After trying many different medications with only moderate improvement, we have come to the conclusion that the best way to help our son is to decrease his stress level. At home, we have done this by taking him off the family chore chart and giving him only one task at a time. We make sure he has quiet time in his room at frequent intervals throughout the day and carefully supervise him at all times. Probably the two most important ways we try to decrease his stress at home are to prevent circumstances and situations that are likely to get Edward into trouble and to maintain a strict routine (which frequently means lots of reminding and refocusing of his attention to the task at hand).

Unfortunately, we have not been able to get adequate accommodations outside of home. Since Edward, now in high school, gets good grades when he does the work and doesn't act or look like a person with an obvious disability, there is a reluctance to accept the fact that he is handicapped. They choose not to understand that, in spite of his high intelligence, his comprehension of basic life skills (e.g., right and wrong, self-responsibility, cause and effect, and social obligation and expectations) is similar to that of a child with autism who is cognitively challenged. His ability to perceive, interpret, and respond to other people's cues is also deficient. Since he is unable to filter stimuli, he often withdraws into himself or behaves inappropriately when he's overwhelmed, the same way a child with autism does. They choose not to see that because of these short circuits he will not learn appropriate attitudes and behaviors simply by being around normally developing peers. It's easier for them to think that Edward is intentionally behaving this way or that he's just odd and that his inappropriate behavior should simply be ignored.

The result of this "head in the sand" attitude about Edward's disability on the part of the educational system is that we have been forced to watch him struggle on a daily basis with situation after situation that confuses, frustrates, and angers him because he doesn't understand what's going on or how to do what's expected of him. Because he can't recognize his feelings, he has no way to deal with them, so his stress level builds, causing more and more inappropriate and aggressive behavior. Since all his energy is spent just trying to get through the day at school, he frequently arrives home exhausted and ready to explode from all the stresses and confusions of the day, and the family bears the brunt of it.

In an attempt to try to help him relieve some of this stress, Edward and I have a talk immediately after school each day. We talk about things that are on his mind, good and bad. I try to explain to him why situations went the way they did and to help him put things in perspective. We also use this time for coaching on situations that are likely to occur in the near future, in hopes that this will help him deal a little better with them and decrease some of his anxiety.

Unfortunately, this doesn't always work, especially if he is angry, stressed, or upset. We have tried to teach him appropriate ways to cope with his feelings, but since he isn't able to recognize what he is feeling, he isn't able to use alternatives when needed. If we encourage him to use them, he becomes very belligerent and angry because he views it as making him do something else he doesn't see a need to do. This only adds to the problem. As Edward becomes more and more stressed, we see a definite increase in random aggression toward his younger brother and sister and, more recently, me. The aggression takes the form of instigation of activities that are likely to cause the smaller person to get hurt, unnecessary verbal attacks, or physical actions that they can't protect themselves against because he's so much bigger than they are. Even though we have him spending more quiet time in his room at these times, the stress continues to build, and eventually Edward begins to hear voices. He begins to do things that are irrational and potentially dangerous, such as stealing, running away, mixing chemicals or body waste products into drinking or grooming products, experimenting with fire, and many other things most of us would never even think of, much less act on.

Naturally, Edward's problems also affect his younger siblings, Nathaniel and Rosa. It is difficult for them to understand why the big brother they love will suddenly and without apparent cause do or say something that hurts or upsets them. Although most of the time Edward's behaviors are merely annoying or years below his age level, the unpredictability of his behavior has caused his younger siblings to be very wary around him. As Nathaniel, now 8, put it, "I wish I knew if Edward was going to act like my big brother or my little brother so I'd know how to act around him. I can't trust him."

It also puzzles them when Edward continues to repeat inappropriate behaviors that they have long since learned are wrong. Even Rosa, at the young age of 5, recognizes that many of Edward's behaviors and attitudes are "little kid." Since our younger children can't begin to comprehend how someone can quote rules word for word, yet not be able to apply them, we have had to come up with other ways to help them keep their balance of right and wrong. We do things like giving Edward exactly the same consequence for breaking a rule as we do the other two. If the consequence for Nathaniel and Rosa is to stand in the corner for 2 minutes for breaking a certain rule, when Edward breaks that rule, he stands in the corner for 2 minutes. While we older and hopefully wiser folks know that since Edward doesn't connect the consequences with his actions, he is not learning from the situation, we are setting a pattern of consistency for our younger children by letting them know that wrong is wrong no matter who did it, and that the consequence will be the same. It also reassures them to know that Edward's inappropriate actions toward them will be addressed. His disability is not an excuse for bad behavior.

Another problem area, especially for Nathaniel, is playing with friends. Since Edward's friendships do not continue outside the school setting, he tends to intrude into whatever activity Nathaniel and his friends are doing and to monopolize the situation. The frequent outcome is that Nathaniel winds up getting excluded altogether, which of course makes him angry. The best way we've found to protect Nathaniel's right to have his own friends is to divert Edward into another activity away from the younger kids unless one of us is able to be close by to step in as needed.

Probably the most frequent area of frustration for both siblings is Edward's preference to sit and do nothing or to "zone" (enter the "safety zone" of television or the computer to the exclusion of all else). They enjoy doing things with other people and can't understand that Edward is much more comfortable when he's not interacting with others. After several unsuccessful attempts to get Edward to play with them, they tend to take it personally even though it's not meant that way. Sometimes we allow Edward some "zone" time. Sometimes we step in and direct Edward and one of the younger children into a physical activity or a mind-challenging game that we keep a constant ear to, just in case intervention becomes necessary.

Probably the easiest thing we do to help minimize the "shut out" feeling Rosa and Nathaniel get from Edward is to encourage them to snuggle with him while he's watching television. Although Edward will likely not respond any more than to occasionally put an arm around one of them, he doesn't object when Rosa climbs up on his lap or Nathaniel leans against him, and they feel accepted. It's not unusual to look in the living room in the hour or so before supper and see all three kids snuggled up on the couch watching Nickelodeon. And peace temporarily reigns.

With all the extra time and supervision Edward continues to require from us as parents, our younger children sometimes feel slighted and less important. To try to alleviate some of these feelings, my husband and I have set aside a story time at the end of each day for Rosa and Nathaniel. They each have about 10 minutes of guaranteed uninterrupted time with each parent. We may read stories, talk, or maybe play a game. During this time, Edward stays in his room doing an activity of his choice. That way we can give the younger children our undivided attention, reassure them that we love them just as much as their brother, and let them know that they are just as important to us.

In addition to dealing with all of this, as parents of a child with Asperger syndrome, we are also included in the negative attitude much of the world has about our son. We have been accused of bad parenting, being overly strict, too easy, overprotective, unreasonable, and demanding by educators, parents of our son's peers, and even family members. We often receive disapproving looks when in public because we cannot talk to Edward in the same manner we do our other children if we want him to hear us. While uninformed people's opinions in this area are a relatively minor concern to us, when paired with the fact that we can't leave Edward alone and we can't get sitters to stay with him, our social life is nearly nonexistent. Simply put, if we can't take Edward with us, at least one of us stays home.

Another part of daily life as Edward's parents is exhaustion. Having to be on constant alert and dealing with the 1,001 annoying things Edward does without realizing it takes its toll. Keeping up with a typical teenager can be taxing, but providing all the additional supervision that Edward needs every day creates a large physical and emotional drain. Unfortunately, nighttime doesn't provide respite either, because Edward frequently can't get to sleep for several hours after he goes to bed, especially when his stress level is up. Knowing the unpredictability of his behavior, we can't sleep until he does. Even then, we sleep lightly, always ready to react.

The largest single concern that always lurks in the back of our minds is our son's future. This concern grows daily as Edward approaches adulthood physically and intellectually, while still remaining a very young child in many of the basic skills necessary to be able to survive and succeed in the outside world. We look ahead and see that despite his intelligence, when our son graduates from high school in 2 years, he will not be ready to deal with the demands of college or even a vocational school on his own. The same is true of employment. We don't want to see him forced to sit at home doing nothing because the world will not give him the acceptance, guidance, and accommodation he needs to be a productive member of society.

We also have to think ahead to the time when we are no longer able to provide what he needs. Unfortunately, at this time, there is no place for people with Asperger syndrome to go for assistance of any type, because they fail to meet all criteria to be eligible. This is a frightening concern our family lives with as we try to bring the plight and potential of individuals with Asperger syndrome to the attention of the public.

Like all families, we have good days and not-so-good days. True, our good days are more stress-filled than the average family's, and our bad days are like living in a war zone, but as in most families, the good days outnumber the bad. We have learned to cherish those infrequent moments when Edward gets all the pieces put together and responds appropriately or with thoughtfulness on his own—moments such as when we walk into a room to find Edward sitting on the couch with a rare expression of peaceful contentment on his face as his two young cousins with autism sleep curled up in his arms. We have also learned to appreciate and find amusement in some of his unique ways of looking at things. We look forward to those infrequent occasions when he realizes he did something well and feels proud of himself. We are impressed when something temporarily opens a window and he writes a poem with clear insight.

Most important, these rare moments remind us that under all the problems and aggravations, there is a good kid who wants very much to be like everyone else. And that gives us the hope and strength to go on for one more day.

Andrew

Andrew's mother describes her young son's development, diagnosis, and education. She also offers suggestions for professionals and parents related to having a child with AS/HFA.

My name is Jo Ellen, and I have a son with Asperger syndrome. A year ago, I had never even heard of this syndrome, but now feel that I have tried to get my hand on every book, article, and piece of information that might help me understand my son and offer him the help that will guide him along in life. I am hoping that in writing down some of my thoughts and feelings, it might help other parents, families, friends, or teachers who are reaching out to children who have Asperger syndrome. Perhaps I can share some of the struggles and triumphs we have experienced with our son, Andrew, and perhaps in some small way it will help you through your journey.

Our son was diagnosed just a few months before his sixth birthday. My husband and I are educated professionals, he an engineer, and I a nurse. Andrew, the oldest child, lives with us and his 3-year-old sister in a middle-class, suburban area. It has been only 7 months since we received the diagnosis. A lot led up to it and a lot has happened since then. Actually, Andrew was one of the youngest children to be diagnosed with Asperger syndrome, according to many professionals with whom we spoke. I worried that it meant he had a very severe case, but I think instead it was more our persistence and concerns that resulted in the diagnosis.

Andrew is a blond, blue-eyed boy who, at age 6½, is a whiz on the computer and loves to look at science and experiment books. He attends an all-day kindergarten program in the public school system, and although he doesn't much like the schoolwork part, he already reads at the third-grade level. He looks like any other kindergartner; it isn't until you are around him more that you begin to notice subtle differences in his personality. For instance, he does not have much eye contact with other kids, and he is very particular about not touching finger paints or anything messy. He rarely raises his hand in school and often daydreams or gets a far-off look in his eyes. He has a hard time interacting with peers and occasionally screams out when he is upset. Lately, he has taken to a sort of self-talk during quiet times, sort of "reliving" conversations with others. He is working on his knock-knock jokes, and we read books together on social situations. He doesn't play much with other children. He has to wear only sweatpants (because they are soft), he much prefers foods that go "crunch," and he won't eat slimy foods. We always thought he was the ideal child—he would always entertain himself so well when he was just a toddler. Little did we know that this was something that might be a sign of things to come.

I thought I would share some things that I have found helpful, at least for me, in working with a child with Asperger syndrome. I will give a brief history up to diagnosis and then share some things that we as a family have found to be helpful.

Andrew was born 5 weeks early after a somewhat complicated pregnancy with preterm contractions. He spent a week in the neonatal intensive care unit because of a possible "seizure-like activity" that was proved negative with a CAT scan. He had no further neurological problems and seemed to develop well. He was slightly behind at the 9-month checkup on some motor skills, but with the premature birth adjustment, he was on target. He was a late walker—14 months—but talked right on schedule. His only real illnesses were frequent ear infections, which were treated with ear tubes. He always preferred to play alone, look at books, and entertain himself. Our friends said we had the "perfect child." He never was much of a climber, never tried to get out of his crib, and was always a good eater. He did, however, do things like line objects up according to size and shape, and he recognized unusual things in his environment, like the tape dispenser could be a number 6 or, when turned upside down, a 9. He began recognizing words at about age 3 to 4 and could put them in their proper context.

We did not have any concerns until Andrew started preschool at age 4. His teacher noticed that he couldn't put on his own shoes. She told us that she was worried about his self-esteem if he couldn't dress himself, but it didn't seem to upset him. She also said that he just was not "normal" like the other kids, that he didn't play with them much, and that his behavior went beyond "unique." Every phone call she made to us was negative, and after a while, I felt that she couldn't see anything positive about our son. After several phone calls to us about our child's "unusual behavior," she suggested we have him tested through the school system. We did as she requested, and they said he was "age appropriate."

As a mother, I wanted to prove that Andrew was truly "normal," so I made an appointment with a developmental pediatrician at the nearby university medical center. The doctor there found him to be healthy and within normal limits; however, he was displaying something she called "opposition behavior"; that is, he was defying us and wouldn't dress himself. She suggested that we see a psychologist to help us with disciplining him.

We made an appointment with a behavioral psychologist, who worked with us on time-out procedures. This seemed to help some; he too could see how bright our son was. Andrew still couldn't dress himself very well, and we had many a frustrating morning trying to get his shoes on. After four or five sessions with the psychologist, he suggested we have our son tested for autism at a multidisciplinary team screening. As a mother, I have to say that I was shocked. My son couldn't possibly have autism! Not my bright, wonderful son! What was this man suggesting, that my son had something major wrong with him?

The day of the testing I was more nervous than I thought possible. I told the speech therapist that I thought Andrew was tired, that he wouldn't perform well, that 3 hours in a row would tire him out, and that I wasn't comfortable with one test that would just label or diagnose him—just like that. She assured me that it would give us only information about how

Andrew fit on the autism spectrum and would show where he did or did not have problem areas.

They gave us the results at the summation conference, just an hour or so after all the tests were completed. Andrew was not autistic. I breathed such a sigh of relief. He did, however, have something called tactile defensiveness and dyspraxia (mild motor-planning problems). I learned that he was nearly 2 years behind on gross-motor skills, and 2 ½ years behind on daily living skills. I went from relief to fear to guilt. After all those mornings of coaxing him to put on his shoes and timing him out for not dressing himself, I learned that he didn't have the motor-planning ability to do it. Boy, did I feel bad as a mother and sad too—making him try to dress himself. The poor little guy was not developmentally able to do it. I also learned that with his tactile defensiveness, he did not like messy things such as painting, touching gooey things, or even eating some slimy foods. We all came home exhausted.

The next step was trying to find appropriate help for him. I was disappointed in the testing site, as they were unable to provide me any therapy or treatment. They told me they were only a testing program, so I started calling occupational therapists listed in our phonebook who worked with children. I found one who worked specifically with children, but due to insurance snags, we had to switch to another program. We were fortunate enough to have a children's hospital in the area and started with them. We have been very happy with the therapist there and have been visiting her for over a year now. She suggested that we retest Andrew for his gross-motor skills, so we had a physical therapist work with him. He was "age appropriate" after a summer of working on a few things like climbing the monkey bars, running, and jumping.

Andrew was now 5 and ready to start kindergarten; however, in light of his "problems," we decided to have him attend a prekindergarten class at a church-run preschool. The teacher was marvelous and made every effort to work with Andrew and us regarding our concerns. He was in a class with eight other boys and a certified teacher. He still didn't seem to play with the other children and often screamed out when a bright light would shine in his eyes. He rarely participated in the lessons, although he was easily reading all the books the teacher had. At recess, he preferred to spend the time up in the lookout fort lost in his own thoughts. The teacher clearly could tell that he was bright; she just didn't know how to teach him.

In October, we had his first parent–teacher conference, and the teacher said she continued to have concerns regarding how he was interacting with the class. She said he seemed very happy playing by himself on the playground or lost in his thoughts in the classroom. She already knew what we had done to date with his testing and therapy and was willing to help with anything that we suggested. I decided to call and see if he could be examined by another developmental pediatrician in town, but the wait was over 5 months. So in the interim we visited yet another behavioral psychologist, who worked with us on time-out tactics again. They worked with Andrew and said he was pretty bright and that we should try more positive praise. They also suggested that we invite other children over, one at a time, and have monitored play sessions. We were to praise Andrew for playing appropriately and time him out when he didn't interact well with the other child. This was challenging, as Andrew only lasted about 10 minutes, and that left Dad or me to interact with the other child for the remainder of the session. We even contemplated trying medication for Andrew's hyperactivity at this time but decided to wait.

Our appointment with the developmental pediatrician finally arrived, and she was pleasant and very low key. She took a thorough history from both my husband and myself and then worked with Andrew for a while. At the end of our session, she said she was not sure—in fact, could not be sure until further testing by a clinical psychologist was completed—but she felt that Andrew had Asperger syndrome.

It was something we had never heard of. I felt great relief knowing that there was a physiological cause of some of Andrew's behaviors. Also, there was a deep sense of sadness—that I had lost my perfect little boy. I wanted to read everything. The doctor said that until the diagnosis was confirmed, she wanted me to read just one article. I remember taking it home, reading it from cover to cover, and saying, "Oh my God—that is Andrew." He didn't have some of the features some children with Asperger syndrome have regarding memorizing dates, facts, or time schedules, but he always did like the United States map and could list most of the states. He definitely had trouble with eye contact and difficulty with social situations. These were his hallmark signs. He was hyperlexic and had some tactile defensiveness, which sometimes occur with Asperger syndrome.

We were able to see the clinical psychologist within just a week, and she spent several hours with Andrew and me doing some paper-and-pencil tests and also some play therapy. She reviewed his history and asked me to return the next day with my husband, leaving Andrew at home. The next morning, we went to her office and she confirmed that our son had Asperger syndrome. Now the tears started to flow. I remember her telling us that we would need to "change our expectations of Andrew." But what did that mean? I then envisioned my beautiful son living at home with us well into his 50s, never getting a job, never marrying—all due to this syndrome and to his inability to understand social rules and participate well in our very social world.

The doctor allowed me to be sad, mad, and frustrated all at the same time. She was very supportive and suggested several articles, and she also left the door open for support sessions for us as needed. To date, I see her every 6 to 8 weeks for ideas on how to deal with Andrew's behavior, problems that arise at school, and ideas on how to cope with our special needs child.

For over a year, Andrew has met at least three times a month with an occupational therapist, who works with his motor planning and tactile defensiveness. She has him paint with shaving cream (which he hates), and she has him make up obstacle courses and tell her how he would execute his way through them (which he loves). She works really well with him, and I am happy to report that just this month, she felt he was age appropriate for most of the skills (e.g., using scissors, writing with a pencil). We continue to work at home with the tactile kinds of things, and he has improved steadily.

We had to make the choice of having Andrew start in the public school system or in the parochial school where he was pre-enrolled for kindergarten. After talking with both schools, we felt that he would be entitled to more services and have a better chance of having his special needs met if we chose the local public school. We met with the school district's administrators, who, just a few weeks before school started, wanted to have Andrew take all kinds of intelligence tests, aptitude tests, and so on. He took them and did very well. The school district examiners were impressed with his excellent reading and comprehension skills but figured that his attention deficit might challenge the teachers. We were lucky that the school district had at least one other child with a diagnosis of Asperger syndrome, so at least the administration understood some of what we were up against.

I met with the teachers Andrew would have. We selected the new all-day kindergarten program to lessen his need for transition and to provide continuity for him. We had to educate the staff about Asperger syndrome, and they continue to work well with him and us as parents. The school had him tested with the occupational therapist on-site, but as expected, he did not qualify for therapy. However, he did qualify for their speech therapist to come into the classroom and work with him on conversational skills with the other children. She even brings games and has him teach another child how to play.

Andrew also started private speech therapy sessions before the school year started. I found a therapist who works well with pragmatics and social skills of speech, and she has helped him on a weekly basis. He likes the games she plays with him and is working on practical things like ordering a soda at McDonald's.

Another thing that I have found to be very helpful is talking with other parents whose children have Asperger syndrome. When we received the diagnosis, I asked our developmental pediatrician to connect me with another mother who had recently gone through this experience of diagnosis and treatment. She found a very positive woman in our community who just 6 months before we met had received the diagnosis of Asperger syndrome for her 10-year-old son. Her ideas, sharing, and support have really been a boost. Also, our community just happened to start a support group for parents of children with Asperger syndrome. We meet monthly, share ideas and frustrations, and laugh at what other parents might be horrified to hear. It has been a wonderful sense of strength to see that the little oddities of your child are not so unusual and that other parents are going through the same kinds of things that you experience.

One thing that I have learned is that you have to grieve the loss of the perfect child. As parents, we all have expectations for our children. I always assumed that our son would be an engineer or scientist. I hoped that he would marry a nice girl and have a family. I don't know if any of these will come to pass; I hope that they all do. Right now, there are days that I am just thankful that we have had a calm day. He gets upset easily if he spills milk on his shirt or makes a mess of any kind. He cannot tie his own shoes (thank goodness for Velcro). He still gets frustrated with zippers and buttoning his own shirt. He is working on buttering his own waffles and cutting his own meat. It continues to be a struggle to get him to do any kind of art or to write. Andrew still has a hard time sitting still at mealtimes (but then again, don't most kids?).

Andrew rarely gets invited to anyone's house, and when he goes, I worry about how he will act or react. He doesn't share toys well and doesn't understand the social skills that most 6-year-olds live by. He doesn't understand teasing and so is the victim of several classmates' pranks. It breaks a mother's heart to see her child be the butt of jokes, but you deal with it. Andrew doesn't understand humor very well, so we watch *America's Funniest Home Videos* on television and talk about why things are funny. We also have selected several knock-knock joke books to give him something to share with other people (and his teachers are great to laugh at his jokes). He has a hard time in new environments, so we try to explain everything as we go along. He isn't able to transfer social rules from one setting to another, for example, "No kicking at school" can't be translated for him to "We don't kick at the playground." We have to remind him in each new setting of how to behave.

Parents deal with getting the diagnosis for a special needs child in different ways. You both start to feel guilty and wonder things like "Did I give this to my child?" Both my husband and I tried to look back to our family trees to see if somehow we passed it down from generation to generation.

Fathers grieve and accept in different ways from mothers—it must be in how we are genetically built. I'm not sure. I, as a mother, needed to grieve, to cry and talk it over with supportive family and friends. My husband, on the other hand, chose to be more self-reflective and to pursue the Internet for up-to-date information. Being in the health care field, I started reading all sorts of studies and technical articles. I wouldn't recommend them for most people, because they have a tendency to present the worst-case scenarios.

It is also hard to decide who you tell and how much they need to know. You would never want to hold back information from those caring for your child, but just how much you tell a neighbor or another child's parents is an individual call. Our families have been supportive and encouraging, and now that they know more of why Andrew gets upset easily or behaves the way he does, they are more accommodating and eager to help him excel in areas in which he can shine.

As I write this, Andrew is halfway through his kindergarten year. The school has 30-minute monthly meetings when we meet with teachers and the behavior specialist to discuss concerns or ideas regarding our son. They say he is doing better socially and has even initiated interactions with some of his classmates. He still doesn't raise his hand to answer questions and doesn't appear to follow a lot of the schoolwork. However, his reading skills are fine, and he has even participated in art class a little more. They do not think that he needs medication for the attention-deficit disorder at this time, and that is just fine by me. They also have started to let him have 20 minutes a day of computer time as a sort of motivational reward.

We continue to see the speech therapist weekly, and I keep a log for her of things to spark a conversation with Andrew. We have good communication with the school, and I am already planning ahead for the first grade.

Suggestions I have for someone who has a child with Asperger syndrome are to keep an open mind and read all you can, especially handouts from your psychologist or therapists. Find someone you can confide in, like a sibling or best friend. These people are invaluable, as are any caring listeners. Spend one-on-one time with your child doing an activity he or she likes and excels at. It gives the child lots of positive reinforcement for things he or she already does well. Look up current sources on the Internet, in the library, or at autism centers. Start a parent support group in your area. It is really great to meet with other parents, and you might be able to help them as much as they help you. Truly, do not try to predict your child's future; just live in the present. Each child with Asperger syndrome is different, and each child is special and unique. The most important suggestions I could give for parents, family members, teachers, or anyone working with these truly special needs children is to be patient, love them a lot, and celebrate their little victories.

 ## Dan*

Dan is a young adult. His parent relates his story, based on the article "The Long Road."

My son, Dan, is 21 and has Asperger syndrome. We have traveled a long road to diagnosis and appropriate treatment. At times, discouragement seemed to overtake us, but we have gone farther now than we ever hoped. Our desire in telling Dan's story is that others will find hope and will determine never to give up!

Adopted at age 2 ½, Daniel was the joy of my life. When we got Dan, we were told that he had some developmental delays and might be mildly retarded. He wasn't speaking yet, had walked late, and was not potty trained. As a speech–language pathologist, I thought I could deal with those issues and more. He was so cute and seemed so needy. He was a perfect match!

Dan was not legally free for adoption. He had an unstable pre-adoption experience and had been in the foster care system for quite a while. However, parental rights had not yet been terminated. We agreed to take Dan as a foster child until he was free for adoption. The legalities went smoothly, and we eventually adopted Dan.

Dan had health and developmental difficulties from the beginning. The day after we brought him home, he started crawling on the carpeted floor,

---

*Adapted from "The Long Road," by Terri Carrington, 2000, *Focus on Autism and Other Developmental Disabilities,* 15(4), pp. 216–220. Copyright 2000 by PRO-ED, Inc. Adapted with permission.

scooting his ear along the rough carpet. He didn't cry or fuss, but he soon began to run a fever. Of course, it was a weekend, and we had no pediatrician yet. We were able to take him to a friend's pediatrician, and he was diagnosed with an ear infection. Already his tympanic membranes were scarred and showed evidence of multiple infections. We checked with the adoption workers and found no evidence of prior treatment for ear infections. Dan had apparently found a way to soothe his ear by rubbing it on the carpet. This started a long course of chronic ear infections, antibiotic treatment, allergy treatments, insertion of tubes, and finally a prophylactic dose of antibiotic every day to curb the infections. Dan's lack of speech development and his clumsiness were attributed to the ear infections. We already had numerous concerns about his development, but the chronic ear infections seemed to explain the concerns away.

Dan's speech and language development was interesting. By the time we got him at age 2½, he had developed an elaborate gestural system interpreted by others fairly easily. The first word didn't come until age 4. He said "watch" and immediately began using it in kernel sentences with a variety of meanings: "Wear watch," "Watch TV," "Watch me." Curiously, he learned to read at about the same time. He loved books and was read to every day, but no formal attempt at teaching reading had been presented. By the time Dan entered kindergarten, he could read just about anything given to him. Speech continued to be problematic, and the diagnosis of dyspraxia was made. He had speech therapy privately and in school.

Dan's play skills were unusual, but because his play seemed so smart, red flags did not go up for us. He preferred constructive play to imaginative play and solitary play to group play. An activity he particularly enjoyed was lining up several wooden puzzles and then placing pieces one at a time and in the same place (e.g., left corner piece) in each puzzle down the line. When finished, he would dump the pieces, turn the puzzles to the side, and start the process over again. We thought he was so clever! Dan spent hours listening to Disney tape and book sets. He enjoyed doing this activity under a table or in some other small space. Electronic items and transportation were all-consuming interests. Dan also seemed to have an uncanny sense of direction. He loved spending hours with globes and maps and always received a new atlas for Christmas.

Emotionally, there were also red flags, although we didn't see them at the time. Dan was affectionate, but indiscriminately so. He would go to anyone. He was as comfortable with a stranger in a grocery store as he was with us. He did show some separation anxiety when left at the church nursery or day care. I remember taking him to a Christmas parade where there was a homeless person sitting on the curb. Dan cuddled up to him as if they were long-lost friends. We didn't know what to do!

School was easy for Dan, at least in the academic sense. He was already reading and showing facility with numbers upon entering kindergarten. We went to a cemetery on Memorial Day that year, and Dan enjoyed walking along the rows of headstones, reading people's names and figuring their ages at death. We were amazed. He continued to do well academically and was placed in the gifted and talented program in first grade.

School was a different story when it came to social issues. Dan had difficulty making friends, but he didn't seem bothered by it. We would have children over to play, but Dan tended to ignore them. We ended up playing with his friends! He was in Boy Scouts and Sunday school and participated marginally. We also tried several sports. Dan had undiagnosed sensory integration problems and visual problems (his eyes didn't converge), so the sports attempts were generally disasters. He almost always received the "most improved player" award, because he didn't have anywhere to go but up.

As Dan progressed in school, he became more and more disenfranchised with other students. He hated working in cooperative groups and going out for recess. He much preferred to spend his recess in the library with his books. Things were better for him at home. He rode his bike and then an all-terrain vehicle. We lived out in the country, and he seemed to enjoy that setting. We had a swimming pool, and Dan was a good swimmer. He enjoyed his time in the pool both by himself and with others.

About sixth grade, in a middle school setting, Dan began to deteriorate rapidly. He became obsessed with germs and developed compulsive behavior related to that. When someone would come too close, Dan would start blowing (to blow away germs). He wanted his clothes sterilized and would not wear underwear that someone else had touched. He became afraid of taking a bath and would cower at the end of the bathtub. Although we now know Dan was experiencing obsessive-compulsive disorder, sometimes seen in people with autism, we interpreted his behavior first as obstinate and then, as it increased in intensity, as paranoia.

By the time Dan reached seventh grade, he was frankly different from his peers, continued to engage in obsessive-compulsive thoughts and behaviors, and was performing poorly in school. A crisis ensued when Dan actually became fearful of his family, took the keys to one of our cars, and drove to a state south of us where we had often camped and vacationed. He managed to drive because he had used our riding lawn mower and his all-terrain vehicle, and we had let him occasionally drive our old truck in our field. He called when he ran out of gas, and we had him picked up by the police. When we arrived at the police station sometime later, we were blessed to deal with an experienced officer who recognized Dan's disorganization and knew something was wrong beyond a youth stealing a car. Dan was released back to our custody.

We contacted our pediatrician, who felt Dan should be hospitalized. This began a long road of dealing with the mental health system. Just a few years ago, autism wasn't recognized as the wide spectrum disorder it is, and Dan certainly did not fit the stereotypic image of a child with autism. The psychiatric hospitalization was lengthy and very scary. Autism was not considered as a diagnosis.

Because of Dan's foster care experience, resulting from parental neglect, and his current unexplainable behavior, Dan was thought to have reactive attachment disorder (RAD). We were unfamiliar with this disorder, but we read everything we could find. Children with RAD fail to bond with caregivers, usually because their early needs were not met. They fail to establish the cycle of bonding, in which there is a need (such as a wet diaper or hunger); they let that need be known by crying and raging; and the need is then met. When early needs are not met, the foundational development of early building blocks (e.g., cause and effect) does not emerge. Without intensive and often controversial and intrusive treatment, development is skewed. These children are thought not to develop consciences, show no remorse, and are egocentric. They become manipulative and even dangerous. If not treated, children who display RAD may be diagnosed as sociopaths and psychopaths as adults—personality disorders thought to be resistant to treatment. We were told there was a poor prognosis for Dan; he would become progressively more dangerous, and he needed to be institutionalized. We reluctantly agreed for him to be placed in a residential treatment center following his hospitalization.

There can't be anything much worse than allowing your child to be placed somewhere other than the home. We weren't sure the placement would meet his needs and didn't feel comfortable with the facility. Unfortunately, it seemed the only answer at the time. Daniel did not do well there.

As we now know, he was misdiagnosed and received inappropriate treatment. He continued to deteriorate, running away from the facility. He found a small truck with keys in the ignition, took it, and drove to our property. The ordeal was terrifying, but there was nothing to do but return the truck and return Dan to the facility. With this scare, it seemed that staff at the facility would have watched Dan more closely, as they were charged to do. However, supervision was careless, and Dan took another vehicle—one of the facility vans—and drove it across state lines, was chased by the police, and rolled the van. Miraculously, he was not hurt. Later, the officers told me they expected a mean juvenile delinquent to emerge from the van. They were surprised when a chubby little kid with hard-to-understand speech and a poor understanding of what had transpired emerged. Dan was jailed overnight, and we were again blessed with officers who allowed us to return Dan to our state. The staff at the facility and I retrieved Dan, and he was taken to juvenile detention. This was the first occurrence of what I call system dumping. When a child's behavior is unexplained or increases in difficulty, he or she often is dumped from one system or one facility to another. There didn't seem to be a framework for problem solving. If a child didn't fit, he or she was simply sent somewhere else. Fortunately, we were able to convince the juvenile authorities to rehospitalize Dan. During that hospitalization, I made an active search for a place that would meet Dan's perceived needs.

The diagnosis of RAD continued, and I found a facility in another state claiming to specialize in the disorder. By this time, we had exhausted the mental health provisions of our insurance policy. Because Dan is adopted, we were able to access adoption subsidy funding, which is negotiable and can be used in a variety of ways to meet a child's needs. Funding was provided for a 6-month stay at the new facility. Although the new facility seemed better than the first one, his treatment didn't seem adequate for the RAD diagnosis. He was not provided with the intensive treatment described in the literature for RAD, and the national consultant who was supposedly working with the facility never saw Dan. The psychiatrist who saw Dan, however, opened the door as to whether something "organic" was causing his symptoms. Unfortunately, this was not pursued. The recommendation continued to be that Dan had a poor prognosis and that he was probably facing a lifetime of institutionalization, if not imprisonment. In the meantime, Dan's father and I divorced, which left me to support Dan alone. I brought him home and enrolled him in school.

At his home school, Dan was placed in a behavior disorder classroom, which again did not meet his needs. This placement did not last long, and Dan found his way to yet another psychiatric hospitalization. Without detailing every hospitalization and placement, Dan eventually totaled 19 hospitalizations and three residential placements. Huge expenditures were required from the adoption subsidy, and a financial strain was put on me as well. The doctors and staff at these placements continued to misdiagnose and provide inappropriate treatment.

It was a long journey to the diagnosis of Asperger syndrome. My own instincts as a speech–language pathologist, and the comments about Dan's status, seemed to say, "Look at autism." A friend who specialized in autism assessed Dan and felt he qualified for an educational diagnosis of autism in our state. Unfortunately, she wasn't taken seriously by the mental health community. At that time and in the place we lived, developmental disability professionals and agencies were reluctant to work with the mental health community, and vice versa. Children who displayed both mental health issues and developmental issues were in a no-man's land of sorts. Working together and sharing resources didn't happen. In fact, it seemed to me that the bottom line quite literally had to do with funding and wanting "someplace else" to pay the bill. It was fortunate that we had access to adoption subsidy funding. This funding source is negotiable and not tied to a program or diagnosis. Its use helped us cross agency and diagnostic lines. Through networking, I learned of a psychiatrist in a neighboring state who had expertise with developmental disabilities as well as psychiatric concerns. We obtained an evaluation from him—at my own cost, but worth it—which concluded that Dan not only qualified for an educational diagnosis of autism, but met the DSM-IV (*Diagnostic and Statistical Manual of Mental Disorders–Fourth Edition;* American Psychiatric Association, 1994) criteria for Asperger syndrome as well. Other mental health practitioners we had consulted at the time looked at Dan and expounded such things as, "He doesn't look autistic to me." Knowledge of autism spectrum disorders is increasing, but many clinicians continue to hold a narrow view of what autism "looks like."

The additional psychiatric report, coupled with the educational diagnostic report, supported our approach to the center for Mental Retardation and Developmental Disabilities, where Dan was accepted as a client. The Regional Center purchases services and we were able to acquire the services of Pathways Supports, a company providing community integration, independent supported living, and psychological services. In fact, the psychologist with Pathways had provided services for Dan off and on for a long time and had been one of the few professionals who had remained supportive and open to our search for an appropriate diagnosis and services. The staff at

Pathways subscribes to the philosophy of positive behavior support. This same psychologist had been a member of the initial group of persons trained in positive behavior support in our state.

One of the tenets of positive behavior support is looking at individual needs and not limiting services to those suggested by a specific diagnosis or by what a particular agency is prepared to supply. Once needs are identified, an individualized program is designed to meet those needs. This was a breakthrough for Dan and our family. We were finally able to access what seemed to work for him. Before, we had been tied to whatever was available in his diagnostic box, whether that fit or not.

Another tenet of positive behavior support was important to Dan's eventual success as well. The program was designed from the beginning to be dynamic and to change as Dan's needs changed. There were proactive plans for crisis intervention and plans to bring him back to original services if more intensive intervention was needed for a time. Other services, which were driven by placements made by diagnosis, ended when needs intensified. "Dan no longer fits our program" was the excuse as Dan hopped from placement to placement. There was no overall plan for Dan's cycles of needing increasing and decreasing levels of services. Each move was seen as a failure on Dan's part, when in fact the system failed to meet Dan's needs. The philosophy of positive behavior support places the child's needs first. Intervention services are tools to meet those needs. Success is measured not by ability to meet the requirements of an established program but by the child's meeting of individually established goals and objectives.

Because Dan was young, and because I wasn't willing to have him live anywhere except with me, we decided to provide an independent supported living arrangement in our home. This seemed workable, even though it was intensive. It certainly was better than institutional options. The road proved to be a rocky one. We initially had 24-hour staff with us. As time went on, the need for staff varied, from times with no staff present to times when we needed to double staff. During this time, my daughter also lived at home. She was in her late elementary–middle school career. In retrospect, the situation was difficult for her, although she did develop lifelong friendships with several of the staff members. When there is more than one child in a family, it is a never-ending balancing act to meet each one's needs even in the best of circumstances. When one child has needs that seem to far exceed the needs of another, life becomes challenging. She suffered as I made "Sophie's Choices" concerning both my children. One issue in particular continues to haunt me, and I have seen reference made to this in the adoption literature. When determining living choices for a very challenging child while considering arrangements for the other, more "normal" children, we need to consider safety paramount. My daughter was, at times, not safe in her own home. This is probably where a choice to provide services away from the home setting needs to be made, if possible. There were several instances where Dan's status deteriorated to the point that we made other arrangements—specifically, psychiatric hospitalization. These times were always difficult, but we were supported by the staff at Pathways. Dan was able to return to the independent supported living situation as his status improved.

There was, finally, a point when support in the home seemed no longer appropriate. It was time for Dan to move to an apartment. He was to be released from his latest lengthy psychiatric hospitalization, and the independent support living situation was moved. Although it was hard to let go, this proved to be the right choice. Dan's improvement was marked but continued to be marred by occasional crises. He eventually made a serious suicide attempt, which resulted in a broken femur. After the femur was repaired in surgery, Dan came home to stay with me and his sister. During his recovery, he again deteriorated, and it was determined that he again needed to leave home. The crisis was severe, and very clear lines were drawn in relation to Dan's living arrangements and our family. This seemed to be a turning point for Dan, and he has lived more or less successfully in supported living since. We continue to use the services of Pathways, but staffing has been reduced to a minimal level, and goals now focus on employment and community integration.

School has been a difficult issue. During Dan's elementary years, he excelled academically and seemed mostly oblivious to social demands. However, in junior high and high school, Dan's lack of social skills and his continuing speech disorder became more evident. Dan struggled and eventually turned school attendance into a daily battle. He finally refused to attend, and forcing him only escalated behavior difficulties. Homebound teaching was provided by the school, and one teacher provided some after-school work for Dan in the school building. The school provided minimal homebound services, because it is only reimbursed for a few hours a week. We eventually homeschooled and prepared Dan to take the test to obtain a general equivalency diploma (GED). He was not a wonderful home school student, but he took the test and scored well. He completed his GED during what would have been the fall semester of his senior year in high school. With that struggle over, we weren't willing to immediately look at postsecondary educational opportunities. (I think we do a nice job, for the most part, of educating and supporting our special needs elementary students. Unfortunately, when students transition to the secondary setting, problems occur for a variety of reasons. Increased academic demands, changing schedules, classes focused more on content than on students, lack of a safe place or home base, and lack of a peer group all contribute to decreased success.)

The student with Asperger syndrome usually deeply wants to interact with others but lacks the skills and social perception to do so. Some students become so frustrated with their lack of social prowess that they actually become severely depressed. This certainly contributed to Dan's continuing mental health difficulties, as it does for many other students who function similarly. Furthermore, subtle language problems and continuing sensory issues compound the inability of these students to do well in school. Often their narrow focus of interest in a particular subject causes others to view them as very bright academically, so expectations are skewed. Sometimes alternative schooling options such as home schooling, enrollment in small private schools, or increased special education supports are beneficial. The most important aspect of these students' education is training for teachers and others who interact with the students so their needs relating to autism are identified and supported. Eventually, Dan tried two community college classes but felt he was unable to complete them. I was impressed, however, with the willingness of the faculty and support personnel to assist Dan. I hope we can try again.

Employment has not been as challenging as school completion. Dan has worked part-time for Pathways in a clerical position for several years. This has not been officially referred to as supported employment, but the nurturing environment at Pathways has contributed to Dan's success there. Asperger syndrome is understood, and Dan's idiosyncratic behaviors have been tolerated, with his uniqueness even enjoyed by other workers. This experience has helped him establish confidence in his ability to work with others and has given him hope that he can be competitively employed. Currently, we are working with vocational rehabilitation to assist Dan in finding full-time competitive employment.

It has been a long road to diagnosis and appropriate services. As I think about the journey, it's appropriate to separate what worked and what did not. We need to look beyond the obvious. Dan's chronic otitis (ear infections) and early disrupted development were obvious explanations for his unusual behavior. If his behavior had been assessed in a systematic way, without preconceived ideas of cause, we might have looked further. The autism red flags were his disordered rates and sequence of development (facility with some developmental tasks and lags in others), his speech–language difficulties (dyspraxia, elaborate gestural system but no functional speech, late speech development that took an unusual course), early untaught reading, multiple sensory issues, narrow focus of interest, lack of facility with social skills, unusual play, more constructive than imaginative play, and superior intelligence as measured on standardized tests.

Many of the diagnosticians we consulted were not familiar with autism. They relied on their impressions and did not consider characteristics outlined in diagnostic guides. Furthermore, many clinicians did not consider autism a spectrum disorder and failed to recognize it in higher functioning individuals like my son.

There was a failure to consider the dual diagnosis of autism and mental health disorders. It is my experience that many children have complex diagnoses and that children with Asperger syndrome are at higher risk for mental health concerns such as depression and obsessive-compulsive disorder.

Practitioners were not willing to look beyond their own areas of expertise or the constraints of their employment setting. The mental health community did not work with the developmental disability and mental retardation agencies. There was an either–or philosophy. Diagnosis—whether appropriate or not—and funding sources drove treatment. Individual needs took a backseat to preset programs.

We took seriously the instincts that Dan's behavior had not been well explained over time. Hints from doctors that something organic was going on, and his resistance to treatment provided, indicated we were missing something. The addition of Asperger syndrome to the DSM-IV and the additional outside evaluations I obtained gave credibility to our thoughts concerning autism.

Adoption subsidy funding, which is not tied to specific programs or agencies, was key in developing supports for Dan. Adherence to the philosophy of positive behavior supports by Pathways Supports and the Regional Center for Mental Retardation and Developmental Disabilities was central to developing appropriate services and to eliminating the hopping from program to program. Alternative schooling options were considered when traditional school enrollment was not appropriate.

As noted, Dan was eventually employed in a supportive environment. This has allowed him to develop confidence and ease in the search for competitive employment. The support of a few professionals, including Dan's adoption worker and the psychologist at Pathways who remained involved over time and through numerous crises, was critical to the overall continuity eventually achieved.

Recently, Dan spoke at the annual conference of the Autism Society of America. He did a great job outlining the long road he has walked. I think he gave hope for an eventual level of success for people with Asperger syndrome. I have learned a great deal from Dan, as have the professionals who have chosen to support him. Being Dan's mom has been worth it!

 ## Jason

Jason is an adolescent with a diagnosis of Asperger syndrome. He shares here the original and largely unedited lyrics to a verse he wrote related to his experiences and frustrations in living with the daunting challenges of a higher functioning autism spectrum disorder. He also offers a perspective on his future. His personal reflection poignantly captures the significant emotional and other challenges connected with high-functioning autism and Asperger syndrome. At the same time, it reflects the optimism that we have found so common among children and families with this challenging condition.

Doomed From a Cause Unseen*

I got cuffs to my wrists and shackles on me.
My life really twists like the waves of the sea.
I'm a living rage, my fist like flail,
I'm an innocent prisoner in a cell.
I got some knuckles and some nasty scenes
where some heads fly clear to New Orleans
but there's an evil shadow that holds the key
to the evil chains that strongly bind me.
He clung to me I didn't cling to him

---

*Poem reprinted with permission of the author.

cause he ticks me off every time he clings to my skin
but I'm not going to let him ruin my life
I got to raise some kids, I got to get a wife.
I'm going to be someone, maybe someone to lead
but my determination weighs a ton and I will succeed.
These rattling chains weigh heavy on my soul
but my desperation glows like a flaming coal.
I'm getting back up, I'm breaking out of this cage.
I shake the bars hard to express my rage.
I rise in my shackles back up again.
I yell out loud in my torcher pin [torture pen].
I bash to the left and I bash to the right
I'm not giving up without a fight.
I got a painful past but a life ahead.
I hope you heard just what I said.
I got a painful past behind my back
but a life ahead that I can't keep slack.

Concluding Thoughts

Individuals with diagnoses of Asperger disorder or high-functioning autism and their parents and families are in a unique position to share perspectives about the impact of their disabilities. The personal stories and reflections in this chapter capture the joys, frustrations, and challenges connected to these demanding disorders. These stories also poignantly capture the hope and optimism that comes with finding services, answers, and acceptance of the individuality and inimitability that comes in the myriad faces of persons on the spectrum. Finally, these narratives relate in the most personal fashion that there is every reason to believe that with the assistance of qualified and committed professionals and knowledgeable and resolute parents and families, individuals with Asperger syndrome or higher functioning autism spectrum disorders will be able to actualize their significant potential and live productive lives, both as students and as adults.

References

Adams, L., Gouvousis, A., VanLue, M., & Waldron, C. (2004). Social story intervention: Improving communication skills in a child with an autism spectrum disorder. *Focus on Autism and Other Developmental Disabilities, 19*(2), 87–94.

American Psychiatric Association. (1994). *Diagnostic and statistical manual of mental disorders* (4th ed.). Washington, DC: Author.

American Psychiatric Association. (2000). *Diagnostic and statistical manual of mental disorders* (4th ed., text rev.). Washington, DC: Author.

American Psychological Association. (2007). *Childhood disorders.* Retrieved December 7, 2007, from http://www.apa.org/divisions/div12/rev%5Fest/children.html#opp_beh

Americans With Disabilities Act of 1990, 42 U.S.C. § 12101 *et seq.* (1990).

Apple, A., Billingsley, F., & Schwartz, I. (2005). Effects of video modeling alone and with self-management on compliment-giving behaviors of children with high-functioning ASD. *Journal of Positive Behavior Interventions, 7,* 33–46.

Arwood, E. L. (1991). *Semantic and pragmatic language disorders* (2nd ed.). Denver, CO: Aspen.

Asperger, H. (1944). Die "Autistischen Psychopathen" im Kindesalter. ["Autistic Psychopathy" in Childhood]. *Archiv fur Psychiatrie und Nervenkrankheiten, 117,* 76–136.

Attwood, T. (1998). *Asperger's syndrome: A guide for parents and professionals.* London: Jessica Kingsley.

Attwood, T. (2007). *The complete guide to Asperger syndrome.* Philadelphia: Jessica Kingsley.

Autism Society of America. (2009). *What are autism spectrum disorders?* Retrieved June 10, 2009, from http://www.autism-society.org

Barnhill, G. P. (2001). Social attribution and depression in adolescents with Asperger syndrome. *Focus on Autism and Other Developmental Disabilities, 16,* 46–53.

Barnhill, G., Hagiwara, T., Myles, B. S., & Simpson, R. L. (2000). Asperger syndrome: A study of the cognitive profiles of 37 children and adolescents. *Focus on Autism and Other Developmental Disabilities, 15,* 146–153.

Barnhill, G. P., Hagiwara, T., Myles, B. S., Simpson, R. L., Brick, M., & Griswold, D. (2000). Parent, teacher, and self-report of problems and adaptive behaviors in children and adolescents with Asperger syndrome. *Diagnostique, 25,* 147–167.

Baron-Cohen, S., Golan, O., Wheelwright, S., & Hill, J. (2004). *Mind reading: The interactive guide to emotions.* London: Jessica Kingsley.

Baron-Cohen, S., Jolliffe, T., Mortimore, C., & Robertson, M. (1997). Another advanced test of theory of mind: Evidence from very high functioning adults with autism or Asperger Syndrome. *Journal of Child Psychology and Psychiatry, 38,* 813–822.

Baron-Cohen, S., Leslie, A., & Frith, U. (1985). Does the autistic child have a theory of mind? *Cognition, 25,* 37–46.

Bauminger, N. (2007). Brief report: Group social-multi-modal intervention for HFASD. *Journal of Autism & Developmental Disorders, 37,* 1605–1615.

Beaumont, R., & Sofronoff, K. (2008). A multi-component social skills intervention for children with Asperger syndrome: The Junior Detective Training Program. *The Journal of Child Psychology and Psychiatry, 49*, 743–753.

Bellini, S. (2008). *Building social relationships*. Shawnee Mission, KS: Autism Asperger Publishing.

Bellini, S., & Akullian, J. (2007). A meta-analysis of video modeling and video self-modeling interventions for children and youth with autism spectrum disorders. *Exceptional Children, 73*, 261–284.

Bellini, S., Peters, J., Benner, L., & Hopf, A. (2007). A meta-analysis of school-based social skill interventions for children with autism spectrum disorders. *Remedial and Special Education, 28*(3), 153–162.

Ben-Arieh, J., & Miller, H. J. (2009). *The educator's guide to teaching students with autism spectrum disorders*. Thousand Oaks, CA: Corwin Press.

Bieber, J. (Producer). (1994). *Learning disabilities and social skills with Richard LaVoie: Last one picked . . . first one picked on* [Videotape]. (Available from Public Broadcasting Service Video, 1320 Braddock Place, Alexandria, VA 22314)

Bledsoe, R., Myles, B. S., & Simpson, R. (2003). Use of a social story intervention to improve mealtime skills of an adolescent with Asperger syndrome. *Autism, 7*(3), 289–295.

Bock, M. A. (2007a). The impact of social-behavioral learning strategy training on the social interaction skills of four students with Asperger syndrome. *Focus on Autism and Other Developmental Disabilities, 22*(2), 88–95.

Bock, M. A. (2007b). A social-behavioral learning strategy intervention for a child with Asperger syndrome. Brief report. *Remedial and Special Education, 28*, 258–265.

Bölte, S., Feineis-Matthews, S., Leber, S., Dierks, T., Hubl, D., & Poustka, F. (2002). The development and evaluation of a computer-based program to test and to teach the recognition of facial affect. *International Journal of Circumpolar Health, 61*(Suppl. 2), 61–68.

Brasic, J. R. (2008). *Pervasive developmental disorder: Asperger syndrome*. Retrieved September 17, 2008, from e-medicine, from WebMD, http://www.emedicine.com/ped/TOPIC147.HTM

Brigance, A. H. (2010). *BRIGANCE comprehensive inventory of basic skills II*. North Billerica, MA: Curriculum Associates.

Brown, L., & Hammill, D. (1990). *Behavior rating profile*. Austin, TX: PRO-ED.

Bruner, J. S. (1966). *Toward a theory of instruction*. Cambridge, MA: Harvard University Press.

Cameron, M. J., Shapiro, R. L., & Ainsleigh, S. A. (2005). Bicycle riding: Pedaling made possible through positive behavioral interventions. *Journal of Positive Behavior Interventions, 7*(3), 153–158.

Cantor, R. M., Kono, N., Duvall, J., Alvarez-Retuerto, A., Stone, J., Alcarcon, M., et al. (2005). Replication of autism linkage: Fine-mapping peak at 17q21. *American Journal of Human Genetics, 76*, 1050–1056.

Carpenter, L. B. (2001). The travel card. In B. S. Myles & D. Adreon (Eds.), *Asperger syndrome and adolescence: Practical solutions for school success* (pp. 92–96). Shawnee Mission, KS: Autism Asperger Publishing.

Carrington, T. (2000). The long road. *Focus on Autism and Other Developmental Disabilities, 15*(4), 216–220.

Cartwright-Hatton, S., Roberts, C., Chitsabesan, P., Fothergill, C., & Harrington, R. (2004). Systematic review of the efficacy of cognitive behaviour therapies for childhood and adolescent anxiety disorders. *British Journal of Clinical Psychology,* *43*, 421–436.

Centers for Disease Control and Prevention. (2008). *Autism information center.* Retrieved September 17, 2008, from http://www.cdc.gov/ncbddd/autism/index

Cesaroni, L., & Garber, M. (1991). Exploring the experience of autism through firsthand accounts. *Journal of Autism and Developmental Disorders, 21*, 303–313.

Chalfant, A. M., Rapee, R., & Carroll, L. (2006). Treating anxiety disorders in children with high functioning autism spectrum disorders: A controlled trial. *Journal of Autism and Developmental Disorders, 37*, 1842–1857.

Charlop-Christy, M. H., & Freeman, K. A. (2000). A comparison of video modeling with in vivo modeling for teaching children with autism. *Journal of Autism and Developmental Disorders, 30*, 537–552.

Church, C., Alisanski, S., & Amanullah, S. (2000). The social, behavioral, and academic experiences of children with Asperger syndrome. *Focus on Autism and Other Developmental Disabilities, 15*, 12–20.

Clarke, S., Dunlap, G., & Vaughn, B. (1999). Family-centered, assessment-based intervention to improve behavior during an early morning routine. *Journal of Positive Behavior Interventions, 1*, 235–241.

Connolly, A. (2007). *KeyMath–3 diagnostic assessment.* San Antonio, TX: Pearson.

Constantino, J. (2009). *Social responsiveness scale.* Los Angeles: Western Psychological Services.

Couteur, A., Lord, C., & Rutter, M. (2003). *Autism diagnostic interview* (Rev. ed.). Los Angeles: Western Psychological Services.

Crooke, P., Hendrix, R., & Rachman, J. (2008). The effectiveness of teaching social thinking to adolescents with Asperger syndrome and high functioning autism. *Journal of Autism and Developmental Disorders, 38*, 3.

Crozier, S., & Tincani, M. (2007). Effects of social stories on prosocial behavior of preschool children with autism spectrum disorders. *Journal of Autism and Developmental Disorders, 37*, 1803–1814.

Delano, M. E. (2007). Improving written language performance of adolescents with Asperger syndrome. *Journal of Applied Behavior Analysis, 40*(2), 345–351.

Dolch, E. W. (1955). *Methods in reading.* Champaign, IL: Garrard Press.

Downing, J. A. (1990). Contingency contracts: A step-by-step format. *Intervention in School and Clinic, 26*(2), 111–113.

Ducharme, J. M., Sanjuan, E., & Drain, T. (2007). Errorless compliance training: Success-focused behavioral treatment of children with Asperger syndrome. *Behavior Modification, 31*, 329–344.

Duke, M. P., Nowicki, S., & Martin, E. A. (1996). *Teaching your child the language of social success.* Atlanta, GA: Peachtree.

Dunn, W. (1999). *The sensory profile: A contextual measure of children's responses to sensory experiences in daily life.* San Antonio, TX: Psychological Corp.

Dunn, W. (2008). A sensory-processing approach to supporting students with autism spectrum disorders. In R. Simpson & B. Myles (Eds.), *Educating children and youth with autism* (pp. 299–356). Austin, TX: PRO-ED.

Durand, V. M., & Crimmins, D. (1992). *Motivation assessment scale.* Topeka, KS: Monaco.

Durrell, D. D., & Catterson, J. H. (1981). *Durrell analysis of reading difficulty* (3rd ed.). San Antonio, TX: Psychological Corp.

Earles-Vollrath, T. L., Cook, K. T., & Ganz, J. B. (2007). *How to develop and implement visual supports.* Austin, TX: PRO-ED.

Ehlers, S., & Gillberg, C. (1993). The epidemiology of Asperger syndrome: A total population study. *Journal of Child Psychology and Psychiatry, 34*(8), 1237–1350.

Ehlers, S., Nyden, A., Gillberg, B., Sandburg, A., Dehlgren, S., Hjelmquist, E., et al. (1997). Asperger syndrome, autism and attention deficit disorders: A comparative study of cognitive profiles of 120 children. *Journal of Child Psychology and Psychiatry and Allied Disciplines, 38*, 207–217.

Ellis, A., Abrams, M., & Abrams, L. (2008). *Theories of personality: Critical perspectives.* New York: Sage Press.

Feldman, J., & Kazdin, A. E. (1995). Parent management training for oppositional and conduct problem children. *The Clinical Psychologist, 48*(4), 3–5.

Frith, U. (Ed.). (1991). *Autism and Asperger syndrome.* Cambridge, UK: Cambridge University Press.

Fry, E. B. (1980). The new instant word list. *The Reading Teacher, 34,* 284–289.

Gagnon, E. (2001). *The power card: Using special interests to motivate children and youth with Asperger syndrome and autism.* Shawnee Mission, KS: Autism Asperger Publishing.

Garcia Winner, M. (2007). *Thinking about you, thinking about me.* San Jose, CA: Think Social Publishing.

Garcia Winner, M. (2008). *A social thinking curriculum for school-age students.* San Jose, CA: Think Social Publishing.

Ghaziuddin, M., Weidmer-Mikhail, E., & Ghaziuddin, N. (1998). Comorbidity of Asperger syndrome: A preliminary report. *Journal of Intellectual Disability Research, 42*(4), 279–283.

Gillberg, C. L. (1992). Autism and autistic-like conditions: Subclasses among disorders of empathy. *Journal of Child Psychology and Psychiatry and Allied Disciplines, 33,* 813–842.

Gilliam, J. E. (2001). *Gilliam Asperger disorder scale.* Austin, TX: PRO-ED.

Golan, O., & Baron-Cohen, S. (2006). Systemizing empathy: Teaching adults with Asperger syndrome or high-functioning autism to recognize complex emotions using interactive multimedia. *Development and Psychopathology, 18,* 591–617.

Goldstein, A. P., & McGinnis, E. (1997). *Skillstreaming the adolescent: New strategies and perspectives for teaching prosocial skills.* Champaign, IL: Research Press.

Grandin, T. (1995). *Thinking in pictures and other reports from my life with autism.* New York: Vintage.

Gray, C. (1994). *Comic strip conversations.* Arlington, PA: Future Horizons.

Gray, C. (1995). *Social stories unlimited: Social stories and comic strip conversations.* Jenison, MI: Jenison Public Schools.

Gray, C. (2004). Social stories 10.0. *Jenison Autism Journal, 15,* 2–21.

Gray, C., & Garand, J. D. (1993). Social stories: Improving responses of students with autism with accurate social information. *Focus on Autistic Behavior, 8,* 1–10.

Gresham, F. M. (1998). Social skills training: Should we raze, remodel or rebuild? *Behavioral Disorders, 24,* 19–25.

Gresham, F. M., & Elliott, S. (2008). *Social skills improvement system.* San Antonio, TX: Pearson.

Griswold, D., Barnhill, G. P., Myles, B. S., Hagiwara, T., & Simpson, R. L. (2002). Asperger syndrome and academic achievement. *Focus on Autism and Other Developmental Disabilities, 17*(2), 94–102.

Guber, P., Peters, J. (Producers), & Levinson, B. (Director). (1988). *Rain Man* [Motion picture]. (Available from MGM/UA Home Video, 2500 Broadway, Santa Monica, CA 90404-3061)

Hagiwara, T., Cook, K., & Simpson, R. (2008). Assessment of students with autism spectrum disorders. In R. Simpson & B. Myles (Eds.), *Educating children and youth with autism* (pp. 61–91). Austin, TX: PRO-ED.

Hagiwara, T., & Myles, B. (1999). A multimedia social story intervention: Teaching skills to children with autism. *Focus on Autism and Other Developmental Disabilities, 14,* 82–95.

Hammill, D., & Larsen, S. (1996). *Test of written language.* Austin, TX: PRO-ED.

Harpur, J., Lawlor, M., & Fitzgerald, M. (2004). *Succeeding in college with Asperger syndrome: A student guide.* London, UK: Jessica Kingsley.

Herschell, A. D., Calzada, E. J., Eyberg, S. M., & McNeil, C. B. (2002). Parent-child interaction therapy: New directions in research. *Cognitive and Behavioral Practice, 9,* 9–16.

Horner, R. H., Carr, E. G., Halle, J., McGee, G., Odom, S., & Wolery, M. (2005). The use of single-subject research to identify evidence-based practice in special education. *Exceptional Children, 71,* 165.

Howlin, P., Baron-Cohen, S., & Hadwin, J. (1999). *Teaching children with autism to mind-read: A practical guide.* New York: Wiley.

Howlin, P., & Yates, P. (1999). The potential effectiveness of social skills groups for adults with autism. *Autism, 3*(3), 299–307.

Hresko, W. P., Reid, P. K., & Hammill, D. (1999). *Test of early language development.* Austin, TX: PRO-ED.

Idol, L., Nevin, A., & Paolucci-Whitcomb, P. (1999). *Models of curriculum-based assessment: A blueprint for learning.* Austin, TX: PRO-ED.

Individuals With Disabilities Education Act of 1990, 20 U.S.C. § 1400 *et seq.* (1990). (amended 1997)

Individuals With Disabilities Education Act of 2004, 20 U.S.C. § 1400 *et seq.* (2004). (reauthorization of IDEA 1990)

Institute of Education Sciences, U.S. Department of Education, What Works Clearinghouse. (2009). Retrieved from http://ies.ed.gov/ncee/wwc

Jones, V. F., & Jones, L. S. (1995). *Comprehensive classroom management: Creating positive learning environments for all students* (4th ed.). Boston: Allyn & Bacon.

Kadesjo, B., Gillberg, C., & Hagberg, B. (1999). Autism and Asperger syndrome in seven-year-old children: A total population study. *Journal of Autism and Developmental Disorders, 29,* 327–332.

Kanner, L. (1943). Autistic disturbances of affective content. *The Nervous Child, 2,* 217–250.

Kaplan, J. S., & Carter, J. (1995). *Beyond behavior modification: A cognitive-behavioral approach to behavior management in the school* (3rd ed.). Austin, TX: PRO-ED.

Kauffman, A., & Kauffman, N. (2002). *Kauffman assessment battery for children* (2nd ed.). San Antonio, TX: Pearson.

Klin, A., Sparrow, S. S., Marans, W. D., Carter, A., & Volkmar, F. R. (2000). Assessment issues in children and adolescents with Asperger syndrome. In A. Klin, F. R. Volkmar, & S. S. Sparrow (Eds.), *Asperger Syndrome* (pp. 309–339). New York: Guilford Press.

Klin, A., Volkmar, F. R., & Sparrow, S. (2000). *Asperger syndrome.* New York: Guilford Press.

Kuoch, H., & Mirenda, P. (2003). Social story interventions for young children with autism spectrum disorders. *Focus on Autism and Other Developmental Disabilities, 18*(4), 219–227.

LeGoff, D. B. (2004). Use of LEGO as a therapeutic medium for improving social competence. *Journal of Autism and Developmental Disorders, 34*, 557–571.

LeGoff, D. B., & Sherman, M. (2006). Long-term outcome of social skills intervention based on interactive LEGO play. *Autism, 10*(4), 317–329.

Lewis, T. J., Scott, T. M., & Sugai, G. (1994). The problem behavior questionnaire: A teacher-based instrument to develop functional hypotheses of problem behavior in general education settings. *Diagnostique, 19*, 103–115.

Lincoln, A., Courchesne, E., Kilman, B., Elmasian, R., & Allen, M. (1988). A study of intellectual ability in high-functioning people with autism. *Journal of Autism and Developmental Disorders, 18*, 505–524.

Lopata, C., Thomeer, M. L., Volker, M. A., & Nida, R. E. (2006). Effectiveness of a cognitive-behavioral treatment on the social behaviors of children with Asperger disorder. *Focus on Autism and Other Developmental Disabilities, 21*, 237–244.

Lopata, C., Thomeer, M. L., Volker, M. A., Nida, R. E., & Lee, G. K. (2008). Effectiveness of a manualized summer social treatment program for high-functioning children with autism spectrum disorders. *Journal of Autism and Developmental Disorders, 28*, 890–904.

Lord, C., & Venter, A. (1992). Outcome and follow-up studies of high-functioning autistic individuals. In E. Schopler & G. B. Mesibov (Eds.), *High-functioning individuals with autism* (pp. 187–199). New York: Plenum Press.

Lotter, V. (1996). Epidemiology of autistic conditions in young children. *Social Psychiatry, 4*, 263–277.

Manjiviona, J., & Prior, M. (1995). Comparison of Asperger syndrome and high-functioning autistic children on a test of motor impairment. *Journal of Autism and Developmental Disorders, 25*, 23–39.

Markwardt, F. (1998). *Peabody individual achievement test–Revised.* San Antonio, TX: Pearson.

McGinnis, E., & Goldstein, A. P. (1997). *Skillstreaming the elementary school child: New strategies and perspectives for teaching prosocial skills.* Champaign, IL: Research Press.

McLoughlin, J., & Lewis, R. (2008). *Assessing students with special needs.* Upper Saddle River, NJ: Pearson.

Mercer, C. D. (1996). *Students with learning disabilities* (6th ed.). Columbus, OH: Prentice Hall.

Mercury-Free Vaccines Act of 2005, H. R. 881, 109 Cong. (2005).

Mesibov, G., Shea, V., & Adams, L. (2001). *Understanding Asperger syndrome and high functioning autism.* New York: Kluwer Academic/Plenum Publishing.

Mruzek, D. W., Cohen, C., & Smith, T. (2007). Contingency contracting with students with autism spectrum disorders in a public school setting. *Journal of Developmental and Physical Disabilities, 19*, 103–114.

Mueller, M., Palkovic, C., & Maynard, C. (2007). Errorless learning: Review and practical application for teaching children with pervasive developmental disorders. *Psychology in the Schools, 44*, 691–700.

Myles, B. S., & Adreon, D. (2001). *Asperger syndrome and adolescence: Practical solutions for school success.* Shawnee Mission, KS: Autism Asperger Publishing.

Myles, B. S., Bock, S. J., & Simpson, R. L. (2000). *Asperger syndrome diagnostic test.* Austin, TX: PRO-ED.

Myles, B. S., Constant, J. A., Simpson, R. L., & Carlson, J. K. (1989). Educational assessment of students with higher functioning autistic disorder. *Focus on Autistic Behavior, 4,* 1–13.

Myles, B. S., Cook, K. T., Miller, N. E., Rinner, L., & Robbins, L. A. (2000). *Asperger syndrome and sensory issues: Practical solutions for making sense of the world.* Shawnee Mission, KS: Autism Asperger Publishing.

Myles, B. S., Ferguson, H., & Hagiwara, T. (2007). Using a personal digital assistant to improve the recording of homework assignments by an adolescent with Asperger syndrome. *Focus on Autism and Other Developmental Disabilities, 22,* 96–99.

Myles, B. S., & Simpson, R. (2001a). Effective practices for students with Asperger syndrome. *Focus on Exceptional Children, 34*(3), 1–14.

Myles, B. S., & Simpson, R. L. (2001b). Understanding the hidden curriculum: An essential social skill for children and youth with Asperger syndrome. *Intervention in School and Clinic, 36*(5), 279–286.

Myles, B. S., Simpson, R. L., & Becker, J. (1995). An analysis of characteristics of students diagnosed with higher functioning autistic disorder. *Exceptionality, 5*(1), 19–30.

Myles, B. S., & Southwick, J. (1999). *Asperger syndrome and difficult moments: Practical solutions for tantrums, rage, and meltdowns.* Shawnee Mission, KS: Autism Asperger Publishing.

National Research Council. (2001). *Educating children with autism.* Washington, DC: Author.

No Child Left Behind Act of 2001, 20 U.S.C. 70 § 6301 *et seq.* (2002).

Norris, C., & Dattilo, J. (1999). Evaluating effects of a social story intervention on a young girl with autism. *Focus on Autism and Other Developmental Disabilities, 14,* 180–186.

Ogletree, B. (2008). The communicative context of autism. In R. Simpson & B. Myles (Eds.), *Educating children and youth with autism* (pp. 267–298). Austin, TX: PRO-ED.

Owens, G., Granader, Y., Humphrey, A., & Baron-Cohen, S. (2008). LEGO therapy and the social use of language programme: An evaluation of two social skills interventions for children with high functioning autism and Asperger syndrome. *Journal of Autism and Developmental Disorders, 38,* 1944–1957.

Phelps-Terasaki, D., & Phelps-Gunn, T. (1992). *Test of pragmatic language.* Austin, TX: PRO-ED.

Piaget, J. (1959). *Judgment and reasoning in the child.* Paterson, NJ: Littlefield, Adams.

Quill, K. (2000). *Do-watch-listen-say: Social and communication intervention for children with autism.* Baltimore, MD: Brookes.

Quinn, C., Swaggart, B. L., & Myles, B. S. (1994). Implementing cognitive behavior management programs for persons with autism: Guidelines for practitioners. *Focus on Autistic Behavior, 9*(4), 1–13.

Rao, P., Beidel, D., & Murray, M. (2007). Social skills interventions for children with Asperger's syndrome or high-functioning autism: A review and recommendations. *Journal of Autism and Developmental Disorders, 38*(2), 353–361.

Reynolds, C. R., & Kamphaus, R. W. (1992). *Behavior assessment system for children* (BASC). Circle Pines, MN: American Guidance Services.

Rinaldi, W. (2004). *Social use of language programme: Infant and primary school teaching pack.* Cranleich, UK: Wendy Rinaldi.

Roberts, G. H. (1968). The failure strategies of third grade arithmetic pupils. *The Arithmetic Teacher, 15,* 442–446.

Rogers, M. F., & Myles, B. S. (2001). Using social stories and comic strip conversations to interpret social situations for an adolescent with Asperger syndrome. *Intervention in School and Clinic, 36,* 312.

Roid, G. (2003). *Stanford-Binet intelligence scales* (5th ed.). Itasca, IL: Riverside.

Roosa, J. B. (1995). Men on the move: Competence and cooperation "conflict resolution and beyond." Kansas City, MO: Author.

Safran, S. (2001). Asperger syndrome: The emerging challenge to special education. *Exceptional Children, 67,* 151–160.

Sansosti, F. J., & Powell-Smith, K. A. (2006). Using social stories to improve the social behavior of children with Asperger syndrome. *Journal of Positive Behavior Interventions, 8,* 43–57.

Sansosti, F. J., & Powell-Smith, K. A. (2008). Using computer-presented social stories and video models to increase the social communication skills of children with high-functioning autism spectrum disorders. *Journal of Positive Behavior Interventions, 10,* 162–178.

Scattone, D. (2007). Enhancing the conversation skills of a boy with Asperger's disorder through social stories and video modeling. *Journal of Autism & Developmental Disorders, 38,* 395–400.

Semel, E., Wiig, E. H., & Secord, W. A. (1995). *Clinical evaluation of language fundamentals* (3rd ed.). San Antonio, TX: Psychological Corp.

Shore, S. (2003). My life with Asperger syndrome. In R. W. Du Charme & T. Gullotta (Eds.), *Asperger syndrome: A guide for professionals and families* (pp. 189–209). New York: Kluwer Academic/Plenum Publishing.

Shure, M. B. (1992). *I can problem solve: An interpersonal cognitive problem-solving program.* Champaign, IL: Research Press.

Siegel, D., Minshew, N., & Goldstein, G. (1996). Wechsler IQ profiles in diagnosis of high-functioning autism. *Journal of Autism and Developmental Disorders, 26,* 389–406.

Sigafoos, J., O'Reilly, M., & de la Cruz, B. (2007). *How to use video modeling and video prompting.* Austin, TX: PRO-ED.

Silvaroli, N. J. (1986). *Classroom reading inventory.* Dubuque, IA: Wm. C. Brown.

Simpson, R. L. (2005). Evidence-based practices and students with autism spectrum disorders. *Focus on Autism and Other Developmental Disabilities, 20,* 140–149.

Simpson, R. L. (2008). Children and youth with autism spectrum disorders: The search for effective methods. *Focus on Exceptional Children, 40*(7), 1–14.

Simpson, R., deBoer-Ott, S., Griswold, D., Myles, B., Byrd, S., Ganz, J., et al. (2005). *Autism spectrum disorders: Interventions and treatments for children and youth.* Thousand Oaks, CA: Corwin Press.

Simpson, R., & Myles, B. (2008). *Educating children and youth with autism.* Austin, TX: PRO-ED.

Skrtic, T. M., Kvam, N. E., & Beals, V. L. (1983). Identifying and remediating the subtraction errors of learning disabled adolescents. *The Pointer, 27,* 323–338.

Smith, I. (2000). Motor functioning in Asperger syndrome. In A. Klin, F. Volkmar, & S. Sparrow (Eds.), *Asperger syndrome* (pp. 97–124). New York: Guilford Press.

Smith, I., & Bryson, S. (1994). Imitation and action in autism: A critical review. *Psychological Bulletin, 116,* 259–273.

Sofronoff, K., Attwood, T., & Hinton, S. (2005). A randomised controlled trial of a CBT intervention for anxiety in children with Asperger syndrome. *Journal of Child Psychology and Psychiatry, 46,* 1152–1160.

Sofronoff, K., Attwood, T., Hinton, S., & Levin, I. (2007). A randomized controlled trial of a cognitive behavioral intervention for anger management in children diagnosed with Asperger syndrome. *Journal of Autism and Developmental Disorders, 37,* 1203–1214.

Sofronoff, K., & Farbotko, M. (2002). The effectiveness of parent management training to increase self-efficacy in parents of children with Asperger syndrome. *Autism, 6,* 271–286.

Sofronoff, K., Leslie, A., & Brown, W. (2004). Parent management training and Asperger syndrome: A randomized controlled trial to evaluate a parent based intervention. *Autism, 8,* 301–317.

Solomon, M., Goodlin-Jones, B. L., & Anders, T. F. (2004). A social adjustment enhancement intervention for high functioning autism, Asperger's syndrome, and pervasive developmental disorder NOS. *Journal of Autism and Developmental Disorders, 34,* 649–668.

Solomon, M., Ono, M., Timmer, S., & Goodlin-Jones, B. (2008). The effectiveness of parent-child interaction therapy for families of children on the autism spectrum. *Journal of Autism and Developmental Disorders, 38,* 1767–1776.

Sparrow, S., Balla, D., & Cicchetti, D. (1984). *Interview edition of the survey form manual: Vineland adaptive behavior scales.* Circle Pines, MN: American Guidance Service.

Spivack, G., Platt, J. J., & Shure, M. (1976). *The problem-solving approach to adjustment.* San Francisco, CA: Jossey-Bass.

Strain, P. S., & Cordisco, L. K. (1994). LEAP Preschool. In S. L. Harris & J. S. Handleman (Eds.), *Preschool education programs for children with autism* (pp. 225–244). Austin, TX: PRO-ED.

Sukhodolsky, D. G., Kassinove, H., & Gorman, B. S. (2003). Cognitive-behavioral therapy for anger in children and adolescents: A meta-analysis. *Aggression and Violent Behavior, 9,* 247–269.

Sundbye, N. (2001). *Assessing the struggling reader: What to look for and how to make sense of it.* Lawrence, KS: Curriculum Solutions.

Swaggart, B. L., Gagnon, E., Bock, S. J., Earles, T. L., Quinn, C., Myles, B. S., et al. (1995). Using social stories to teach social and behavioral skills to children with autism. *Focus on Autistic Behavior, 10*(1), 1–16.

Tantam, D. (2000). Adolescence and adulthood of individuals with Asperger syndrome. In A. Klin, F. Volkmar, & S. Sparrow (Eds.), *Asperger syndrome* (pp. 367–399). New York: Guilford Press.

Thompson, T. (2007). *Making sense of autism.* Baltimore, MD: Brookes.

Thorndike, R. L., Hagen, E., & Sattler, J. (1985). *Stanford-Binet intelligence scale* (4th ed.). Chicago: Riverside.

Tiger, J., Bouxsein, K., & Fisher, W. (2007). Treating excessively slow responding of a young man with Asperger syndrome using differential reinforcement of short response latencies. *Journal of Applied Behavior Analysis, 40,* 559–563.

Tincani, M. (2007). Beyond consumer advocacy: Autism spectrum disorders, effective instruction, and public schools. *Policy and Law Briefs, 43,* 47–51.

Todd, T., & Reid, G. (2007). Increasing physical activity in individuals with autism. *Focus on Autism and Other Developmental Disabilities, 21*(3), 167–176.

Tsatsanis, K. D., Foley, C., & Donehower, C. (2004). Contemporary outcome research and programming guidelines for Asperger syndrome and high-functioning autism. *Topics in Language Disorders, 24,* 249–259.

Volkmar, F., & Klin, A. (2000). Diagnostic issues. In A. Klin, F. Volkmar, & S. Sparrow (Eds.), *Asperger syndrome* (pp. 25–71). New York: Guilford Press.

Wallace, G., & Hammill, D. (1994). *Comprehensive receptive and expressive vocabulary test*. Austin, TX: PRO-ED.

Wechsler, D. (1989). *Wechsler preschool and primary scale of intelligence* (Rev. ed.). San Antonio, TX: Psychological Corp.

Wechsler, D. (1991). *Wechsler intelligence scale for children* (3rd ed.). San Antonio, TX: Psychological Corp.

Wechsler, D. (2002). *Wechsler individual achievement test.* San Antonio, TX: Pearson.

Wetherby, A., & Prizant, B. (2000). *Autism spectrum disorders: A transactional developmental perspective.* Baltimore, MD: Brookes.

Wiig, E. H., & Secord, W. (1989). *Test of language competence* (Exp. ed.). San Antonio, TX: Psychological Corp.

Wilde, L. D., Koegel, L. K., & Koegel, R. L. (1992). *Increasing success in school through priming: A training manual.* Santa Barbara, CA: University of California.

Winebrenner, S. (2001). *Teaching gifted kids in the regular classroom: Strategies and techniques every teacher can use to meet the academic needs of the gifted and talented.* Minneapolis, MN: Free Spirit.

Wing, L. (1981). Asperger's syndrome: A clinical account. *Psychological Medicine, 11,* 115–130.

Wing, L. (1991). The relationship between Asperger's syndrome and Kanner's autism. In U. Frith (Ed.), *Autism and Asperger syndrome* (pp. 37–92). Cambridge, UK: Cambridge University Press.

Woodcock, R. (1998). *Woodcock reading mastery tests* (Rev. ed.). San Antonio, TX: Pearson.

Woodcock, R., McGrew, K., & Mather, N. (2001). *Woodcock-Johnson III tests of achievement.* Itasca, IL: Riverside.

Woods, M., & Moe, A. (2007). *Analytical reading inventory.* Upper Saddle River, NJ: Pearson.

World Health Organization. (2007). *International statistical classification of diseases and related health problems* (10th rev.). Geneva, Switzerland: Author.

Zachman, L., Barrett, M., Huisingh, R., Orman, J., & Blagden, C. (1991). *Test of problem solving–adolescent.* East Moline, IL: LinguiSystems.

Zachman, L., Huisingh, R., Barrett, M., Orman, J., & LoGiudice, C. (1994). *Test of problem solving–elementary* (Rev. ed.). East Moline, IL: LinguiSystems.

Index

About the Authors

Richard L. Simpson is a professor of special education at the University of Kansas. He has also been a special education teacher, school psychologist, and coordinator of a community mental health outreach program. His other professional experiences include directing several University of Kansas and University of Kansas Medical Center demonstration programs for students with autism spectrum disorders and coordinating several federal grant programs related to students with autism spectrum disorders and other disabilities. He has authored numerous books, articles, and tests on the topic of students with Asperger disorder, autism spectrum disorders, and other disabilities.

Brenda Smith Myles has worked in a variety of roles in support of children and youth with autism spectrum disorders, including as a university professor and direct-service educator. She is the recipient of the 2004 Autism Society of America's Outstanding Professional Award and the 2006 Princeton Fellowship Award. She has written numerous articles and books on Asperger syndrome and autism. She served as the co-chair of the National ASD Teacher Standards Committee. She is on the National Institute of Mental Health's Interagency Autism Coordinating Committee's Strategic Planning Consortium and the Autism Society of America's Panel of Professional Advisors. Myles is also on the executive boards of several organizations, including the Organization for Autism Research.